Growth of Trade, Commerce and Public Sector Undertaking : An Indian Perspective

Dedicated

to

My loving Parents

Parbati Devi & Mukunda Padhy

who are no more on this earth but their blessing have sustained me to pen this book.

Growth of Trade, Commerce and Public Sector Undertaking : An Indian Perspective

Suresh Prasad Padhy

UPPAL PUBLISHING HOUSE
N E W D E L H I - 1 1 0 0 0 2 (India)

UPPAL PUBLISHING HOUSE
3, Ansari Road, Darya Ganj, New Delhi - 110002
Phones : 23273756, 23286571, Fax : 91-011-23286571
E-mail : uppalbooks@vsnl.net

First Published 2007
ISBN : 81-7658-036-8

Printed in India

Published by B. S. Uppal for Uppal Publishing House, 3, Ansari Road, Daryaganj, New Delhi and Typeset by Versha Computers Centre, Daryaganj, New Delhi and Printed at **ARORA OFFSET PRESS**

Contents

Preface

The path of curiosity is a public way. I urged myself to traverse this way. Hence this book.

The history of human kind is basically a history of struggle, experiments, new inventions, and human enterprise. Rousseau's "noble savage" has mentored generations of individual enterprise culminating in the modern day public enterprise system. Weber's bureaucratic theory, and Maslow's need priority model, had its own dose of criticism. I have tried to access various sources to trace the origin and growth of individual enterprise and commerce from the ancient times. The readers will surely find it eminently interesting to take a journey into those ancient times where men's livelihood & survival depended on interactive enterprise rather than hunting to keep one's family alive.

In our day and time public enterprises, mostly in the third world, face the challenges of globalization, privatization, and WTO released activities. Only time will tell, the extent to which they would be able to cope up with the changing times. I remember the famous dictum "Old order changeth yielding place to new".

This being my maiden endeavor, I shall deem my efforts worth while, if the readers get an insight into on the origin and growth of trade, commerce and public sector not only in India but the world over.

Different historical and economical evidences have been quoted extensively from different books, literatures, periodical, journals, articles from encyclopaedia Britannica government publications and the articles down loaded from internet, in an attempt to make the book a complete one.

I take this opportunity to thank my wife Anila and daughter Sarmistha for their moral support and encouragement in bringing this book. I am also grateful to my parents and well wishers, but for whose supports, I would not have been able to bring out this book.

New Delhi-110001 **Suresh Prasad Padhy**

Abbreviations

AGM	:	Annual General Meeting
BC	:	Before Christ
BIFR	:	Board for Industrial and Financial Reconstruction
CAG	:	Comptroller and Auditor General of India
CBI	:	Central Bureau of Investigation
CD	:	Cassette Decoder
CENVAT	:	Central Value Added Tax
CEO	:	Chief Executive Officer
CG	:	Capital Goods
CIF	:	Capital For Imports
CMP	:	Common Minimum Program
COPU	:	Committee on Public Undertakings
CSO	:	Central Statistical Organisation
DDT	:	Dichloro Dyphenyle Trichloro Ethane
DGS&D	:	Director General Supplies and Disposal
EOU	:	Export Oriented units
EPZ	:	Export Processing Zones
ERC	:	Electricity Regulatory Commission
FDI	:	Foreign Direct Investment
FERA	:	Foreign Exchange Regulation Act
FII	:	Financial Institutional Investments
GNP	:	Gross National Product
GSI	:	Geological Survey of India

IRDA : Insurance Regulatory & Development Authority
ISI : Indian Standards Institution
IT : Information Technology
KVIC : Khadi and Village Industries Centers
MOU : Memoranda of Understanding
MRP : Maximum Retail Price
MRTPA : Monopolies and Restrictive Trade Practices Act
MW : Mega Watt
NEP : New Economic Policy
NIDC : National Industrial Development Corporation
NPC : National Productivity Council
OGL : Open General Licence
POL : Petrol Oil & Lubricants
PSE : Public Sector Enterprises
PSU : Public Sector Undertaking
R&D : Research and Development
RIDF : Rural Infrastructure Development Fund
RBI : Reserve Bank of India
SEBI : Securities and Exchanges Board of India
SIA : Secretariat for Industrial Approval
SICA : Sick Industrial Companies Act
SIDBI : Small Industries Development Bank of India
SIDO : Small Industries Development Organiasation.
SSI : Small Scale Industries
TAME : Taking Ancient Mythology Economically
TELCO : Tata Engine & Locomotive Company
TRAI : Telephone Regulatory Authority of India
TV : Television
UTI : Unit Trust of India
VCF : Venture Capital Funds
VCR : Video Cassette Recorder
VRS : Voluntary Retirement Scheme

1

Ancient Indian Commerce

Indian Magnificence

The East gave impetus to the West according to belief of Romans. It is in the valley of the Nile, the Euphrates, the Yangtse Kang and the Indus that one would first witness the misty dawn of civilization, the beginning of knowledge and progress. Whatever light or civilization that existed there, was confined to the Eastern basin of the Mediterranean being constantly fed by the Orient. The civilization of India is one of the oldest, but, like all of them, has come to a dead end: but it has lived to revive and we may hope never to die again. The contact of the west has shaken the "fixity" and restored her old dynamic power.

The magnificence of India lies in its puritanism, a unique concept followed by other civilizations. It has been synonymous of truth and non-violence. Its geographical position just fitted her to be the early cradle of civilization. Nature has given her that isolation which has been the envy of many of tribal societies which are ever in scarch of a secure abode to develop their capacity and make the most of nature's gifts. Severed from China and Tibet on the North by the Himalayan mountains, on the East from Burma by the Tenasserim and on the west from Afghanistan by Karakoram and Hindukush ranges, the entire peninsula forms a world in miniature in itself, formed by strong natural defences provided by mountains forming a wall on the North-West and the sea, a moat on all other sides.

This inverted triangle conserves the most varied and most abundant of natural resources. Animal life is not only abundant in India, but it is remarkably varied. The variety of animals inhabiting India and its dependencies is very large, far surpassing, for instance, that of the species found in the whole of Europe, although the superficial area of Europe exceeds that of the Indian empire by about one-half. Equally rich is her diversity of flora and fauna and her climate that makes possible the existence of such variegated animal life. The richness of vegetable life is unbounded. All these factors have from time immemorial combined to bestow upon her the economic self-sufficiency, which has been the privilege of a few nations on the face of this planet today.

Given the materials, man can hardly be expected to remain inactive for the economic motive is the strongest and the most dynamic of all. He tries at once to exploit the environment for his well being and the early inhabitants of India were no exception to the rule. It would be a mistake if we take a modern average Indian as a prototype of his stalwart ancestor. He may resemble him perhaps in features but that's all. The semblance ends there. The India of antiquity within the span of time in which he held the undisputed possession of the country accomplished much more than could be expected of primitive. As of now, there have been scanty records of his deeds but whatever little is available does speak volumes.

Of the multifarious achievements of the ancient Indians, important as they are, we are not concerned. We have to centre our attention on their economic activity alone.

At the outset, it would be better to take note of the lampposts or the sources that will help us in our survey. On the nature's side, there is a lamentable paucity. The Hindus are loquacious on everything except the economic activity of their life and the reason is not far to seek. Education was monopolized by a class of people who were more or less "drones in the hive, gorging at a feast to which they [had] contributed nothing". The Brahmin, the intellectual caste of India, enjoyed "the conspicuous leisure" and "the conspicuous consumption" vicariously; consequently the economic activity of the ancient Hindus found no exponents and no mention in the literature, which is purely sacerdotal. This also explains why India did not produce any literature on the Science of Economic as such. Hence, one would be compelled to depend entirely on foreign authorities and their scanty reference to India's commerce.

Before one would launch on the subject of commerce, it would be better to hastily survey economic development of Ancient India. There is no authority on the subject that can take us back to the pre-Buddha times. The Buddha *Jatakas*-the birth-stories of Buddha-are the earliest source on the subject and contain literary references to the economic organisation of the Indian society, which may be supposed to have existed from times very remote from the dates of these *Jatakas*. However *Arthasastra* written by Kautilya (321BC-296 BC), is the science of *artha*, or material prosperity, which is one of the four goals of human life. By *artha*, Kautilya meant "the means of subsistence of man," which is, primarily, wealth and, secondarily, earth. The work is concerned with the means of fruitfully maintaining and using the latter-i.e., land. It is a work on politics and diplomacy. The author was concerned with central control by the king of a realm of fairly limited size, and he spoke of the way a State's economy was organized, how ministers should be chosen and war conducted, and how taxation should be arranged and distributed. "The Government should collect taxes as a bee collects honcy from the flowers" was the dictum propounded by Kautilya. Great emphasis was placed on the importance of a network of runners, informers, and spies, which, in the absence of a ministry of public information and a police force, functioned as a surveillance corps for the king, focusing particularly on any external threats and internal dissidence. This book not only revealed that, as early as during 300 BC, there was not only a concept of taxation policy formulated by the government but also the ways and means to control unproductive expenditure by the State.

Agricultural Organisation

It has been noticed that from ancient times, Hindus have been living a village life. The number of families in a village varied from 30 to 1000. No isolated houses were to be found. Houses existed in clusters. Agriculture is known as the highest occupation and the Indian proverb puts the merchantman second to the farmer and the soldier occupies the last place in social gradation.

The farmers and their families, some times got land cultivated by hired labour. The traditional feeling was apparently against land transfer. Yet, it was noticed that land was rented out for cultivation. Independent landholder was regarded respectfully, but work on the farm of a capitalist was greatly disapproved. There is no evidence to say definitely whether there was feudalism at all in village community.

There was a great deal of co-operation among villagers for building and repairing roads and tanks and municipal buildings. The sovereign claimed an annual *tilha* on raw produce. This was levied, and in kind amounted to 1/6th, 1/8th, 1/10th or 1/12th of the total produce. Grain, pulse, and sugarcane were the chief products. Vegetables, possibly also fruit and flowers were cultivated. Rice was reckoned as the staple article of food. Agriculture was a common occupation for even we see the Brahmin figuring as a goatherd and both as a small and large landholder without losing his caste. The love of the ancient Hindu and for that matter of the modem for agriculture transcends that of the ancient Greek and is just manifested in the worship of the cow.

The origin of cow worship is as much economic as that Roman practice of not offering wine to the Gods from unpruned vines. The cow and for that matter all draft animals, is the soul of the farmers. The cow gives birth to oxen, which are absolutely necessary to the cultivation of the farm. If we kill the cow for meat, we jeopardize our agricultural prosperity. With full foresight, the ancient Hindus tabooed cow-flesh and thus prevented cow killing. But man hardly pays any attention to dry rulings. It must have religious sanction; hence the grotesque mythology around the cow in old Hindu religious literatures.

Organisation of Labour, Industry and Commerce

Hindus are credited to the fact that slavery paid a very little role in their economic life. Individuals become slaves for four principal causes namely, capture, judicial punishment, voluntary self-degradation and debt. But there is considerable evidence to show that kind treatment was the rule and manumission was always possible. Besides few slaves there was a considerable amount of free labour paid in money or food. From among the industrial classes, the following are mentioned:

(a) The *vaddhaki* is a genuine term and is an embodiment of a carpenter, ship-builder, cart-maker and an architect.

(b) The *Kammara* is a generic term for a metal craftsman producing "iron implement, from a ploughshare or an axe or for that matter, an iron house, down to a razor, or the finest of needles, capable of floating in water, or again, statues of gold or silver work."

(c) The *Pasanakottaka* is a generic term for a mason "not only quarrying and shaping stones, but as capable of hallowing a cavity in a crystal, a matter probably of requiring superior tools."

A considerable degree of Organisation characterized all the trading industries. Certain trades were localized in special villages, both suburban and ancillary to the large cities, or themselves forming centres of traffic with surrounding villages, *e.g.* the wood-work and metal work industries and pottery, within the cities trades appear to have been localized in special streets, *e.g.* those of ivory workers and of dyers. The trades were well regulated and were superintended by one or two headmen, who were the chiefs or syndics of municipal and industrial Organisation of the cities. There were numerous guilds *(Seniyo)* under the headship of a President *(Pramukha)* or elder or older man *(Jeistha)*. Carpenters, smiths, leather workers, painters, and experts in various arts had their grids. Even the seamen garland-makers and caravan traders had their own. There was a tendency towards hereditary occupation. But the caste system in all its hideous rigorousness was not present and even Brahmins were often occupied in low professions. It is true that such a system created well organized professionals in various fields. It brought out the best from a person. The father taught his son the skill he perfected in his lifetime through experience. The transfer of skill from father to son went on for generations. It resulted in production of finer and perfect materials that were unique in whole of the world. But this situation gave rise to one of the ugliest and bizarre systems called as caste system. This tore apart the social fabric in its entirety and the country has not been able to wriggle out of such a system even now and still paying for the foolish system that was introduced centuries before.

There was little riverine traffic. It was mostly conducted by the caravans, though there was mention in many old mythological texts that such kind of traffic was prevalent in Dwarka kingdom when Lord Krishna shifted his place of residence from Mathura to Dwarka. The old scripts also extensively mention that Lord Krishna widely traveled in ships, killed a rover known as Panchjanya, and released the son of his teacher, Sandipani from the clutches of another demon in an island. It is also told that the conch that Lord Krishna was using belonged to Panchajanya, the rover, who was killed by Him. These go to show that there might have been some kind of riverine traffic prevalent in those old and ancient times though no clear historical evidence is available to that effect. The industrial centers were connected by good roads, which greatly facilitated traffic. The Ramayana refers to a road starting out from Ayodhya, the capital of King Dasharatha, known presently as Oudh to Rajagriha, the capital of Kekayas, in the vicinity of the Himalayan mountains situated on the River Bias, the ancient Vipasa known to the Greeks as the Hypasis passed through Hastinapur, the capital of the Kurus. Alexander's information regarding the roads in ancient India was perhaps the most accurate and the greatest source for the surveyors to measure the Indian Roads. This source also reveals that a road ran from Penkelaotis (Pushkalavati) near the modern Attock passed on through Takshila to Patalipurta (Patna) after crossing the river Bias. Another road joined Pushkalavathi and Indra-prastha (Delhi) and, after connecting Ujjayini (Ujjain), descended down the Vindhya range, went into the Deccan through Pratisthana after crossing the rivers Narmada and the Tapti. There were the internal highways of traffic and cavalcade of the Caravans carried it on. Early in India the external and internal commerce had assumed such importance that one finds mention in the Buddha Jataka a league of caravan leaders. The caravan leader or Sattravaha in Pali headed the caravan on its journey and was looked to "for directions as to halts, watering, precautions against robbers, and in many cases as to routes, fords, etc." The journey of the Caravan was mostly by night.

Trade in early India was not entirely individualistic. There is enough evidence to show that the corporate commercial activity and partnerships in Trade were occasional. There was very little government control of business and that too only so far as it concerned the Royal purchases. The prices of articles of Royal purchases were fixed by a Royal valuer who would "also assess the merchants for the duty of a twentieth, presumably *ad valorem,* on each consignment of native merchandise, and of a tenth *ad valorem* plus a sample, on each consignment imported from overseas. Finally, he would have to assess merchants for their specific commutation of the " rajaksaya " viz. one article per month sold to the king at a certain discount."

Later on however prices came to be fixed, for Manu says that the king on every 5th or 9th day fixed the rates for the purchase and sale of marketable commodities.

The introduction of money in India, whether it was borrowed or invented at home, has been shrouded in conjecture, but whatever may be said on this, it is true that the use of money in India was known very early. The whole of the Buddhist literature testifies to the fact that the ancient systems of simple barter as well as of reckoning value of cows, or rice measures had for the most part been replaced by the use of metal currency, carrying well understood and generally accepted exchange value. Currency counted of coins but was not regulated by Royal authority. There was gold coinage for the most part and all marketable commodities and services had a value expressible in terms of cash. Banking was not very highly developed. There was no taboo on loaning of money and according to Gautama, interest was sought in six different ways.

With such high type of economic development, it is but natural that there should be commercial expansion of colonization by the Early Hindus. Isolation of India had been a trump card with them and they used it as often as they could. Environmental conditions did delimit the activity of peoples, but it would be foolish to say with Hirder "that history is geography set in motion." One might hold to the truth in the statement that geographic conditions have condemned India to her lot and yet condemn the hyperbole in it.

One may agree, if he likes with Montesquieu when he ascribes the "fixity" of oriental manners, customs and religion to its warm climate. One would believe in buckle when he holds nature's overpowering mountains and forests in all their stupefying greatness as are to be found in India responsible for the abnormal workings of imagination and superstition or one may follow the scientific geographer when he asserts that India has been condemned to isolation on account of her geographic location, isolated from China by the Himalayas mountains and from Persia and Afghanistan by the Hindu Kush mountains. She has a long waterfront, but the eastern and the Western Ghats that fringes the coast from within and cut off the call of the ever-beckoning sea to maritime activity.

All these allegations, perhaps, have a modicum of truth in them, but it would be a mistake to make strong arguments out of them. Barriers, no matter how strong, are never insuperable to man. He has tried everywhere to control them and has succeeded in his effort.

Hemmed in from all sides, the early Indians burst asunder all impediments, natural or otherwise, and launched into the Indian Ocean at a very early date. The Indian Ocean has much in common with the Mediterranean. Zimnurn argues, "land locked on all sides, the Mediterranean seems in summer as gentle as an inland lake. It is in fact double-natured a lake when the Gods are kind and the ocean when they are spiteful." The Indian Ocean, which is, but the enlarged Mediterranean Sea with its southern coast removed is neither an ocean nor a lake but is only half an ocean. The enclosed character of its northern part deprives it of the hydrospheric and atmospheric peculiarities of a true ocean and the winds and currents ran over it in an unorganised way owing to being in close proximity of lands. The Northeast and Southeast monsoons soon enabled the merchants to drag forth in the mid-ocean instead of hugging to the coast. From the dawn of history, the Northern Indian Ocean was a thoroughfare. Alexander the Great's rediscovery of the old sea route to the orient sounds like a modern event in relation to the grey ages behind it. Along these thoroughfare Indian colonists, traders and priests carried the elements of Indian civilisation to the easternmost Sunda isles, and oriental wares, sciences and religions moved westward to the margin of Europe and Africa. The Indian Ocean produced a civilisation of its own, with which it coloured a vast semi-circle of land reaching from Java to Abyssinia, and more faintly, owing to the wider divergence of race, the further stretch from Abyssinia to Mozambique. The Hindus became the dominant commercial nation of the Indian Ocean long before the great development of Arabian Sea power, and later shared the trade of the East African coast with the merchants of Oman and Yemen. Today they form a considerable mercantile class in the ports of Muscat, Aden, Zanzibar, Pemba and Natal.

With this preliminary disquisition about the natural resources and the economic development of India, it would be better if her commercial intercourse were traced from very early times with other countries of ancient civilization.

To begin with Egypt, at the outset, it would be better to premise that the evidence of a commercial intercourse between India and other countries at the dim dawn of history is very flimsy and is embedded in tradition or in articles excavated from early ruins. The evidence, however, ripens into positiveness with the advance of time. Situated in the most rarely endowed location in the world, the Egyptians were economically independent of the rest of the people, and it is even said that they prided economic self-sufficiency to such an extent that they tabooed foreign intercourse; but this is carrying things too far and though we have no positive records to disprove the statement, the foreign articles found in the process of excavation form a strong proof against it.

It is a matter of great controversy whether or not the Egyptians had direct trade with India. Hypercriticism has ranged on both sides. Herodotus says that Sesostris, whom the Gardiner Wilkinson identifies with Ramses II, fleeted out a strong fleet and sailed beyond the straits into the Indian Ocean conquering all the coastal countries while his land forces carried their sword as far as the Ganges.

Long before the exodus of the Israelites from Egypt, India had commercial intercourse with her and the port of Philoteras was the emporium of that early trade. Whether they (the Egyptians) had a direct communication with India at the same early epoch, or they received supplies through Arabia with the merchandise of that country, it is not possible now to determine. But even indirect trade had potential of opening to them a source of immense wealth. However, there have been positive testimony from the tombs of Thebes, at the early period of Joseph's arrival that the productions of India did actually reach Egypt. This is evident from: (1) that the spices which the Ishmaclities were carrying to sell there; (2) the amethysts, hacmatile, lapis'lazuti, and other objects found at Thebes at the time of the Third Thothmus; and (3) succeeding pharaohs argue that the intercourse was constantly kept up.

Maritime Trade and Commerce in the coastal states of India

India has a long coastline and it is difficult to believe that the coastal states did not have any trade and commerce with neighbouring countries. It is incontrovertible that it had a long history of trade and commerce. Prominent among them is Orissa which had the distinction of having maritime commerce with other counties. Orissa, famous as Kalinga in ancient times, has a long maritime history and tradition which had developed owing to its close association with the sea, stretching to a length of more than 500 kilometers on its Eastern front, beginning from river Ganges in the North to Godavari in the South. It is said that it had close maritime trade and commerce with the countries namely; Java, Sumatra, and Borneo. The glorious tradition is intimately linked with some of its religious practices and national festivals. Although Orissa lost its maritime trade activities during the British period, the Oriyas today remember their ancient tradition of the maritime activities by observing "Boita Vandana Utsava" a national festival of Oriyas that reminds it of its glorious past and unfolds a brilliant chapter of Orissan history. This festival is being celebrated throughout Orissa with great pomp and devotion in the early hours of the full moon day of Kartika.

The maritime activities of the people of ancient Orissa (Kalinga) starting from the ports at Kalingapattanam, Palur, Chitrotpala, Dhamra, and Tamralipta, down to far off eastern lands of Simhala, Java, Sumatra, Bali, Borneo, Shyern, Indochina, Brahmadesh (Burma) for trade and colonization, are vividly described by eminent scholars like Dr. R. C. Mazumdar, R. D. Banerjee and Radha Kumuda Mukherjee. The story of the pilgrimage of Dantakumar and Hemamala from Dantapur in Kalinga to island of Sinhala; the description of the sea-voyages from the ports of Tamralipta and Chelitalo to Simhala, China and other places as given by the famous Chinese pilgrim Huen-stang, in 645 A.D. and ceremonial taking off the original manuscript of "Gandavyuha" by the celebrated Buddhist scholar Prajna from the King of Odra to the Chinese Emperor on a sea-voyage in 794 A. D. bear ample testimony to the maritime activities of the people of Kalinga in the days of yore.

These historic facts are further corroborated with the numerous stone carvings depicting shipping activities seen today in the facades of Konark, Bhubaneswar and Jagannath temples and literary evidences in this country. The traces of Kalinga architecture in the monuments of Far East speaks the influence wielded by our ancient heritage.

The Buddhist literature Seuki, Dathadhatuvamsa and Lalitavistara record the existence of a number of ports in ancient Orissa. Ptolemy has also given a very interesting description of Orissan ports. Arthasastra of Kautilya renders a very bright description of shipping activities and administrative layout of the department of trade and commerce during his time. He had mentioned that the voyage in the high sea should take place from Asadha (June) to Kartika (October). Somadeva's Kathasarita Sagara and Acharya Dandi's "Dasakumara Charita" also record the ancient sea-voyages from the port of Tamralipta.

There was a time when the present Bay of Bengal was known as "Kalinga Udadhi" or Sea of Kalinga due to predominance of the Oriya sailors and navigators over this part of the Indian Ocean as is described by late P. C. Rath in his learned paper published in the Journal of Kalinga Historical Research Society (Vol. 1/4). In spite of repeated attacks of the Arabian sailors, which started from the 8th Century A.D., and keen competition from the Portuguese, Dutch, English and French sailors on the high seas, the sailors of Orissa, although gave up sea-voyages, yet, practically monopolized the coastal navigation till the beginning of last century. An interesting account of such navigation is found in the sea-voyage of Vidyarnava and Lilavati from Varuna Pattanam (modern Baruan in Andhra Pradesh) to Purusottama Kshetra, Puri is described in the historical kavya Gangavamsanucharita Champu written by Vasudeva Rath Somayaji in 1762 A. D.

The author describes the sea-voyage of Vidyarnava and Lilavati on a pilgrimage to Puri to witness the famous Car Festival enroute the river Mahendratanaya at Varuna Pattanam and Chilka Lake. Vidyarnava consoles his frightened wife Lilavati bringing a reference to the bravery of the Oriya sailors on sea, who in large numbers cross the high tides for trade and commerce. After spring festival of Lord Jagannath, Vidyarnava and Lilavati took their return journey through sea-route to Vijayanagaram via Khallikote, Vikrampur, Athagarh, Kodala, Langalaveni, Raghunath Sagara, Pittala on the bank of the river Rusikulya, Paralakhimundi, Ghodahad, etc. Vidyarnava describes Chilika Lake as "a sea of thousand boats". Another interesting account is derived from Vidyarnava's words to his wife infusing into her courage and detesting her from the fear of wild sea beings. The copper plate grant of Maharajadhiraj Gopashandra of 5th Century A. D. contains beautiful description on sea wherein the sea has been conceived as the form of God and placed at a high venerable position. Besides these Sanskrit works, description of sea voyages are also found in the works of celebrated Oriya poets, Narasingha Sena (1530 A. D.), Dinakrushna Das (1650 A. D.), and Kavi Samrat Upendrabhanja (1685 A. D.). Their works, namely, "Parimala", "Prastava Sindhu", "Rasa Kalolla", and "Lavanyabati", abound with innumerable references which are reminiscent of the maritime activities of Orissa till to the pre-British period.

The Story of Ta-a-Poi

The story of adventures on the sea as narrated in popular poem "Ta-Poi" of the 18th Century A. D. is briefly narrated here to have an idea about sea-voyage in Orissa. The story runs like as follows:

> "The Brahmin widow tried a foul play with the innocent girl Ta-Poi by instigating her to demand for a golden moon and silver basket for her plaything instead of ordinary bamboo one. The parent no doubt acceded to the request of their darling daughter Ta-Poi but could not fulfill her wish due to pre demise.
>
> The brothers however took up the vow, but the real task of looking after the girl fell on their wives when they left for sea. The Brahmin widow again appear on the scene, poisons the minds of the wives of the brothers who tortured Ta-Poi instead of looking to her comfort. Ta-Poi moved in the woods uncared for looking after the goats.
>
> Misery mounts when a goat missed in the forest. Ta-Poi unable to find out the lost is severely beaten. Ta-Poi is accused of killing the goats by her evil sister-in-laws, and punished. The brothers on return after the trade came to know of the sad plight of their dear sister and punished their wives".

Notwithstanding the authenticity of this folk story, one can be reminded of the sea-trade of Orissa.

The rivers of ancient Orissa namely, Rupanarayan, Kapisha, Suvarnarekha , Vaitarani, Brahmani, Mahanadi, Prachi, Rushikulya, Vansadhara and Nagavali bore the route for inland navigation between the western hilly tract and the eastern seashore. On their banks many towns flourished as centers of trade and commerce. Sambalpur, Sonepur, Bhudo, Kantilo and Cuttack on the bank of Mahanadi, Kakatpur on the Prachi river and Chelitalo on the Chandrabhaga in Konark, Varakote, Bhimanagari, Jenapur and Dhamra on the Brahmani river; Anandapur and Jajpur on the bank of river Vaitarani; Jaleswar and Pipili on the river Suvarnarekha and Palur on the river Rusikulya, and Kalinganagaz on the bank of Vansadhara are silent witness of the glorious past.

Effect of culture in the wake of commerce

Commerce and culture have always been both sides of the same coin. Whenever there have been an upward swing in the relationship between the countries, especially in trade and commerce, it has been the culture that has got the boost. This is truer of ancient times than of the modern. The caravans of the olden times were not only the carriers of wares but also of civilization. Commerce and culture were going side by side. They disseminated and universalised it. This commercial intercourse with India greatly affected the architectures of Egypt so much so that "James Fergusson *(History of Architecture,* 7,142-3) notes about the Axons "the idea Egyptian, but the details Indian. An Indian nine-storied pagoda, translated in Egyptian in the first century of the Christian era!" He notes its likeness to such Indian temples as Bodh-Gaya, and says, it represents "that curious marriage of Indian with Egyptian art which we would expect to find in the spot where the two people came in contact, and enlisted architecture to symbolize their commercial union." It was not only the culture but also the sculpture, scientific knowledge, language, life style, rather the civilisation which followed suit.

It would be worth while to note here the relation of the Dravidians, the earliest inhabitants of India, though by no means aborigines, with the people of western Asia. As Gustavopert says, "It is established now, beyond any doubt, through the decipherment of the Cuneiform inscription that the Turanian Empires had advanced to a high degree of culture. This civilization, though tainted with strange materialism, proved it nevertheless that they were able to develop to a high degree of perfection certain branches of arts and science. To these Turanians, who differed much among each other in idiom belong also to the Dravidians of India of our days, who in those times occupied Ariana and Persia. In Europe, these Turanians appear to be represented by the Esthonians, and in many places of western and central Asia, they formed the substratum of the population, while they supplied in China the ground work of the civilization of the Celestial Empire." These Turanians "had founded empires throughout the old world. The home of the Turanians is assumed to have been the country round Lake Aral. Thence they spread over the greatest part of Asia, reined there paramount for at least 1500 years. "The Egyptians, the Assyrians the Acadians, the Sumerians, the Phoenicians are all branches of the same Turanian race." About 250 years after the Egyptian empire had been established, i. e. 2500 B. C., and after the Akkadian dynasty had reigned for a long period in Babylon, the Aryans invaded Chaldea, and pressing at the same time on the Kannanites of the Persian Gulf and the Dravidians in Persia, drove the former towards the North-west and the latter to the South-east to India. The Aryans when they invaded Indiá, met with a stubborn resistance from these Dravidians due to which they did not go beyond the frontiers of the Punjab till the fifteenth century before Christ. Next in importance and chronology comes the intercourse between India the kingdom of India. In spite of the evidences to be found in the Bible, writers have been very little disposed to credit it for historical purpose. The evidence is too strong to be slighted. Suited in the mainland, Judea was not in a position to develop a direct trade with India. She had no waterfront at all and consequently no harbours. She had entirely to depend upon the Egyptians and the Syrians who controlled the sea and the trade routes of India. The galleys of India brought their goods to Yemen or Arabia Felix. Yemen was the great mart for Indian goods, it was a distributing centre and from it the Egyptian Vessels took Indian commodities to Syria by the caravan or to Egypt. "From the very earliest ages, the refined civilization of Egypt and Syria sought with avidity the spices, the aromatics, the metals, the precious and scented woods, the gems, the ivory in a kind, all the valuable merchandise which the rich soil of India supplied in abundance." King Solomon, however, when he came to the throne, tried to get the control of Indian trade. He saw that the Egyptian power was on its decline and realized that importance of utilizing Idumacans sea port on the Red Sea, which he had inherited as the conquest of his father, for materialising his plans of direct trade relations with India. But since the Jews had not been experienced in the art of navigation, he had to seek the cooperation of Hirain, the king of the Phoenicians. The Phoenicians were the pioneers in navigation. Whether they dealt directly with India is a subject of great controversy. However, Robertson is favourably inclined towards this theory. After showing how the poverty of the land compelled the Phoenicians to subsist by commerce, he goes on to say, " among the various branches of their commerce, that with India may be regarded as one of the most considerable and most lucrative as by their situation on the Mediterranean, and the imperfect state of navigation, they could not attempt to open a direct communication with India by sea. The enterprising spirit of commerce prompted them to wrest from the Idumacans some commodious harbours towards the bottom of the Arabian Gulf. From there, they held a regular intercourse with India on the one hand, and with the eastern and southern coasts of Africa on the other. The distance, however, from the Arabian Gulf to Zyre, was considerable, and rendered the conveyance of goods to it by land carriages so heavy and expensive that it became necessary for them to take possession of Phinocolura, the nearest port in the Mediterrancan to the Arabian Gulf, thither all the commodities brought from India were conveyed overland by a route much shorter, and more practicable, than that by which the productions of the East were carried at a subsequent period from the opposite shore of the Arabian Gulf to the Nile. At Rhinocolura they were re-shipped, and transported by an easy navigation to Tyre, and distributed throughout the world. This, as it is the earliest route of communication with India of which no one has any authentic description, had so many advantages over any ever known, before the modern discovery of a new course of navigation to the east, that the Phoenicians could apply to other nations with the productions of India in greater abundance and at a cheaper rate, than any people of antiquity". Another evidence supporting the view of Robertson was found to be in the fact, that the Phoenicians introduced their letters in India a direct proof of their intercourse. King Solomon, stimulated or otherwise by the neighbouring Phoenicians, joined hands with Hiram, king of Tyre and built a fleet at Elath and Eziongeher. Manned by Phoenician sailors, it sailed to Qphir and brought back many treasures, which two kings shared between themselves. The location of Qphir is another unsettled topic. But for all practical purposes Prof. Lassen had closed the controversy by identifying it with Abhira in the province of Gujarat in India. With the interval of three years, the voyage was repeated and the ships laden with all precious articles to enrich the country so much so that "the king made silver to be in Jerusalem as stones, and cedars made her to be as Sycamore trees that are in the vale for abundance". Thus all the advantages of trade were secured for the people with exposing to the dangers attendant upon it. Consequently in the words of Dean Stanley (Senai and Palestine, p. 261), "to describe the capital as a place where shall go no galley with oars, neither shall gallant ship pass by" (Isaiah XXXIII 21) is not, as according to western notions it would be, an expression of weakness and danger, but of prosperity and security."

The trade between India and Judea does not date with Solomon, it enjoys considerable antiquity; mentions of Qphir are to be found long before the time of Solomon in the I Chronicles XXIX, 4, I kings XXII 48, and in Isaiah, XIII 12). These Biblical evidences may be supplemented by linguistic evidences, such as the Hebrew word *tuki*, which is, but a little changed form of the poetical word Tokei, i e. the Tamil-Malayalam language for peacock or the Hebrew word *Ahalim* or *Aholoth*, a corruption of the Tamil-Malayalam word, *Aghil.*

The rise of Babylon marks the high watermark in the ancient commercial activity of India. Situated at the confluence of the Euphrates and the Tigris, joining the Persian Gulf with the Mediterranean and being a meeting place of upper and lower Asia, Babylon was destined to be the great emporium of the eastern and western trade. It was the meeting place of routes from all parts of the ancient world. "There's ample evidence," says Kennedy, that "warrants us in the belief that maritime commerce between India and Babylon flourished in the seventh and sixth, more especially in the sixth century B. C. It was chiefly in the hands of the Dravidians, although Aryans also had a share in it, and as Indian traders settled afterwards in Arabia and on the eastern coast of Africa, and as we find them settling at this very time on the coast of China, we cannot doubt that they had their settlements in Babylon also. But the sixth and seventh centuries are the culminating period of Babylonian greatness. Babylon, which had been destroyed by Senkacherib was rebuilt by Esarhaddon. Babylon, which had fused her importance and her fame to the sanctity of her temples' flow, appears before us all of a sudden as the greatest commercial mart of the world. There was no limit to her power. She arose and utterly overthrew her ancient rival and oppressor Nineveh. With Nebuchadnezzar, she became the wonder of the world. But the secret of her greatness lay in her monopoly of the treasures of the east, in the shouting of the Chaldeans in their ships and smart orientals who frequented her bazars. It moved the envy of the nations. Pharaoh Necho (612-596 B.C.) vainly sacrificed his subjects in order to reopen the canal, which was made from the Nile to the Red Sea: and dispatched Phoenician fleet round Africa in the hope of discovering a new world for commerce. Since long, the rivalry of the Spaniards and the Portuguese for the treasures of India was anticipated which was equalled by rivalry of Babylonians and Egyptians when the world as yet was one and twenty centuries younger." This commercial intercourse told very decidedly on the literature of India. Sea played an immense role and *'Mokar'* the monster fish was constantly alluded to. The Vedic deities fell in the back ground and the Hindu mind of the times soared high in inventing fantastic cosmogonies as is to be found in the *Vishnu Purana*, where it is said that "the Supreme Being placed the Earth on the summit of the ocean, where it floats like a mighty vessel and from its expansive surface does not sink beneath the waters". The entire literature smacks of commercialism and is essentially different in nature from the early Vedic literature so much so that Prof. Max Muller in his *History of Ancient Sanskrit Literature* says, " there is throughout the Brahmans, such a complete misunderstanding of the original intention of the Vedic hymns that we can hardly understand how such an estrangement could have taken place unless there had been at some time or other a sudden and violent break in the chain of tradition". This "estrangement can be accounted by foreign influence which follows the footsteps of commerce". The focus of this foreign influence upon India was, therefore, in the sixth, seventh and eighth centuries and certainly not later than the time of Buddha, for this great teacher found all India believing in metempsychosis, (rebirth) which is not a Vedic doctrine and must, therefore be an exotic one. Buddha in the *Kevaddhu Sutta* of the *Digha* (fifth century B.C.), says by way of simile "Long ago ocean going merchants were wont to plunge forth upon the sea, on board a ship, taking with them a shore sighting bird. When the ship was out of sight of land, they would set the shore sighting bird free. And it would go to the east and to the south and to the west and to the north, and to the intermediate points, and rise aloft. If, on the horizon, it caught sight of land, thither it would go back to the ship again." Rhys Davids comments that "such a Semitic would scarcely be made use of in inordinacy talk, unless the habit referred to were of some standing and matter of general knowledge".

The decline of Babylon, however, was as sudden as her rise and dates from the reign of king Darius (579-484 B. C.). From the fifth century on, one no longer could find the commercial tablets that were so numerous in earlier times. The Persian conquest not only destroyed Babylon but also extended to Egypt. The canals built for riverine traffic decayed and dams impeded the flow of the rivers as a result the Arabs became the claviers of trade and Yemen interests the splendour of Babylon and Palmyrs. The Chaldeans (astrologers) also, in spite of the sweeping expeditions of Darius, continued their trade by establishing their colonies at Gerrha and other places.

The conquests of Darius brought under his rule a vast Empire, which became contiguous to that of the empire of Alexander. It was quite impossible for the two emperors, full of earth hunger, to remain as good neighbours, friction was bound to arise and Alexander, waiting for an opportunity, set out on his career of conquest. In one sweep, he destroyed the empire of Darius and extended his dominion over Egypt, Central Asia and the northern parts of India. The motives of Alexander's gigantic expedition are a matter of conjecture. Vindication for humiliation suffered at the hands of Darius has been put forth as one of them. Prof. Lassen, however, radically enough, ventures to say that greed of gold was the object of Alexander's expedition and that it was whetted by the presence of Indian goods in Greece. The commercial intercourse with Greece, as with Judea, had left its impression upon the language of the two trading people. "Thus the Greek name for rice *(oryza)*, ginger *(zingiber)*, and cinnamon *(karpion)* have a close correspondence with their Tamil equivalents, viz., *arisi*, *inchiver*, and *karava* respectively; and this identity of Greek with Tamil words clearly indicates that those were Greek merchants who conveyed these articles and their names to Europe from Tamil land. Again, the name *Yavan*, the name by which these Western merchants were known, which in old Sanskrit poetry is invariably used to denote the Greeks, is derived from the Greek word *Jaonis*, the name of the Greeks in their own language." Other words that may be added to this group of words, having a common origin, are the parallel words for ivory or elephant in Greek as "*Elephas*" and in Egyptian as "*Ebu*" and "*Ebha*" in Sanskrit, which, in the opinion of Prof. Lassen, indicate a common Sanskrit origin.

Whatever may have been the motives of Alexander, it is quite certain that, having known India intimately, he did conceive the idea of bringing the two countries in close commercial relation. Alexander found that the Phoenicians of Zyre, who to the rest of the world supplied Indian commodities, monopolized this rich trade of India. His envy of the Phoenicians was considerably heightened by his personal knowledge of the prosperity of India, the country he had hitherto not visited, which was so populous and well cultivated, or abounded in so many valuable productions of nature and of art, as that part of India through which he had let his army in. But when he was informed in every place, probably with exaggerated description, as to how much India was interior to the Ganges, and how far all that he had hitherto beheld, was surpassed in the happy regions through which that great river flows, it was not strange that his eagerness to view and to take possession of them should have prompted him to assemble his soldiers, and to propose that they should resume their march towards that quarter where wealth, dominion, and fame awaited them. The northern part of India, which Alexander subdued, was given over by him to Porus, his ally and is, said to have contained "no fewer than four thousand towns". "Even in the most restricted sense" comments Robertson, "that can be given to the vague indefinite appellations of nations and towns, an idea is conveyed of a very great degree of population. As the fleet (of Alexander) sailed down the river (Indus), the country on each side was found to be in no respect inferior to that of which the government was committed to Porus."

The memoirs or journals of his generals Ptolemy, Aristobulus, and Nearchus opened the knowledge of India to Greece and to Europe. Having conquered Egypt, Alexander thought of opening a direct trade between India and Greece. With this object in view, he founded the city of Alexandria after his own name, which became the greatest emporium of trade in ancient times and continued to be so in spite of many vicissitudes. He cherished many a dreams of permanently joining India to his empire and some of it, not all of them, would have been realized had he lived longer. Unfortunately he died soon after he established his empire, which within a short time crumbled to pieces. The governors of the different provinces parceled out among themselves the whole empire.

Goaded by ambition, emulation and personal curiosity / animosity they fought among themselves for supremacy. It would be erroneous to suppose that the commercial relation between India and Greece ceased because of the fall of Alexander's empire. On the contrary, the relations became closer. Seleucus, the most enterprising and ambitious general of Alexander, after seizing for himself the Persian Empire, sought to join to his dominion the provinces of India conquered by Alexander. Seleucus was alive to the commercial gains to be derived by such a conquest and was determined to carry out his plans by means of his vast armies. But his adversary was more than a match for him. Chandragupta (Sandracottus of the Greeks) was ruling India as a benevolent despot. Amidst all medievalism he was a modern man endowed with both brain and brawn. Seleucus realized the superior strength of his enemy and wisely concluded peace and to cultivate friendly relations between the two, he sent Magasthenes as an ambassador to the court of Chundragupta. Magasthenes was followed by Daimachus to continue the friendly relations. The Greeks maintained their intercourse with India through the (Graceo)-Bactrian kingdom for a long time though there have been very scanty means to judge its magnitude and charter. The Chinese historians tell "that about one hundred and twenty-six years before the Christian Era, a powerful horde of Tartars, pushed from their native seats on the confines of China, and obliged to move towards the west by the pressure of a more numerous body that rolled on behind them, passed the Taxartes, and pouring in upon Bactria, like an irresistible torrent, overwhelmed that kingdom, and put an end to the dominion of the Greeks there, after it had remained established for nearly one hundred and thirty years". Though the land communication was thus interrupted, Alexandria continued to be the emporium of sea trade between Greece and India. Ptolemy, the son of Lagus, during his governorship greatly encouraged the Indian Commerce. His son Ptolemy Philadelphus, in order to carry the articles of India directly to Alexandria, started constructing a canal joining the Red

Sea and the Nile. The project, however, was too big and was abandoned. He, however, built a city on the west coast on the Red Sea and called it Berenice and it continued to be the staple town for Indian trade.

But while the monarchs of Egypt and Syria laboured with emulation and ardour to secure all their subjects with all the advantages of the Indian trade, a power arose in the west which proved fatal to both. The Romans, by the vigour of their military institutions, and the wisdom of their political conduct, having rendered themselves masters of all Italy and Sicily, soon overturned the rival republic of Carthage during A. C. 55, subjected Macedonia and Greece, extended their dominion over Syria, and at last turned their victorious arms against Egypt, the only kingdom remaining of those established by the successor of Alexander the Great.

With the subjugation of Egypt, the lucrative commerce from India flowed into Rome, but this was not the only way. There was another trade route for the Indian commodities into the west. It was a land route and was intended by Solomon to concentrate the Indian trade in Judea. It passed the town of Tadmore or Dalmyra situated midway between the Euphrates and the Mediterranean. After the subjugation of Syria by Romans, Palmyra became independent and grew to be a populous and flourishing town. It became a distributing center. But the Roman cupidity knew no bounds. At the slightest sign of ill feeling on the part of Zenobia, the queen of Palmyra, the Romans took the city and included it within their empire.

But the inclusion of Palmyra was not enough for the Romans to monopolize the Indian trade, for another power, equally strong, was rising in the east. The Parthians had dominated central Asia and had made the boundaries of their empire contiguous with that of the Romans. The struggle between Parthia and Rome extended from 55 to 20 B. C. but the struggle for supremacy remained indecisive. The warfare between 55 and 20 B. C. had left the two empires with a wholesome respect for each other and Augustus left it as a principle of imperial policy that the west bank of the Euphrates was the proper limit for the Roman empire, beyond which the power of Rome could not with advantage be extended. The policy of the Roman Empire during the two centuries following the Christain era was to encourage direct sea trade with India, cutting out all overland routes through Parthia and thus avoiding the annoyance of fiscal dependence on that consistent enemy of Rome . Under the Pax Romana, trade between India was greatly fostered and grew tremendously in importance. Guides to the ports of the India and itinerary of land travels and caravans started to be written for the benefits of the merchants. It was during the middle of the first century A. D. that Hippolus, a Greek Egyptian, discovered the regularity of the Indian monsoon and thus facilitated the voyage of the traders. It was also about this time that a Greek merchant wrote The Periplus of the Erythrean Sea or guide to the Indian Ocean. It was the most authentic document one had for the study of the Indian commercial activity. Another Greek adventurer, Isodore of Charax travelled round the Parthian kingdom and gave a full account of the Caravan trade along the land route. Before this, it had to receive the oriental goods from the hands of the others. The Arabs concealed all information relating to India to perpetuate their monopoly and the Parthian tolls greatly augmented the "value of the Indian commodities," so that all this rich trade that flowed to Rome paid its tolls to the empire of Parthia and to the Arab kingdoms, unless Rome could develop and control a sea-borne trade to India. "But this discovery of the monsoons by Hippolus, the Columbus of modern times, fulfilled much felt want of the Romans". Great shiftings of national power followed this entry of the Roman shipping into the Indian Ocean. One by one, Petia and Gerrha, Palmyra and Parthia itself, their revenues sapped by the diversion of accustomed trade, fell into Roman hands. The Homerite kingdom in South Arabia fell upon hard times, its capital was ruined, and some to its best men northward and as the Ghassanids bowed the neck to Rome. Abyssinia flourished in proportion as its old enemy declined. If this state of things had continued, the whole course of later events might have changed. Islam might never have appeared, and a greater Rome might have left its system of law and government from the Thames to the Ganges. But the logic of history was too strong. Gradually the treasure that fell to the Roman arms was expended in suppressing insurrections in the conquered provinces, in civil wars at home, and in a constant drain of specie to the East in the settlement of adverse trade balances; a drain which was very real and menacing to a nation which made no notable advance in production or industry by means of which new wealth could be created.

Trade with Rome

As regards the Roman's trade with India there is a thesaurus of information though by no means unquestionable. The first kind of evidence is the number of emissaries sent to Rome from India and Ceylon.

The first emissaries came from Ceylon is recorded by Pliny. It is impossible to determine its exact date, but certain circumstantial evidences would warrant every one in placing it somewhere between A. D. 41 and 54. He was sent to Claudis and reached him at a time when more serious events, such as the intrigues of Agrippina and Messalina's violent death too much occupied the minds of the Roman historians to make an adequate mention of it. Chundra Muka Siwa, King of Ceylon, who ruled, sent the emissary from 44 to 52 A. D. Other emissaries soon followed. The second came to Trojan in A. D. 107, third to Antonius Pius A. D. 138, fourth to Julian A. D. 361 and the fifth to Justinian A. D. 530. The natives of India, made no mention of these emissaries. They were recorded by Roman historian and barely so, consequently, it was very difficult to infer regarding the objective of these emissaries. They, however, served to demonstrate that intercourse between India and Rome was constant and alive and continued "during the reign of Servius, his son Commodus, and the pseudo antoninus", when both Alexandria and Palmyra were occupied with commerce and were prosperous. Roman intercourse with India was at its height. Then Roman literature gave more of its attention to Indian matters and did not, as of old, confine itself to quotation from the historians of Alexander or the narratives of the Seleucusian Ambassadors, but drew its information from other independent sources.

Other evidences, mostly of a literary character, strengthen the same conclusion. Dr. Hirth in his *China and the Roman Orient* quotes Sung-Shu, a Chinese historian 500 A. D. writing about the period 420-478 A. D. saying: "As regards Ta-tsin (Syria) and Iien Chu (India) far out on the western ocean, we have to say that, although the envoys of the two Han dynasties have experienced the special difficulties of this road, and traffic in merchandise has been effected, the goods have been sent out to the foreign tribes, overcoming the force of winds, driving them far away across the waves of the sea. There are lofty ranges of mountains quite different from those we know and a great variety of populous tribes having different names and bearing uncommon designations, they being of a class quite different from our own. All the precious things of land and water come from them, as well as the gems made of rhinoceros horns and chrysoprase, serpent pearls and asbestos cloth, there being innumerable varieties of these curiosities and also the doctrine of the abstraction of mind in devotion to the Lord of the world (Buddha), all this having caused navigation and trade to be extended to these parts."

Another Chinese historian Ma-Touanlin, in his Researches into Antiquity says, "India (A. D. 500-16) carries on a considerable commerce by sea with Ta-Tsin, the Roman empire and the Ansi or Ase".

A writer of considerable acumen makes bold to say after the destruction of Palmyra, direct trade between India and Rome never existed. "The Romans", he says, "established their trading station at Adule, the chief port of Ethiopia" and "though under Constantine there was much economic prosperity, yet the Roman trading activity never extended beyond Adule ".

Archaeological discoveries and historical references however point to quite the opposite conclusion. Vincent Smith remarks: "There is good reason to believe that considerable colonies of Roman subjects engaged in trade were settled in southern India during the first two centuries of our era, and that European soldiers, described as powerful *Yavanas*, and dumb *Mlecchas* (barbarians) clad in complete armour, acted as body-guards to Tamil kings, while the large ships of the *Yavanas* lay off Muziris (Cranganore) to receive the cargoes of pepper paid for by Roman gold". Not only were there Roman trading colonies but that "Roman soldiers were enlisted in the service of the Pandas and other Tamil kings". And "during the reign of the Panda Aryappadai -Kadaretha - Nedunj - Cheliyan, Roman soldiers were employed to guard the jobs of the fort of Madura". Numismatics evidences also bear out the intimate commercial relations between India and Rome.

This intimate commercial intercourse between Rome and India is very readily accounted for by the fact that "from the time of Mark Antony to the time of Justinian, i. e. from B. C. 30 to A. D. 550, their political, importance as allies against the Parthians and Sassanians, and their commercial importance as controllers of one of the main trade routes between the east and the west, made the friendship of the Kusans or Sakas, who held the Indus Valley and Bactria, a matter of highest importance to Rome". With this short sketch of the trade relations of India with foreign countries, it would be better now to consider the articles of commerce and trade routes and the important ports of India. The *Periplus, Ptolemy's Geography* and the *Christian Topography* were the chief sources that furnish with information on the articles of commerce and the ports of India.

The *Periplus* mentions the following as articles of export:

(1) Spikenard,
(2) Cortus,
(3) Bdellium,
(4) Ivory,
(5) Qugate

(6) Lycircm,
(7) Cotton cloth of all kinds,
(8) Silk cloth,
(9) Mallow-cloth,
(10) Yarn,
(11) Long pepper,
(12) Diamonds,
(13) Sapphires,
(14) Tortoiseshell,
(15) Transparent stones of all kinds,
(16) Pearls
(17) Malabathrum
(18) Incense
(19) Indigo

Under imports it mentions:

(1) Wine
(2) Copper
(3) Tin
(4) Lead
(5) Coral
(6) Thin clothing and inferior clothes of all kinds
(7) Sweet clover
(8) Flint and crude glass
(9) Antimony
(10) Gold and silver coins accruing from the favourable balance of trade.

The *Periplus* or the marine guidebook to the Indian Ocean mentions the following trading ports of India:

(1) Barygaza or the modem Baroach, the principle trading centre of western India. It mentions two inland towns connected with Baroach, Paitlian and Tagara;
(2) Souppara-modern Supara near Bassein;
(3) Kalliean-the present Kalyan;
(4) Semulla-presumably modern Chembur;
(5) Mandagora;

(6) Palaipatami;
(7) Melizeigara;
(8) Tyndis;
(9) Muziris; and
(10) Nelkynda.

Ptolemy's Geography describes the whole seacoast from the mouths of the Indus to those of the Ganges, and mentions many towns and ports of commercial importance. These are, among others, Syrastra (Surat), Monoglosson (Mangrol) in Guzerat, Ariake (Maharashtra), Soupara, Muziris, Bakarei, Maisoli (Masli-patnam), Kounagara (Konarak), and other places.

Certain of the Tamil poets have beautifully described some of the commercial ports and towns in southern India. One of them says, "The thriving town of Muchiri, where the beautiful large ships of the *Yavans*, bringing gold, come splashing the white foam on the waters of the Periplus which belongs to the Cherala, and return laden with pepper." "Fish is bartered for paddy, which is brought in baskets to the houses," says another. "Sacks of pepper are brought from the houses to the market, the gold received from ships, in exchange for articles sold, is brought to shore in barges at Muchiri, where the music of the surging sea never ceases, and where Kudduvan (the Chera king) presents to visitors the rare products of the seas and mountains." The description given of Kaviripaddinam (the Kamara of the Periplus and Khaberis of Ptolemy) or Pukar is equally important and inspiring. It was built on the northern bank of the Kaveri river, then a broad and deep stream in which heavily laden ships entered from the sea without slacking sail. The town was divided into two parts, one of which, Maruvar-Pakkarn, adjoined the seacoast. Near the beach in Maruvar-Pakkarn were raised platforms and godowns and warehouses where the foods landed from ships were stored. Here, the goods were stamped with the Tiger stamps (the emblem of the Chola kings) after payment of customs duty, and passed on to merchants' warehouses. Close by were the settlements of the *Yavana* (foreign) merchants, where many articles were always exposed for sale. Here were also the headquarters of the foreign traders, who had come from beyond the seas and who spoke various tongues. Vendors of fragrant pastes and powders, of flowers and incense, tailors who worked on silk, wool, or cotton, traders in sandal, aghil, coral, pearl, gold, and precious stones, grain merchants, washer men, dealers in fish baits, butchers, blacksmiths, braziers, carpenters, coppersmiths, painters, sculptors, goldsmiths, cobblers, and toy-makers all had their habitation in Maravar-Pakkam."

The trade routes from India to the west may be conveniently divided under two heads, as

(1) The land routes and

(2) The marine route.

It is truly said that individual migration is a habit of civilized man. Ancient folks, because of their strong gregarious instinct or because of want of security, always moved in bands. This habit of theirs is well depicted in their methods of trade. Compelled to be peddlers, fear of competition was never too strong to break the trading. Caravan which moved from place to place with their loaded animals under conditions so unfavorable that easygoing modern man with all the keen business instinct in him, will rather quit worshipping the mammon rather than undergo the difficulties ill-compensated by gain. Speaking of the Caravan, Harbur says, "The very course of the Caravan was not a matter of free choice, but of established custom. In the vast steppes' of sandy deserts, which they had to traverse, nature had sparingly allotted to the travelers a few scattered places of rest, where, under the shade of palm trees, and beside the cool fountains at their feet, the merchant and the beast of burden might enjoy the refreshment rendered necessary by so much suffering. Such places of repose became center parts of commerce, and not infrequently the sites of temples and sanctuaries, under the protection of which the merchants prosecuted his trade, and to which the pilgrims resorted. Being subject to these conditions the Caravan route was never a straight one, it was always zigzag and when we look at maps of ancient trade we are struck with a network of small roads meeting and crossing each other at various points. However we may decipher two main trade routes from India to the Mediterranean. The northern most followed the river Oxus and encircling the northern basin of the Caspian Sea converged on the Black Sea and thence to Constantinople. The middle one rather followed a straight path, with many bifurcations, which meet at market. It starts on along the southern basin of the Caspian Sea through, Tebriz, Erzewm Trebizond and through the Black Sea to Constantinople. These were the two main land trade routes between the India and the west."

"There were also two marine routes though one of them was only halfway marine. Of these one was the Red Sea route. Ships from Indian ports crossed the Indian ocean either to southern Africa or sailed upwards, and touched at the ports of southern Arabia and Aden and through the *St. of Babel-mandeb* (the gate of Tears) ploughed the waters of the Red Sea, touching at Jedda on the Arabian coast and Bernice on the Egyption coast. From Bernice, Caravan took goods to Thebes and Kos where they were gained through the Nile to Alexandria and from thence to Europe. The other marine route lay through the Persian Gulf. Ships sailed from Baroach and kept bugging close to the land and touched at Masket and at Ormuz through the Gulf of Oman to Bassora. From Bassora at the mouth of the Persian Gulf, the goods were taken by the Caravan along the shores of the Euphrates and Tygris through Babylonia to Antioch on the mediterranean."

These two marine trade routes continued up to the present title, but the story of the land trade routes is entirely different. The closure of the routes changed the course of the destiny of the countries that were closely interlinked with trade, commerce, and culture. They were closed and remained closed forever and the history of their foreclosure is perhaps the only event in the Asiatic continent that profoundly affected the history of Europe.

2

Growth of Public Sector in India

On the consolidated background of the Mauryan age, the period under review shines as the formative phase of Indian civilization from different standpoints-social-economic- religious-cultural-educational and ethical. The different crosscurrents, often almost unperceivable, were highly active during these days, at the end of which the fluid state of culture, in the broader sense, ended up in crystallization.

It has been a travesty that as the Indian history is written, it is no more dependent on the speculations and conjectures based on literary sources only. The evidences, gathered through excavations, have attributed a scientific and more reliable character to it. Simultaneously, there are many other factors like Internet facility, huge modern libraries, etc, which have played a very significant role. It is the modern approach to history, diametrically opposite to that of the colonial, which used to set all attention on the political aspect, the rest given only a passing glance.

This changed attitude has brought in its turn a remarkable boom in the entire activities concerning the subject. The reading, teaching, research-works, and publications-everything centering around history tend to assume a mere realistic character as they seek the facts relating to the society, religion, economy, education, culture, morality and like which, are equally important component parts of a civilization, along with the political life. The process enables us to secure a bird's eye view to form a total conception of the past saga of Indian civilization and culture. The job of the historian is, however, complicated and difficult enough, since the literary evidences, often highly technical and scrappy, have to be corroborated, corrected, and supplemented by the archaeological data, whenever the latter are found. Fortunately, we are in a somewhat better position than our predecessors, the precursors of ideology, who had to build the total foundation through enormous toil on their own. Now, there is an attempt at analysing the information related to trade and the traders of Northern India, including the Western and Eastern parts of the country.

There was no political activity within the five centuries (circa 200 B.C. to 320 A.D.) in between the decline and dismemberment of the Mauryan Empire and the rise of the Gupta Dynasty. They witnessed the downfall of the successors of Ashoka, the rise of petty principalities of local rulers and the tribal chiefs, and the intrusion of foreign hordes the Bactrian Greeks, the Sakas, the Pahlavas, and the Kushanas through the Northwestern passes in a continuous process.

Gradually, the foreigners occupied certain territories, demanded allegiance of the local people, introduced some new elements in the indigenous life-style and eventually got merged in the mainstream of the society. The same days witnessed strong waves of heterodox religions, particularly Buddhism and Jainism, sweeping over the plains of Northern India, creating considerable upheavals in the country.

The Mauryan rule, in the preceding age, had bequeathed certain positive gifts to its subjects that were of great significance. It brought an extensive territory under a single political authority, established a well-knit and uniform system of administration throughout the empire, and furnished another bond of unity, the use of Prakrit language all over the area governed.

Compared to the strong, stable and secure life under the Mauryan rule, this period may apparently seem to be lacking in remarkable political events, and consequently, in interest. But these five centuries are full of historical value, as they have left documents in literature as well as other objects that are replete with facts, both interesting and important. On the consolidated background of the Mauryan age, the period under review shines as the formative phase of Indian civilization from different standpoints social-economic-religious-cultural-educational and ethical. The different crosscurrents, often almost unperceivable, were highly active during these days, at the end of which the fluid state of culture, in the broader sense, ended up in crystallization. The process eventually reached its culmination in many respects during the following age, ruled by the imperial Guptas.

Beginning with a brief sketch of the economic backdrop of the period under consideration, the most significant information appears to be that state control over land introduced in Kautilyan days, was withdrawn in the age of Manu (the author of *Manu-samhita,* the law book). Consequently, individual enterprise in farming found encouragement. The intensification of agriculture provided the economic base for the growth of towns and cities, especially in the Ganges valley. Big cities like Pataliputra, Sravasti, Saketa, Kausambi, Rajagrha, Varanasi, Mathura, Takshasila and Pushkalavati gradually became centers of politico-socio-eco-religious exchange of ideas. These were the nuclei of the affluent and the natural habitat of the Sethi-Gahapati (the extremely rich banker, and the merchant-householder with enormous wealth). The flexibility of a market economy was facilitated by three innovations. Those were "the use of a script, the consequent issuing of letters and pledges, and the introduction of money in the form of silver and copper punch-marked coins, issued initially, it has been suggested, by traders' guilds". Traders, making transaction in money and bankers, deriving huge wealth from usury, began to acquire considerable power and influence, though the latter practice did not find favour in the earlier Brahmanical works, which put certain restrictions upon the Brahmans in this connection.

Another remarkable factor helping the growth of cities was a rapid rise of Jainism and its prohibition on agricultural professions and restrictions on ownership of land. Thus, trade became the chief occupation of the Jainas. In the centuries immediately before and after Christ, a great impetus was received by India's overland and maritime trade particularly with the West. It must be admitted that in the preceding times Kautilya showed favourable disposition to foreign trade. Piracy was put down, trade routes secured, and the fashionable foreign trade world of Rome began to demand on an unprecedented scale of Oriental luxuries of every kind. But the point of interest lies in the fact that unlike South India, North of the Vindhya Range produced no great quantities of goods of the kind demanded by the Mediterranean market. It was particularly as a channel for trade in transit from remoter sources that North-Western India came into the present context. As for overland trade, the direct passage from Indus delta to the West would have been the so-called Silk-Route, across Iran to Syria. Astride this route, stood Parthia, who, often at war and always in rivalry with the Roman Empire, blocked the Orient trade, occasionally closing the Western part of the Silk-Route. The main lines of traffic with Alexandria, the focus of the Orient trade lay through West Pakistan and Northern India, where geographical and political factors combined to facilitate them. By the beginning of the Christian era, the Kushanas consolidated their rule, particularly in the Northwestern parts, with principal centers at Pushkalavati and Mathura, both of them being able to secure the profits of the overland trade with central Asia. The Kushana rulers even modeled their gold coinage on the weight-standard of Roman Aureus in order to consolidate the position of advantage for India in international trade and commerce.

One of the great trade routes of ancient India linking the East-West Trans was the Asian silk-Route at Balkh which turned South-Eastwards to Kabul river and India through the clefts in the Hindukush. It was the easiest highway from Central Asia to North-West India. Besides raw silk and silk yarn, silk cloth was also brought on foot from Bactria to Barygaza. The numerous valuable objects discovered in course of excavations at Taxila and Begram bear evidence of this close trade-relationship. Within the subcontinent, overland and maritime trade with the South (Dakshinapatha) was being explored. It was especially with the growth of land borne trade that the caravan-merchants or the Sarthavahas (Pali Sathavaha) came into existence and eventually occupied a pre-eminent position in society. The inland traders covered long distances, for example between Takshasila and Varanasi.

Indian shipping itself developed considerably from the early days. Some time during the middle of the second century B.C., the first Indian, a shipwrecked sailor, reached Alexandria. The subsequent expansion in trade is marked by the rules for merchandise, shipping and port dues, found in the *Code of Manu*. In the *Yuktikalpataru* of Bhoja Narapati, an interesting treatise on shipping, detailed directions for shipbuilding have been given, and ships- 176 cubits long, fitted with cabins- are referred to. It should be borne in mind that the maritime trade in the Western Indian Ocean was not restricted to luxury goods only, but was sustained by subsistence items and agricultural products. The Indian trans-oceanic voyaging was often an extended form of inland trade networks.

On the Roman part, the sea-route to India was advantageous, both politically and economically. It was free from the overland encounters with adversaries in the east, and was faster, and therefore cheaper.

The epoch making discovery of the Southwest monsoon-wind blowing regularly across the Indian Ocean took place around 45 A.D. The discoverer was a Captain named Hippalus. This event transformed the entire character of the sea borne trade between India and Rome, which has left a curious impression on the pages of the *Periplus,* the Greek merchant's handbook. An important Indian harbour mentioned by the author was the market town Barbaricum on the middle mouth of the Indus. The inland behind it was the Scythian capital Minnagara.

The next one was the ancient harbour of Barygaza (Sanskrit-Brgukachchha, modern Bharuch or Broach), the most famous of the Indian ports trading with the West, until it was eclipsed by its southern rivals after 47 A.D. The fertile coast country between Broach and the Indus has been referred to as Syrastrene, obviously Saurashtra or modern Surat. The wealthy cities of Central India maintained access to the port through the arterial valleys of the Narmada and the Tapti, and quite easy land-routes from Rajputana and Northern India helped the supply of commodities to the same. The commerce of the Western Indian coast was so lucrative that Bharuch (Barygaza) and Sopara had trade settlements or "station" in the "Gulf", the presence of foreign citizens being of course entrepreneurial in nature. It is also indicated by the fact that the merchants were able to pay the extremely high rates of interest of about 25%, as evidenced by the Vienna Papyrus of mid-second century A.D., undoubtedly by reaping enormous profits from the Indo-Roman trade.

A careful analysis of the articles of trade enables to explain the background, which facilitated the growth and affluence of the goldsmiths, merchants and perfumers, frequently mentioned as donors, particularly in Western Indian inscriptions. It showed that Indians were not averse to consumerism. South of Barygaza, Calliena (modern Kalyana, near Bombay) has been mentioned in the book. Once a port offering trading facilities, at the time of *The Periplus*, was being obstructed for its use by the local ruler.

But the use of the phase "anthemsmon emporium" (privileged market) about this port indicates clearly the special legal provisions for trading here. In the eastern part, the author mentions Dosarene with its trade in ivory. After this he becomes very vague though he mentions a harbour at the mouth of the Ganges (probably Tamralipta), whence came the Benares muslin, and Chinese silks. The conflict for control of the external trade of Barygaza between the Saka Kshatrapas and the Satavahanas had been mentioned in *The Periplus* and presumably that explains partly the beginning of the decline of this trade.

Origin of Industrial Revolution

"Old order changeth, yielding place to new", an old dictum came to be true gradually. Feudalism that held the society for such a long time, started declining as an economic system toward the end of middle age. It (feudalism) was a major stumbling block in economic development. It was always a rule of 'haves' over the 'have-nots', of the 'powerfuls' over the 'weaks' and of the 'oppressors' over the 'oppressed'. Renaissance and other factors like, education, trade, and economic well-being hastened the process of change. The rise of towns and cities and the growth of trade centers stimulated the production of manufactured goods. The demands for goods were on rise, which hitherto were known as luxury items. People started enjoying the city life and the purchasing power of the people was on rise. The desire and the ability to spend more gave rise to a new form of economic boom. This gave a big boost to the industry and to the economy. Simultaneously, there was a need for technological up-gradation and new innovations had to follow. These new discoveries and innovations that revolutionized the society and the pace of development, both in the industry as well as in the economy, were on the rise. Faster pace of development having far-reaching effects in the history of the world were heralded by "Industrial Revolution". The desire to produce more goods at low cost to make more profits led to Industrial revolution. It began in England during 1750. It was then that some machines took over the works of men and animals in the production of goods and services. Though there had been concerted efforts in different civilizations to upgrade the technology, it came at a faster pace during Industrial evolution that dramatically changed the living pattern of the common men. The transportation system also developed at a much faster pace. In 1814, George Stephenson invented steam engine, which vastly improved the movement of goods and commodities. As early as 1853, the first railroad was laid in India during Lord Dalhousie's time. Similarly, the need to transport goods and raw material led to improvement of roads and canals. There was a revolution in the agriculture sector also. Though the revolution in agriculture sector started prior to the Industrial revolution, the changes in the farming methods, the technological up-gradation, and developing cash crops took place during this period only. Farmers adopted intensive manuring and the practice of crop rotation to maintain soil fertility. The Industrial Revolution spread to other countries as well. France began developing iron industry by importing iron ore and coal. Similarly, Germany also started producing steel. England gained supremacy over world trade as their goods and commodities were cheaper in comparison to that of other countries. This led to intense rivalry and competition among different countries. Edward Baines, in his book *The History of Great Britain, 1835* and Richard Hooker, an eminent economist during their period, have described the origins of Industrial Revolution in England and Industrial Revolution in eighteenth century Europe in an article, a synopsis of which has been reproduced here under.

The Origin of Industrial Revolution in England

For nothing England has not been told as the country of great fortune. It is this country that gave birth to democracy, liberty, and allowed complete freedom to its citizens. The political and moral advantages of England, as a seat of manufactures, were not less remarkable than its physical advantages. The arts were the daughters of peace and liberty. In no country had these blessings been enjoyed in so high degree, or for so long a continuance, as in England. Under the reign of just laws, personal liberty and property had been secure; mercantile enterprise was allowed to reap its reward; capital was allowed to be accumulated in safety; the workmen were sincere and honest and, thus protected and favoured, the manufacturing prosperity of the country had struck its roots deep, and spread forth its branches to the ends of the earth.

In the eighteenth century, a series of inventions transformed the manufacture of cotton in England and gave rise to a new mode of production — the factory system. During these years, other branches of industry effected comparable advances, and all these together, mutually reinforcing one another, made possible further gains on an ever-widening front. According to David Landes, in his *The Unbound Prometheus, 1969*, the abundance and variety of these innovations almost defy compilation, but they may be subsumed under three principles: the substitution of machines — rapid, regular, precise, tireless — for human skill and effort; the substitution of inanimate for animate sources of power, in particular, the introduction of engines for converting heat into work, thereby opening to man a new and almost unlimited supply of energy; and use of new and far more abundant raw materials, in particular, the substitution of mineral for vegetable or animal substances. These improvements constitute the Industrial Revolution. The Industrial Revolution of the late 18th and early 19th centuries was revolutionary because it changed and revolutionized the productive capacity of England, Europe and United States. But the revolution was something more than just new machines, smoke-belching factories, increased productivity and an increased standard of living. The macro and micro economic concept pertaining to the general well-being also got transformed and allied with the mundane developments.

It was a revolution, which transformed English, European, and American society down to its very roots. Like the Reformation or the French Revolution, no one was left unaffected. Everyone was touched in one way or another — peasant and noble, parent and child, artisan and captain of industry. The Industrial Revolution serves as a key to the origins of modern Western society. As Harold Perkin, in the *Origins of Modern English Society, 1780-1880 (1969)* has observed, "the Industrial Revolution was no mere sequence of changes in industrial techniques and production, but a social revolution with social causes as well as profound social effects." Indeed, this revolution resulted in profound changes in the entire gamut of human civilization-social-political, and economic.

The Industrial Revolution could be said to have created the European working-class. It made the European middle-class as well. In the wake of the Revolution, new social relationships appeared. As Ben Franklin once said, "time is money." Man no longer treated men as men, but as a commodity, which could be bought and sold on the open market. This "commodification" of man was what bothered Karl Marx and his solution was to transcend the profit motive by social revolution.

The Industrial Revolution began in England sometime after the middle of the 18th century. England was the "First Industrial Nation." It was England which first executed "the takeoff into self-sustained growth." By 1850, England had become an economic giant. Its goal was to supply two-thirds of the globe with cotton spun, dyed, and woven in the industrial centers of northern England. England proudly proclaimed itself to be the "Workshop of the World," a position that country held until the end of the 19th century when Germany, Japan and United States overtook it. In order to expand the business, England started colonizing more and more countries, and took control of not only the business but also the general administration of the area.

More than the greatest gains of the Renaissance, the Reformation, Scientific Revolution or Enlightenment, the

Industrial Revolution implied that man now had not only the opportunity and the knowledge, but also the physical means to completely subdue nature. No other revolution in modern times can be said to have accomplished so much in so little time. The Industrial Revolution attempted to effect man's mastery over nature. This was an old vision, a vision with a history. In the 17th century, the English statesman and "Father of Modern Science", Francis Bacon (1561-1626), believed that natural philosophy; what we call science, could be applied to the solution of practical problems, and so, the idea of modern technology was born. For Bacon, the problem was that man could not enjoy perfect freedom if he had to constantly labour to supply the necessities of existence. His answer was clear, the machines. These labour saving devices would liberate mankind, they would save labour which then could be utilized elsewhere. "Knowledge is power," said Bacon, "and scientific knowledge reveals power over nature".

The humanity was in cross road. It had to change from Neolithic feudalistic concept to a modern and progressive society. The vision was all-important. It was optimistic and progressive. Man was going somewhere. His life had direction. This vision was part of the general attitude known as the idea of progress that was the history of human society was a history of progress, forever forward, forever upward. This attitude was implicit throughout the Enlightenment and was made reality during the French and Industrial Revolutions. With relatively few exceptions, the philosophers of the 18th century embraced this idea of man's progress with intensity. It was unmatched in this century. Human happiness, improved morality, an increase in knowledge was now within man's reach. This was indeed the message, the vision, of Adam Smith, Denis Diderot, Voltaire, Thomas Jefferson and Ben Franklin.

"Tremble all ye oppressors of the world," wrote Richard Price and tremble they did. The American and French Revolutions, building on enlightened ideas, swept away enthusiasm, tyranny, fanaticism, superstition, and oppressive and despotic governments. "Sapere Aude!" exclaimed Kant, "Dare to know"! With history and superstition literally swept aside, man could not only understand man and society, man could now change society for the better. These are all ideas, glorious, noble visions of the future prospect of mankind. By the end of the 18th century, these ideas became tangible. The vision was reality. Even Karl Marx understood this when he wrote, "Philosophers have only interpreted the world in various ways; the point, however, is to change it."

The glorious products of science, *viz,* engines and machines, began to revolutionize the idea of progress itself. If a simple machine could do the work of twenty men in a quarter of the time formerly required, then it would bring about perceptible change in the concepts of natural phenomena, like earth, fire and water and supernatural powers. When the Industrial Revolution was viewed alongside the democratic revolutions of 1776 and 1789, optimism so generated was enormous. Heaven on Earth seemed reality and no one was untouched by the prospects. But, while the Industrial Revolution brought its blessings, there was also much misery. Revolutions, political or otherwise, are always mixed blessings. If we can thank the Industrial Revolution for giving us fluoride, internal combustion engines, and laser guided radial arm saws, we can also damn it for the effect it has had on social relationships. We live in the legacy of the Industrial Revolution, the legacy of the "cash nexus," as the mid-19th century English critic Thomas Carlyle (1795-1881) put it, "where the only connection between men is the one of money, profit and gain". The Industrial Revolution also brought out an unending arms race, which endangered the growth of civil society. The World wars are the best examples. Since the conclusion of second world war more people have been killed due to internal hostilities, wars and strife. In such cases more and more sophisticated weapons are used putting the civilization in peril.

The origins of the Industrial Revolution in England are complex and varied and, like the French Revolution, the Industrial Revolution is still a subject of a vast historical debate over origins, developments, and growth and end results. This debate has raged among historians since at least 1884, when Arnold Toynbee (1852-1883), an English historian and social reformer, published the short book, Lectures on the Industrial Revolution in England. Toynbee was in a fairly good position to assess the revolution in industry. England had, by the 1880s, endured more than a century of industrialization.

Still, like any revolution, the Industrial Revolution leaves many questions;

i. Whether the revolution in industry is simply an issue of new machinery or mechanical innovation?
ii. Whether young boys and girls did work and live shoulder to shoulder for more than twelve hour a day?
iii. Whether industrial capitalism was nothing more than a clever system devised by clever capitalists to exploit the labour of ignorant workers?
iv. Whether the revolution in industry was the product of conscious planning or did it appear spontaneously?
v. Whether such a revolution has been able to reduce poverty, distrust among the communities, and peace?
vi. Whether the revolution did bring about a wedge between the concepts of old and new methods of human development?
vii. Whether such a revolution brought about a domino effect on the religious beliefs of a person or a society?
viii. Whether it was instrumental in bringing about socio-politico-economic changes in the society?
ix. Whether it was instrumental in bringing about a change in quality of life?

It would be difficult on one's part to get closer to the answers to these important questions even though one goes for an entire course of study on the subject. However, it was crystal clear that the Industrial Revolution accomplished a structural change in the economic organization of English and European society. This was what made the Revolution revolutionary. In other words, England, then the Continent and the United States, witnessed a shift from a traditional, pre-modern, agrarian society to that of an industrial economy based on capitalist methods, principles and practices.

In general, the spread of industry across England was sporadic. In other words, not every region of England was industrialized at the same time. It has always the cluster approach. In some areas, the factory system spread quickly, in others not at all. Such a development also applies to the steam engine — one would think that once steam engines made their appearance that each and every factory would have one. But this was clearly not the case. The spread of industry, or machinery, or steam power, or the factory system itself was erratic. Late 20th century developments in technology were perhaps most responsible for this attitude. We know that technology supplies a constant stream of products that are "new and improved." We know that the moment we bring home a top of the line computer that within six months it would become not necessarily obsolete but "old".

Historians are now agreed that beginning in the 17th century and continuing throughout the 18th century, England witnessed an agricultural revolution. English and Dutch farmers were the most productive farmers of the century, and were continually adopting new methods of farming and experimenting with new types of vegetables and grains. They also learned a great deal about manure and other fertilizers. In other words, many English farmers were treating farming as a science, and all this interest eventually resulted in greater yields. It is not the question whether the English farmers are more enterprising than his French counterpart. English society was far more open than French. There were no labour obligations of the lord. The English farmer could move about his locale or the country to sell his goods while the French farmer was bound by direct and indirect taxes, tariffs or other kinds of restrictions. During 1700, eighty per cent of the population of England earned its income from the land. A century later, that figure had dropped to 40%. An open society and economy indeed brings about rapid economic progress in comparison to a closed one. Hence a society or a nation must keep its doors and windows open and allow fresh wind to be circulated. To put it in other words, unless one allows ingress or egress of water in a tank, the stagnant water may stink.

The wind of change resulted in the marked improvement in terms of performance, infusion of new ideas, better quality of product and lowered the cost of production. The result of these developments taken together was a period of high productivity and low food prices. And this, in turn, meant that the typical English family did not have to spend almost everything it earned on bread (as was the case in France before 1789), and instead could purchase manufactured goods.

There are other assets that helped make England the "first industrial nation." Unlike France, England had an effective central bank and well developed credit market. The English government allowed the domestic economy to function with few restrictions and encouraged both technological change and a free market. England also had a labour surplus, which, thanks to the enclosure movement, meant that there was an adequate supply of workers for the burgeoning factory system.

England's agricultural revolution came as a result of increased attention to fertilizers, adoption of new crops and farming technologies, and the enclosure movement. Jethro Tull (1674-1741) invented a horse-drawn hoe as well as a mechanical seeder, which allowed seeds to be planted in orderly rows. A contemporary of Tull, Charles "Turnip"

Townsend (1674-1738), stressed the value of turnips and other field crops in a rotation system of planting rather than letting the land lay fallow. Thomas William Coke (1752-1842) suggested the utilization of field grasses and new fertilizers as well as greater attention to estate management.

In order for these "high farmers" to make the most efficient use of the land, they had to manage the fields as they saw fit. This was, of course, impossible under the three field system, which had dominated English and European agriculture for centuries. Since farmers, small and large, held their property in long strips, they had to follow the same rules of cultivation. The local parish or village determined what ought to be planted. In the end, the open field system of crop rotation was an obstacle to increased agricultural productivity. The solution was to enclose the land, and this meant enclosing entire villages. Landlords knew that the peasants would not give up their land voluntarily, so they appealed by petition to Parliament, a difficult and costly adventure at best. The first enclosure act was passed in 1710 but was not enforced until the 1750s. In the ten years between 1750 and 1760, more than 150 acts were passed and between 1800 and 1810, Parliament passed more than 900 acts of enclosure. While enclosure ultimately contributed to an increased agricultural surplus, necessary to feed a population that would double in the 18th century, it also brought disaster to the countryside. Peasant farmers were dispossessed of their land and were now forced to find work in the factories, which began springing up in towns and cities.

England faced increasing pressure to produce more manufactured goods due to the 18th century population explosion; England's population nearly doubled over the course of the century and more and more colonies came into the fold. And the industry most important in the rise of England as an industrial nation was cotton textiles. No other industry could be said to have advanced so far so quickly. Although the putting out system (cottage industry) was fairly well developed across the Continent, it was fully developed in England. A merchant would deliver raw cotton at a household. The cotton would be cleaned and then spun into yarn or thread. After a period of time, the merchant would return, pick up the yarn and drop off more raw cotton. The merchant would then take the spun yarn to another household where it was woven into cloth. The system worked fairly well except under the growing pressure of demand, the putting-out system could no longer keep up.

There was a constant shortage of thread so the industry began to focus on ways to improve the spinning of cotton. The first solution to this bottleneck appeared around 1765 when James Hargreaves (1720-1778), a carpenter by trade, invented his cotton spinning jenny. At almost the same time, Richard Arkwright (1732-1792) invented another kind of spinning device, the water frame. Thanks to these two innovations, ten times as much cotton yarn had been manufactured in 1790 than had been possible just twenty years earlier. Hargreaves' jenny was simple, inexpensive and hand-operated. The jenny had between six and twenty-four spindles mounted on a sliding carriage. The spinner (almost always a woman) moved the carriage back and forth with one hand and turned a wheel to supply power with the other. Of course, now that one bottleneck had been relieved, another appeared; the weaver (usually a man) could no longer keep up with the supply of yarn. Arkwright's water frame was based on a different principle. It acquired a capacity of several hundred spindles and demanded more power waterpower. The water frame required large, specialized mills employing hundreds of workers. The first consequence of these developments was that cotton goods became much cheaper and were bought by all social classes. Cotton was the miracle fiber; it was easy to clean, spin, weave and dye and was comfortable to wear. Now millions of people, who had worn nothing under their coarse clothes, could afford to wear cotton undergarments.

Although the spinning jenny and water frame managed to increase the productive capacity of the cotton industry, the real breakthrough came with developments in steam power. Developed in England by Thomas Savery (1698) and Thomas Newcomen (1705), these early steam engines were used to pump water from coalmines. In the 1760s, a Scottish engineer, James Watt (1736-1819) created an engine that could pump water three times as quickly as the Newcomen engine. In 1782, Watt developed a rotary engine that could turn a shaft, and drive machinery to power; the machines to spin and weave cotton cloth. Because Watt's engine was fired by coal and not water, spinning factories could be located virtually anywhere.

Steam power also promoted important changes in other industries. The use of steam-driven bellows in blast furnaces helped iron makers switch over from charcoal (limited in quantity) to coke, which is made from coal, in the smelting of pig iron. In the 1780s, Henry Cort (1740-1800) developed the peddling furnace, which allowed pig iron to be refined in turn with coke. Skilled ironworkers ("peddlers") could "stir" molten pig iron in a large vat, raking off refined iron for further processing. Cort also developed steam-powered rolling mills, which were capable of producing finished iron in a variety of shapes and forms. Aided by revolutions in agriculture, transportation, communications and technology, England was able to get the distinction of becoming the "first industrial nation." Historians had to recognize this reality. However, there were a few others less-tangible reasons, which deserve consideration. These are perhaps cultural reasons. Although the industrial revolution was clearly an unplanned and spontaneous event, it never would have been "made" had there not been men who wanted such a thing to occur. There must have been men who saw opportunities not only for advances in technology, but also the profits those advances might create. The English people saw little problem with making money, nor with taking their surplus and reinvesting it. Whether this attribute has something to do with their "Protestant work ethic," as Max Weber put it, or with a specifically English trait is debatable, but the fact remains that English entrepreneurs had a much wider scope of activities than did their Continental counterparts at the same time.

Industrial Revolution in Eighteenth Century Europe

Though Industrial Revolution left many a question unanswered in had tremendous impact on the post-revolution era. Richard Hooker an eminent economist in one of his articles delineated the causes and consequences of Industrial Revolution and emphasized the far- reaching effects in the modern-day world. According to him, the phenomenon which had "the most far-reaching impact and influenced transformation of human culture, since the advent of agriculture eight or ten thousand years ago, was the Industrial Revolution of eighteenth century Europe". The consequences of this revolution changed irrevocably human labour, consumption, family structure, social structure, and even the very soul and thoughts of the individual. This revolution involved more than technology; to be sure, there had been industrial "revolutions" throughout European history and non-European history. In Europe, for instance, the twelfth and thirteenth centuries saw an explosion of technological knowledge and a consequent change in production and labour. However, the Industrial Revolution was more than technology, impressive as this technology was. It effected every aspect of human life, behaviour, thought process and activity. What drove the Industrial Revolution were profound social changes, as Europe moved from a primarily agricultural and rural economy to a capitalist and urban economy, from a household, family-based economy to an industry- based economy. The individual approach was transformed to collective wisdom. This required rethinking of social obligations and the structure of the family. The abandoning of the family economy, for instance, was the most dramatic change to the structure of the family that Europe had ever undergone, and still has to struggle with the unforeseen and sudden changes that came in the way. The European economy was overwhelmingly an agricultural economy, up to 1750. Largely wealthy and frequently aristocratic landowners owned the land. They leased the land to tenant farmers who paid for the land in real goods that they grew or produced on that land. Most non-agricultural goods were produced by individual families that specialized in one set of skills: wagon-wheel manufacture, for instance. Most capitalist activity focused on mercantile activity rather than production. There was, however, a manufacturing industry growing up around the logic of mercantilism.

While explaining the reason as to why the Industrial Revolution took place, globalization of European economy becomes a compulsion explanation. European trade and manufacture stretched to every continent, except Antarctica. This vast increase in the market for European goods in part drove the conversion to an industrial, manufacturing economy. Why other nations didn't initially join this revolution is in part explained by the monopolistic control that the Europeans exerted over the global economy. World trade was about making Europeans wealthy, not about enriching the colonies or non Western countries. In the process of search for wealth, the European countries colonized number of countries and ruled over them for centuries. They fought among themselves to capture colonies to expand their business. Prominent among them was England, who was able to colonize a number of countries including a major portion of Asian sub-continent. The Industrial Revolution brought about economic prosperity in the European countries, but brought miseries in the colonies. They exploited the natural wealth of those colonies at a nominal price, but sold the finished products in the same colony at a much higher cost. The process neither created any job nor added to economic prosperity of the colonies. The small scale industries in these colonies were almost wiped out, giving way to the big and large- scale industries of European countries. It resulted in massive unemployment, poverty, and misery in the colonies. Some attribute to Industrial Revolution the reasons of substantial increase in the population of Europe; this belief of historians was never questioned. Population growth, however, is a mysterious affair to explain; most often it occurs when standards of production rise. So whether the Industrial Revolution was started off by a rise in population, or whether the Industrial Revolution caused a rise in population is hard to guess. It is the same egg- and-chicken story. But inquisitiveness in a man always leads to scientific inventions. Even though either of the two may not be true, it's clear, that the transition to an industrial, manufacturing economy required more people to man this manufacture. Similarly, in the undeveloped countries, people living below the poverty line, tend to produce more children, who could be employed to earn and sustain the family. While the logic of a national economy founded centrally on the family economy and family production is more or less a subsistence economy, most production is oriented around manufacturing economy; a person's productive labour needs to produce more than they need to keep life going. This surplus production is what produces profits for the owners of the manufacture. This surplus economy sometimes not only makes population growth possible, but also desirable.

a. England

It is hard to pinpoint precise reasons for beginning of the Industrial Revolution, though historians generally propose a number of reasons. Among the most compelling is the exponential increase in food production following the enclosure laws of the eighteenth century. Parliament passed a series of laws that permitted lands that had been held in common by tenant farmers to be enclosed into large, private farms worked by a much smaller labour force. While this drove peasants off the land, it also increased agricultural production and increased the urban population of England, since the only place displaced peasants had to go were the cities. The English Parliament, unlike the monarchies of Europe, was firmly under the control of the merchant and capitalist classes, so the eighteenth century saw a veritable army of legislation that favoured mercantile and capitalist interests.

Because of the strong role of Parliament in English government and the incredible influence of capitalists and mercantilists, social values had also been steadily shifting in England. In continental Europe, the aristocracy represented the fullest embodiment of social values. They believed that they were born with higher virtues than the common people, who, because of their birth, would never attain these virtues to the same level. They also believed that the pursuit of money was a characteristic of common people; the non-aristocratic classes accepted the mercantile and capitalist revolutions throughout Europe, but in England was a middle class bourgeoisie revolution.

The diminished role of the aristocracy in English government and society, however, allowed for a steady shift in values; the values of the mercantile and capitalist classes slowly became the norm. The most important of these values was the pursuit of wealth. Adam Smith's *The Wealth of Nations* proposed that the only legitimate goal of national government and human activity is the steady increase in the overall wealth of the nation. This is not an idea that would have flown two hundred years earlier.

Mercantilism had thrived in England in ways that it hadn't on the continent. In particular, the English had no internal tariffs or duties on commerce, which wasn't true of any of the continental European states. Moving goods around in continental Europe was an expensive affair as one had to pay taxes and duties every hundred miles or so. Moving goods around in England was cheap, and hence profits soared. In addition, England had come to monopolize overseas trade. Every time England fought a war in the eighteenth century, it always acquired new overseas territory. It completely monopolized trade with the North American colonies. In fact, one-half of all British exports went to America in the 1780's. But it also began to control the South American and, most importantly, the Indian trade. In India, the Britishers entered as small-time merchants. Then they formed a company called as East India Company at Kolkata during 1600. Then they spread their area and captured the whole of India and ruled the country for more than 200 years. They could spread the business with protection. All this trade produced the largest merchant marine in the world as well as a navy to protect this merchant marine fleet. Like Periclean Athens, England shot to the forefront of the new capitalist economy, primarily through its navy.

The technological innovations followed these social and economic changes. The first major technological innovation was the cotton gin. Cotton is a plant grown in America and India; it was a small industry through much of the seventeenth century, but exploded in the middle of the Eighteenth. Most of the cotton was produced in British colonies. Because it was a labour intensive agriculture, it fueled the traffic in African slaves to the colonies; the cotton shroud that fell over the history of Africa. The first innovation in cotton manufacture was the fly-shuttle, which greatly speeded up the process of weaving cotton threads into cloth . That wasn't enough, though, for cotton had to be stretched out or spun into threads to begin with. This process was done slowly, one thread at a time, by a machine called a spinning wheel. This slow process was mechanized by James Hargreaves, a carpenter, in what is usually pointed to as one of the typological major technological innovations of the Industrial Age: the "spinning jenny" patented in 1767, was a series of simple machines rather than a single machine, and it spun sixteen threads of cotton simultaneously. These two qualities like, multiple machines in a single machine as well as a machine that was designed not just to speed up work, but to do the work of several labourers simultaneously, was the hallmark of all subsequent technological innovations. In 1793, the American, Eli Whitney, invented the cotton gin, which mechanized the separating of seeds from cotton fibers. These innovations made cotton incredibly cheap and infinitely expandable. Since cotton clothing was tougher than wool, the manufacture of cotton clothing shot through the roof. By the end of the eighteenth century, the manufacture of thread and cloth was slowly moving out of the family economy into large factory mills, though this transition could not be fully realized until the middle of the nineteenth Century.

While the spinning jenny is frequently pointed to as the first, major technological innovation of the Industrial Revolution, the invention that really drove the revolution in the eighteenth century was invented several decades earlier: the steam engine. Along with the growth in the cotton industry, the steel industry began to grow by leaps and bounds. This was largely due to a quirk in English geography: England sits on vast quantities of coal, a carbon based minerals derived from ancient life forms. Coal burns better and more efficiently than wood and, if you have lots of coal, it is infinitely cheaper. The English figured out that they could substitute coal for wood in the melting of metals, including iron, and blissfully went about tearing coal from the ground while manufacturers in Europe looked on jealously.

Mining coal, however, was not an easy task. As you drew more and more coal out of the ground, you had to mine deeper and deeper. The deeper the mine, the more it fills with water. In 1712, Thomas Newcomen built a simple steam engine that pumped water from the mines. It was a single piston engine, and so it used vast amounts of energy. Because of its inefficiency, nobody could think of any use for it besides pumping water.

A Scotsman, named James Watt, added a separate cooling chamber to the machine in 1763, since this cooling chamber condensed the steam so the cylinder itself didn't have to be cooled. Patented in 1769, Watt's steam engine had the efficiency to be applied to all kinds of industries. He was not, however, good at doing business and it was only when he had teamed up with the businessman, Matthew Boulton, that the steam engine began to change the face of English manufacture. By 1800, Watt and Boulton sold 289 of these new engines; by the middle of the next century, the steam engine replaced water as the major source of motive power in England and Europe. The changes that the steam engine wrought, however, is a story for another day.

And it is here, with 289 steam engines pumping and steaming around England that one would leave the story of the Industrial Revolution, half completed. The nineteenth century saw exporting of the Industrial Revolution to Europe in the decades after 1830, and the explosion of factory-based, technology driven manufacture. The Age of Absolutism and the waning years of the Enlightenment saw Europe just beginning a new phase in its history, one that would irreparably severe it from the traditions and certainties of the past. There came the age with new opportunities not only in terms of wealth, but also to carry forward the civilization to a new era of scientific inventions and discoveries, and to create a new world order having better quality of life, coupled with higher socio-economic achievements. In spite of criticisms, the 'Industrial Revolution' transformed the society in its entirety, a revolution that was long due to the people. It not only castigated dogmas, faiths and blind beliefs, but also revolutionized the whole society, through scientific inventions in the fields of technology, medicine, as well as social sciences.

3

Theoretical Aspects of PSU

Definition of Public Sector Undertaking

Public Sector Undertaking has been defined as "any undertaking over which the public authorities may exercise directly or indirectly a dominant influence by virtue of their ownership of it, their financial participation therein, or the rules, which govern it". This definition has been used by the European Commission in Directive 80/723 of 25 June 1980 concerning the transparency of financial relations between Member States and public undertakings. It has now become the reference point for all Community legislations applicable to public undertakings.

It follows from this definition that dominant influence of a public authority, and not public ownership, is now considered to be the main criterion of the public undertaking; influence being exerted, irrespective of ownership, through the power to appoint top decision-makers in the undertaking or the ability to control major decisions through special rights for public authority representatives.

At the same time, a public undertaking must have:

(1) a degree of autonomy vis-à-vis the public authorities,
(2) an economic purpose: i.e. to produce and sale goods or services, and
(3) operating methods similar to those of private undertakings.

Public Sector Undertaking has also been defined as a "Business organization wholly or partly owned by the State and controlled through a public authority". Some public sector undertakings are placed under public ownership because, for social reasons, as it is thought the services or product should be provided by a State monopoly. Utilities (gas, electricity, etc.), broadcasting, telecommunications, and certain forms of transport are examples of this kind of public enterprise. The concept of public sector enterprise is in vogue for more than a century. Still it requires to be conceptualized in a scientific manner. Pointing out the vague and varying nature of public sector, Dr.Laxminarayan, a noted scholar on the subject, has observed "It is surprising that considering the vital importance of public enterprise in the economy and literature produced on the subject, the meaning of public enterprise continues to remain vague and varying. Although sometimes it is meant to cover the whole of the public sector, including the public services, and quite as often, it is confined to Central Government industrial and commercial enterprises organized as autonomous corporations and companies." S.S.Khera has defined public sector enterprises as "the industrial, commercial and economic activities carried on by Central Government or by a state government and in each case either solely or in association with private enterprises, so long as it is managed by a self contained management. The *Encyclopedia Britannica* defines public sector enterprise as "an undertaking that is owned by a national, state or local government, supplies services or goods at a price, and is operated on a more or less self supporting basis." Prof. A.H.Hudson remarks, "it is to public enterprise that is assigned the greater part of the task of laying the basis upon which the structure of a dynamic and diversified economy is to arise". N.N.Mallay defines public enterprises as "autonomous or semi-autonomous corporations and companies established, owned and controlled by the State and is engaged in industrial and commercial activities". Dr. Laxmi Narayan defined public sector enterprise as "an activity of the government, whether Center, state, or local, involving manufacturing or production of goods, including agriculture, or making available service for a price: such activity being managed directly, that is departmentally, or through an autonomous body with the government having the majority ownership, that is, more than 50% of the equity." From the definitions quoted above, it can be safely concluded that the primary ingredients of a public sector undertaking would be as follows:

(a) ownership,
(b) nature of the activities,
(c) area of operation,
(d) control of the Government-state-Central and local.

As per the provisions of law regarding extent of ownership of a public enterprise, the government should have a majority ownership, i.e., more than 50% equity in the enterprise. After the enactment of the Indian Companies Act, 1956, the government should hold 51 per cent or more shares in any undertaking, directly or indirectly, only then any undertaking would be called a public enterprise. But this concept may not be true in case of all public sector enterprises, because some of the enterprises are being controlled by government statutorily, even with out any financial participation in the said enterprise. Thus, at times, the Government may not have financial participation at all, but the area of activity of the said enterprise, and the extent and nature of its control on the said enterprises determine it status.

As far as the question relating to the nature of activities is concerned, in every definition the main stress has been laid on business activities involving manufacturing or producing of goods, including agriculture or rendering services in consideration for a price. It is implied that the articles or the services should not be provided free of charge. In this connection, it would not be out of context to mention here that those services, which are provided free of cost, do not come within the operation and purview of public enterprises. As such, social services, including health and education sector, regulatory functions, judicial administration, administrative activities, as well as sovereign executive functions of the government departments, do not come within the purview of public enterprises. To quote Dr. Laxmi Narayan, "An activity to be within the functional domain of the public enterprises must promise break-even over a period of time. If it were to be subsidized perpetually, it cannot be termed as public enterprise." He pointed out further that "some non economic activities, like universities and hospitals, some times charge a fee for their services, but it does not cover and it is also not intended to cover the cost, such activities are not public enterprises, though owned and managed by the state." Thus only those enterprises come within the range of the public enterprises, which market goods and services purely on a commercial basis in consideration of a price and not on a subsidized basis. There are also certain undertakings in the form of authorities, which are engaged in the sovereign executive functions of the State and develop public utilities infrastructures like communications, sports, as well as develop green areas to maintain ecological balances, including land management, and simultaneously pursue an economic purpose, having operating methods similar to those of private sector undertakings, but these continue to be under the general control and supervision of the Government without any financial participation therein. Though these authorities pursue an economic purpose, some services are rendered to the general public at a subsidized cost and even free of cost. Such authorities are the creatures of the statute. The general control and supervision of such authorities continue to bc with the Government, including the authority to appoint the top executive functionaries having decision making powers.

As regards operation of public enterprises, it is important to mention here that these undertakings must be managed and controlled by the government. These units may be run by the government directly in the form of government departmental undertakings or as a corporate body in the form of public corporation or in the form of a government company. Thus on a thorough reading of the definitions on the subject, the public enterprises can be defined as "any business, commercial activity or public utility services, owned, controlled and operated by the government." In this context, the word government may include Central, state or any public body or local authorities. To cite an example, the Department of Culture and Tourism under the Ministry of Tourism and Culture, Government of India, is not a public sector, as it does not enter into any business of goods and services, but Hotel Corporation of India, under the same Ministry, is a public sector unit as it provides services at a cost, and operates with a profit motive. Thus, it implies that:

- It is not a Department of Government engaging itself in the sovereign executive functions of the State;
- The goods and services are neither provided free of cost nor subsidized; and
- Majority equity is not with any private individual or concern (s).

To conclude, it may be observed that the concept of public enterprises may be used in a more broader sense and would include all those undertakings which are owned, run and controlled by Central, state, public body, or local self government, individually or taken together and engaged in any economic, commercial, or public services activities, having an intention of making profits. These units may be in the form of departmental units, corporations, companies, autonomous bodies or authorities. It does not matter, even if, in some of the enterprises government does not have any financial participation at all.

The provision of these services by public enterprises is a common practice in India and elsewhere. In the United States, private companies are generally allowed to provide such services subject to strict legal regulations. In some countries, industries-such as railways, coal mining, steel, banking, and insurance-have been nationalized for ideological reasons, while another group-such as armaments and aircraft manufacture-has been brought into the public sector for strategic reasons. In communist countries, most forms of production, commerce, and finance belong to the State; in many newly independent and less-developed countries, there is a very large public-enterprise sector. In Europe, the prevailing pattern is a mixed economy, with the public enterprises operating side by side with private corporations, though the trend is gradually changing for more private participation. In Great Britain, during the early years of the 20th century, the post office, utilities, armaments, and the Port of London belonged to the public sector; to them were later added various forms of public transport, thus markedly widening the role of the State sector. Under the Labour government (1946-50), a massive nationalization programme was effected, embracing coal mining, the iron and steel industry, the gas industry, railways, and long-distance road transport. During the Conservative regime of Prime Minister Margaret Thatcher (1979-90), many public enterprises were privatized. The post-war French government undertook a similar extensive nationalization programme that included banks, insurance companies, finance houses, and manufacturing concerns. Many were subsequently privatized. The United States has few public enterprises. They include, ironically, one of the world's models for such undertakings, the Tennessee Valley Authority, established in 1933. In 1970, the U.S. postal system- until then a department of the executive branch of the federal government- became a government owned corporation. Thus in all most all the countries of the world, State interference has become the *sine qua non* for the sound and balanced economic development. In India, the Government, during pre- 1991 periods, was quite keen for the expansion of public sector, mainly for removing the regional imbalances, and for strengthening and safeguarding the overall socio-economic interest of the society. The other reasons for such colossal rise in the public sector in India has been attributed to prevention of concentration of wealth with a few, growth of infrastructure when private players were either reluctant or were not capable for such massive investment, to maintain regional balance, and to bring about a socio-economic change by providing employment to the deprived sections of the society. The growth of public sector in independent India has been phenomenal and has been guided by the Industrial Policy Resolution, 1956, which gave the public sector a strategic and commanding role in the economy. Public enterprises are by definition intended to be operated in the public interest. This gave rise to a number of organizational and commercial issues. One problem is how to reconcile the need for close political control with the need for sufficient management autonomy. The public corporation form, used extensively in Great Britain and widely copied in other parts of the world, is created by a special act of Parliament that defines its powers, management structure, and relationship with government bodies. As a corporation, it has legal entity. The Treasury meets its capital requirements, but it is supposed to meet its current expenses from its normal commercial operations. Its employees are not civil servants, and the minister in-charge often appoints the top management. Another administrative form that is popular in parts of the world is the state company, which is simply an ordinary joint-stock company, whose shares are owned wholly or partly by the State. Public enterprises are usually intended to pay their way in the longer term, and yet they may be subject to political constraints in their pricing policy that could be in conflict with that objective. Conversely, for social reasons, they may receive hidden subsidies or enjoy additional protections which are not available to competitors. Such factors tend to distort the normal commercial operations of the corporation or the company and often lead to managerial disorientation.

Partly because of these non commercial considerations, public enterprises may appear to be highly inefficient and, in times of difficult trading conditions, may be a drain on public resources. Public sector undertakings have huge social obligations, which are conspicuously missing with the private sector organizations. Moreover, these are answerable to Parliamentary House Committee, Administrative Ministry, the Minister in-charge of the department, the Court of Law, CAG, anticorruption departments, and so on, which are conspicuously missing in any private sector enterprises. In view of this, the measurement of efficiency of a public enterprise is no easy matter. However, when it produces a marketable product, such as coal or steel that competes with other products, the normal commercial criterion of profit may be adopted to assess its performance. In the case of a utility enjoying monopoly power, economists have developed concepts like cost-benefit analysis as a performance measurement tool. In recent years many state enterprises in the developed world have been given financial targets that take into account both social and commercial responsibilities.

Provision of Services by Enterprises

Enterprises provide certain classes of services to the public, including common carrier transportation (buses, airlines, railroads, motor freight carriers, pipelines, etc.); telephone and telegraph; power, heat, and light; and community facilities for water, sanitation, and similar services. In most countries such enterprises are State-owned and State-operated, but in the United States these are mainly privately owned and are operated under close governmental regulation. The classic explanation for the need to regulate public utilities is that they are enterprises in which the technology of production, transmission, and distribution almost inevitably leads to complete or partial monopoly-that they are, in fact, natural monopolies. The monopolistic tendency arises from economies of scale in that particular industry, from the large capital costs typical of such enterprises, from the inelasticity of demand among consumers of the service, to the considerations of the excess capacity necessary to meet demand peaks at a very short notice, and other considerations. It is often also the case that the existence of competing parallel systems of local telephones or natural gas, for example would be inordinately expensive, wasteful, and inconvenient. Given the tendency to monopoly and the potential therefore of monopolistic pricing practices, public regulation has for more than a century been applied to certain classes of business. In practice, regulation aims to ensure that the utility serves all who apply for and are willing and able to pay for its services, that it operates in a safe and adequate manner, that it serves all customers on equal terms, and that its rates are just and reasonable. Such regulatory bodies are, indeed, a mandatory requirement in order to ensure that the consumers get a better deal in countries where there has been a liberalized economy or in the process of doing so. All states have now got regulatory commissions, and the Central government has several, including the Telephone Regulatory Authority of India (TRAI), Electricity Regulatory Commission (ERC), and the Securities and Exchange Board of India (SEBI). Consumer forums have also been strengthened to guard the interests of consumers against the arbitrary action of the manufacturers and service providers.

There are sets of principles and techniques by which the ownership and allocation of economic resources are decided and organized by society. There are two main types of modern economic system, the private or free enterprise economy and the Centrally controlled and planned economy. Neither of these is to be found in practice in its pure form; in reality, all economic systems contain varying degrees of each. The basis of the private enterprise system is the belief that when each member is allowed to pursue his rational self-interest the maximum common good will be generated. In effect, the greatest common good is simply a sum of its constituent parts, and anything that interferes with the pursuit of individual rational self-interest will reduce that sum. The mechanism that assures that the pursuit of myriad private goals will produce public good is the market, which impersonally sets prices for both, the factors of production-like land, labour, and capital- and the products of industry. With the factors of production in private hands, the proportions in which these factors are combined to produce different goods and services are determined through the price mechanism. If something is supplied in quantities greater than what are required, the price will fall or production will be reduced, or both results will occur. If there is unsatisfied supply for the demand for any product, the price will rise and, with profits in prospect, production will be stimulated. The Central planning approach is based on the observations that the private enterprise system accepts patterns of unequal wealth and income distribution and that, moreover, because of technological and other developments, some producers attain a size and importance that destroy the competitive conditions required for the operation of the market mechanism. The other observation in support of the Central planning also revolves round the theory that private enterprise system, leading to free market economy, would destroy the small scale industries, leading to large scale unemployment and the benefits of such a free market economy do not percolate to the common people. The answer, for proponents of central planning, is public ownership of the means of production and the central determination and control of what is produced. In this way, inequalities of wealth and income are to be reduced or eliminated and economic activities organized according to agreed upon social and political objectives. The developed economies of Western Europe, North America, and Japan are described as private enterprise systems, while those few countries which still follow communism, have centrally planned and controlled economies. (Developing countries have no established pattern; in many the rival philosophies coexist, often uneasily, with each other.) Most developed free enterprise countries, however, recognize the criticisms of the pure market economy and accept the need for a degree of State involvement. In many of these countries, there is a degree of State ownership of economic enterprises, mainly in public utilities and some basic industries. In addition, all governments take an active role in influencing the nature and tempo of economic growth by controlling such key economic variables as the money supply, interest rates, government expenditure and borrowing. In most cases, government action in these areas reflects a judgment relating to political, social, or economic objectives, but it is radically different from the prescriptions of the central-planning doctrine stemming from the belief that freedom of enterprise is the most efficient way of maximizing economic growth. Although the extent of State involvement varies from country to country and may change with successive governments, Western countries agree that private enterprise is to be preferred on both philosophical and practical grounds. Centrally controlled economies begin with the assumption that State determination of economic goals and detailed State control of economic activities are desirable as a matter of principle. In centrally controlled economies, State ownership of the means of production is the rule. Resources are allocated to investment, and the output of goods and services is decided and organized in accordance with a detailed economic plan that attempts to ensure, by administrative direction rather than incentive, that all parts of the economy and every enterprise perform according to a complex set of officially determined interlocking objectives. In practice, this has proved to be impossible. Despite a vast planning and controlling bureaucracy, the fulfillment of each of thousands of objectives cannot be guaranteed, yet such is the rigidity of the system that failure in one aspect will compromise the integrity of the entire plan. Lack of incentive, leads to non involvement and insincerity. Moreover, the famous dictum of Lord Acton that "power corrupts and absolute power corrupts absolutely" becomes a reality. Central planning system obviously devolves absolute powers with the functionaries and bureaucrats, and in the absence of a transparent system and accountability, the system leads to corruption, degeneration and inefficiency. After the Stalinist era, Yugoslavia, Hungary, and China were among the communist countries that experimented with limited degrees of individual enterprise and decision making to overcome the inflexibility of the system without compromising State control over the basic aims of economic development. After the Soviet Union abandoned its control over Eastern Europe in 1989, the Eastern European nations retreated from the rigid controls of central planning and adopted the economic model that had been pioneered by Hungary in the late 1960s. In subsequent years, the Eastern European countries came to rely more and more on private enterprise and the price mechanisms of the free market. Meanwhile, the collapse of the Soviet Union and its communist government in 1991 was accompanied by the complete breakdown of that country's system of central planning. New governments in Russia and other former Soviet republics then began to make the difficult transition to an economic system based largely on private ownership and market price mechanisms. The demise of the Soviet Union left the world with only a few nations still relying on undiluted central planning and complete State ownership of the means of production.

Economics System

No one for certain can say the process of creation of universe, though some theories have been propounded by scientists. The humankind has passed through countless ages witnessing marathon manoeuvring of the creations of nature. The changes in human nature as well as life style are bewildering. Although a wide range of institutions and social customs have been associated with the economic activities of society, only a very small number of basic modes of provisioning could be discovered beneath this variety. Indeed, history has produced three such kinds of economic systems-like those based on the principle of tradition, those organized according to command, and the rather small number, historically speaking, in which the central organizing is the market. The very paucity of fundamental modes of economic organization calls our attention to a central aspect of the problem of economic "systems"; namely, that the objective to which all economic arrangements must be addressed has itself remained unchanged throughout human history. This unvarying objective is the coordination of the individual activities associated with provisioning. Such activities would range from hunting and gathering in primitive societies to administrative or financial tasks in modern industrial systems. What may be called "the economic problem" is the orchestration of these activities into a coherent social whole; coherent in the sense of providing a social order with the goods or services it requires to assure its own continuance and to fulfill its perceived historic mission. Social coördination can, in turn, be analyzed into two distinct tasks. The first of these is the production of the goods and services needed by the social order, a task that requires mobilization of society's resources, including its most valuable and most resistive resource, human effort. Of nearly equal importance is the second task, the appropriate distribution of the product. This task must not only provide for the continuance of society's labour supply, but must also accord with the prevailing values of different social orders, all of which favour some recipients of income over others like, men over women, aristocrats over commoners, haves over have-nots, property owners over non-owners, or party members over nonmembers. All modes of accomplishing the basic tasks of production and distribution rely on social rewards or penalties of one kind or another. Tradition-based societies depend largely on communal expressions of approval or disapproval. Command systems utilize the open or veiled power of physical coercion or punishment, or the bestowal of wealth or prerogatives. The third method, i.e., the market, also brings pressures and incentives to bear, but the stimuli of gain and loss are not usually within the control of any one person or group of persons. Instead, they emerge from the 'workings' of the system itself, and, on closer inspection, those workings turn out to be nothing other than the efforts of individuals to gain pecuniary rewards by supplying the things that others are willing to pay for. There is a paradoxical aspect to the manner in which the market resolves the economic problem. In contrast to the conformity that guides traditional society or the obedience to superiors who orchestrates the command of society, behaviour in a market society is mostly self-directed. The unintended outcome of this competitive engagement of self-seeking individuals is the creation of the third, and by all odds the most remarkable, mode of solving the economic problem. Not surprisingly, these three principal solutions are distinguished by the distinct attributes they impart to their respective societies. The coordinative mechanism of tradition, resting as it does on the perpetuation of social roles, is marked by a characteristic changelessness in the societies in which it is dominant. Command systems, on the contrary, are marked by their capacity to mobilize resources and labour in ways far beyond the reach of traditional societies, so that societies with command systems typically boast of large-scale achievements, such as the Great Wall of China, the Egyptian pyramids or the myriad temples and places of worship depicting architectural splendour, set up by the ruling clans of India during different periods of civilizations. The third of the systems, in which the market mechanism plays the role of energizer and coordinator, is in turn marked by yet another historical attribute, resembling neither the routines of traditional systems nor the highly personalized achievements of command systems. The mark of the market is the galvanic charge imparted to economic life from the energies unleashed by its competitive, gain-oriented setting. This charge is dramatically illustrated by the trajectory of capitalism, the only social order in which the market mechanism has played a central role. In *The Communist Manifesto*, published in 1848, Karl Marx and Friedrich Engels wrote that in less than a century, the capitalist system had created "more massive and more colossal productive forces than have all preceding generations together." They also wrote that it was "like the sorcerer, who is no longer able to control the powers of the nether world whom he has called up by his spells." That creative, revolutionary, and often disruptive capacity of capitalism can be traced in no small degree to the market system that performs its coordinative task.

Economic System

From Commercial to Industrial Capitalism

Transition to capitalism from traditionalism has never been smooth sailing. But commercial capitalism proved to be only transitional. The succeeding form would be distinguished by the pervasive mechanization and industrialization of its productive processes, a change that would not only vastly alter the social and physical landscape but would also set into motion new dynamic tendencies for the system. The transformative agency was already present, observable in a few coal mines where steam driven engines invented by Thomas Newcomen pumped water out of the pits. The diffusion and penetration of such machinery-driven processes of production during the first quarter of the next century has been traditionally called "the Industrial Revolution", although historians today stress the long germination of the revolution and the many phases through which it passed. There is no doubt, however, that a remarkable confluence of advances in agriculture, cotton spinning and weaving, iron manufacture, machine tool design, and harnessing of mechanical power began profoundly to alter the character of capitalism in the last years of the 18th century and the first decades of the 19th.The alterations did not affect the driving motive of the system or its reliance on market forces as its coordinative principles. Their effect was rather on the social complexion of the society that contained these new technologies and on the economic outcome of the processes of competition and capital accumulation. This aspect of industrialization was most immediately apparent in the advent of the factory as the archetypal locus of production. In Smith's time the individual enterprise was still small. The opening pages of 'The Wealth of Nations' describe the effects of the division of labour in a 10-man pin factory, but by the early 19th century the increasing mechanization of labour, coupled with the application of water and steam power, had raised the size of the work force in an ordinary textile mill to several hundreds, by mid-century in the steel mills to several thousands, and by the end of the century in the railways to tens of thousands. The increase in the scale of employment brought a marked change in the character of employment itself. In Smith's day, the social distance between employer and labourer was still sufficiently small that the very word "manufacturer" implied an occupation (a mechanic) as well as a capitalist like position. By the time of the "dark satanic mills" of the 1830s, a great gulf had opened between the manufacturers, who were now a propertied business class, and the men, women, and children who tended their machines for 10- and 12-hour stints. It was from the spectacle of mill labour, described in unsparing detail by the inspectors authorized by the first Factory Act of 1802, that Marx drew much of the indignation that animated his analysis of capitalism. More importantly, it was from this same factory setting and the urban squalor which industrialization brought, that capitalism derived much of the social consciousness-sometimes revolutionary, sometimes reformist-that was to play so large a part in its subsequent political life. The degradation of the physical and social landscape was the aspect of industrialization that first attracted attention, but it was its slower acting impact on economic growth that was ultimately to be judged as its most significant effect.

A single statistic may dramatize this process. Between 1788 and 1839, the output of pig iron in Britain rose from 68,000 to 1,347,000 tons. For the significance of these numbers to be grasped, they must be translated into the huge multiplication of iron pumps, iron machine tools, iron pipes, iron rails, and iron beams that this increase in pig iron production made possible, and this multiplication of iron implements must, in turn, be translated into the strength and speed that they lent to production itself. This was the means by which the first industrial revolution promoted economic growth, not immediately but with gathering momentum. Thirty years later, this effect would be repeated with even more spectacular results when the Bessemer converter (Sir Henry Bessemer: British inventor and metallurgist who developed the Bessemer process (1813-1898)) ushered in the age of steel rails, ships, machines, girders, wires, pipes, and containers. The most important consequence of industrialization of capitalism was, therefore, its powerful effect on enhancing what Marx called "the forces of production"; the source of what is now called standard of living. The Swiss economic demographer Paul Bairoch has calculated that gross national product per capita in the developed countries rose from $180 in the 1750s (in dollars of 1960 purchasing power) to $780 in the 1930s and then to $3,000 in the 1980s, whereas the per capita income of the less developed countries remained unchanged at about $180-$190 from 1750 to 1930 and thereafter rose only to $410 in 1980. The single most important explanation for this difference is that the first group of countries became industrialized and the second did not. A second major effect of the industrialization of the system was its increasing economic instability. Market systems are intrinsically susceptible to perturbations, because of mismatches and miscalculations in individual markets. Such disturbances bring relatively small effects in an economy of small enterprises, but they can have major repercussions as the scale of enterprises becomes larger. The difference can be likened to the contrast between a sand pile and a girdled structure: the sand pile absorbs blows without collapsing because of the adjustment of its many small particles, while a girdled structure can fail if a single beam buckles. Not surprisingly, then, one side effect of industrialization was the effort to minimize or prevent such shocks by linking firms together into cartels or trusts or simply into giant integrated enterprises. Although these efforts dampened the repercussions of individual miscalculations, they were insufficient to guard against the effects of speculative panics or commercial convulsions. By the end of the 19th century, economic depressions had become a worrisome and recurrent problem, and the Great Depression of the 1930s rocked the entire capitalist world. During that debacle, the gross national product (GNP) in the United States fell by almost 50 percent from its peak to its trough; business investment fell by 94 percent, while unemployment rose from 3.2 percent of the civilian labour force to 24.9 percent. Of all the reasons that account for the extraordinary increase in instability from 1830 to 1930, none is more persuasive than the increase in scale from pin factories to giant enterprises. From industrial to state capitalism, the problem of instability takes on further importance insofar as it is a principal cause of the next structural phase of the system. The new phase is often described as State capitalism because its outstanding feature is the enlargement in size and functions of the public realm. In 1929, for example, total U.S. expenditure on account of federal, state, and local government came to less than 10 percent of the GNP; as of the 1970s, this amounted to roughly one-third. This increase is observable in all major capitalist nations, many of which have reached considerably higher ratios of government disbursements to GNP than the United States. At the same time, the function of government changed as decisively as its size. Already, by the last quarter of the 19th century, the emergence of great industrial trusts had provoked legislation in the United States (although not in Europe) to curb the monopolistic tendencies of industrialization. Apart from these antitrust laws and the regulation of a few industries of special public concern, however, the functions of the federal government were not significantly broadened from Smith's vision. Prior to the Great Depression, for example, the great bulk of federal outlays went for defense and international relations, for general administrative expenditure and interest on the debt, and for the Post Office. The Great Depression radically altered this limited view of government in the United States, as it had earlier begun to widen it in Europe. The provision of old-age pensions, relief for the hungry and poor, and a dole for the unemployed were all policies inaugurated by the administration of President Franklin D. Roosevelt, following in the footsteps of similar enlargements of government functions in Britain, France, and Germany. From 1970s forward, such new kinds of federal activities-under the designation of social security, health, education, and welfare expenditures-grew to be 20 to 50 percent larger than the traditional categories of federal spending. Thus, one very important element in the advent of a new stage of capitalism was the emergence of the public sector as a guarantor of public economic well being, a function that would never have entered Smith's imagination. A second and equally important departure was the government's assumption of responsibility for the general course of economic conditions themselves. This was a change of policy orientation that also emerged from the challenge of the Great Depression. Once regarded as a matter beyond remedy, the general level of national income came to be seen by the end of the 1930s as the responsibility of government, although the measures taken to improve conditions were on the whole timid, often wrongheaded (such as highly protectionist trade policies), and only modestly successful. Nonetheless, the appearance in that decade of a new economic accountability for government constitutes in itself sufficient reason to describe capitalism today in terms that distinguish it from its industrial, but largely unguided, past. The concept of capitalistic economy has changed. Provision of infrastructure has now been the responsibility of the State. In order to develop infrastructure, State should not shy to go for huge investments either through its own resources or through private participation. There is little doubt that capitalism in the 21st century will undergo still further structural alterations. Technological advances are rapidly reducing to near insignificance the once formidable barriers and opportunities of economic geography. Among the startling consequences of this technological leveling of the world have been the displacements of the economic center of the globe from the Atlantic to the Pacific and the threat of large displacements of high tech manufacture from Europe and North America to low wage regions of Southwest Asia, Latin America, and possibly Africa. Another change has been the unprecedented growth of international finance to the point at which the total value of transactions in foreign exchange is estimated to be at least 20 times that of all foreign movements of goods and services. This boundary-blind internationalization of finance, combined with the boundary-defying ability of large corporations to locate their operations in low wage countries, poses a challenge to the traditional economic sovereignty of nations, a challenge arising from the new capabilities of capital itself. A third change again involves the international economy, this time through the creation of new institutions for the management of international economic trade. A number of capitalist nations have met the challenges of the fast-growing international economy by joining the energies of the private sector, including organized labour, with the financial and negotiating powers of the State. This "corporatist" approach, most clearly evident in the organization of the Japanese economy, may become a common structural characteristic of capitalism in the 21st century, not only in managing foreign trade and production but also in dealing with domestic problems, such as inflation. These still emergent trends seem likely to exert their pressures toward further growth of the governmental guiding role within capitalism. It is not necessary, however, to venture risky predictions about the future. Rather, it seems more useful to conclude with two generalizations. The first emphasizes that capitalism, in all its variations, continues to be distinguished from other economic systems by the priority accorded to the drive for wealth and the centrality of the competitive mechanism that channels this drive toward those ends that the market rewards. The second generalization is that this driving force and constraining mechanism appear to be compatible with a wide variety of institutional settings, including substantial variations in the relationships between the private and public sectors. It is to this very adaptability that capitalism appears to owe its continued vitality.

4

Economics Development

A Survey of Development Theories: Role of Governments and Markets

As per earlier thinking on development, it was assumed that the market mechanisms of developed economies were so unreliable in developing economies that governments had to assume central responsibility for economic activity. This was to be done through economic planning for the entire economy, which in turn would be implemented by active government participation in the economy and pervasive controls over all private sector economic activity. Government participation took many forms. Public sector enterprises were established to manufacture many commodities, including steel, machine tools, fertilizers, heavy chemicals, and even textiles and clothing. Government marketing boards assumed monopoly power over the purchase and sale of many agricultural commodities, and government agencies became the sole importers of a variety of goods, and they often became exporters as well. Controls over private sector activity were even more extensive. Price controls were established for many commodities. Similarly, elaborate import licensing procedures complicated, if not eliminated imports and the importing of commodities was not given priority in official plans; investment licenses were required before factories could be expanded; capacity licenses regulated maximum permissible outputs; and comprehensive regulations governed the conditions of employment of workers. The consequence, frequently, was that indigenous entrepreneurs often found it more financially rewarding to devote their energies and ingenuity to the task of procuring the necessary government import licenses and other permits and exploiting the loopholes in government regulations than to the problem of raising the efficiency and productivity of resources. For public sector enterprises, political pressures often resulted in employment of many more persons than could be productively used and in other practices conducive to extremely high cost and inefficient operations. The consequent fiscal burden diverted resources that might otherwise have been used for investment, while the inefficient use of resources dampened growth rates. Related to the belief in market failure and in the necessity for government intervention was the view that the efficiency of the price mechanism in developing countries was very small. This was reflected in the view of foreign exchange shortage, in which it was thought that there are fixed relationships between imported capital and domestic expansion. By the end of the 1950s, the experience gained from efforts to promote economic development showed great differences among developing countries. Some had broken away relatively quickly from the import substitution, government control and ownership pattern that had been the early development wisdom. Others persisted with the same policies for several decades. India initially tried to wriggle out from the policy of import substitution, and government control, which was also reflected in 1948 Industrial Policy Resolution, but gave in to and persisted with the policy till 1991, due to reasons that no private entrepreneur came forward to capitalize on the government policy. A great deal was learnt from the experiences of different developing countries.

Centrally Planned Systems

No survey of comparative economic systems would be complete without an account of centrally planned systems, the modern descendants of the command economies of the imperial past. In sharpest possible contrast to those earlier tributary arrangements, however, modern command societies have virtually all been organized in the name of socialism, that is, with the function of command officially administered on behalf of the broad masses of the population. Socialist central planning needs to be differentiated from the idea of socialism itself. The latter draws on moral precepts of concern for the needy that can be discovered in the Judeo-Christian tradition and derives its general social orientation from Gerrard Win Stanley's 'Diggers Movement' during the English Civil Wars in the mid-17th century: "The Earth," Winstanley wrote, "was made by Almighty God to be a Common Treasury of livelihood to the whole of mankind . . . without respect of persons." Socialism as a means of orchestrating a modern industrial system, did not receive explicit attention until the Russian Revolution in 1917. In his brochure *The State and Revolution*, written before he came to power, Lenin envisaged the task of coordinating a socialist economy as little more than delivering production to central collecting points from which it would be distributed according to need-an operation requiring no more than "the extraordinarily simple operations of watching, recording, and issuing receipts, within the reach of anybody who can read and who knows the first four rules of arithmetic." After the revolution, it soon became apparent that the problem was a great deal more difficult than it was thought to be. The mobilization of manpower required the complex determination of appropriate amounts and levels of pay, and the mobilization of foodstuffs from the countryside posed the awkward question of the degree to which the "bourgeois" peasantry would have to be accommodated. As civil war raged in the country, these problems intensified until production fell to a catastrophic 14 percent of pre-war levels. By the end of 1920, the system was on the verge of collapse. To forestall disaster, Lenin instituted the New Economic Policy (NEP), which amounted to a partial restoration of capitalism, especially in retail trade, small-scale production, and agriculture. Only the "commanding heights" of the economy remained in government hands. The NEP resuscitated the economy but opened a period of intense debate as to the use of market incentives versus moral persuasion or coercive techniques. The debate, which remained unresolved during Lenin's life, was brought to a conclusion at his death in 1924, when Joseph Stalin rose to power and rapidly forced the collectivization of the economy. Private agriculture was converted into collective farming with great cruelty and loss of life, all capitalist markets and private enterprises were quickly and ruthlessly eliminated, and the direction of economic life was consigned to a bureaucracy of ministries and planning agencies. By the 1930s, a structure of centralized planning had been put into place that was to coordinate the Russian economy for the next half century. Soviet planning at the center of the planning system was the Gosplan (gos means "committee"), the top economic planning agency of the Soviet state. Above the Gosplan were the political arms of the Soviet government, while below it were smaller planning agencies for the various Soviet republics. The Gosplan itself was staffed by economists and statisticians charged with drawing up what amounted to a blueprint for national economic activity, usually for a five to seven year period. This blueprint translated the major objectives determined by political decision (electrification targets, agricultural goals, transportation networks, and the like) into industry-specific requirements (outputs of generators, fertilizers, steel rails, etc.). These general requirements were then referred to ministries charged with management of industries in question, where the targets were further broken down into specific outputs (quantities, qualities, shapes, and sizes of steel plates, girders, rods, wires, and so forth) and where lower-level goals were fixed, such as budgets for firms, wage rates for different skill levels, or managerial bonuses. Planning was not, therefore, entirely a one-way process. General objectives were indeed transmitted from the top down, but as each ministry and factory inspected its obligations, specific obstacles and difficulties were transmitted from the bottom up. The final plan was, thus, a compromise between the political objectives of the Central Committee of the Communist Party and the nuts-and-bolts considerations of the echelons charged with its execution. This coordinative mechanism worked quite well when the larger objectives of the system called for a kind of crash planning that resembled a war economy. The Soviet economy achieved unprecedented rapid progress in its industrialization drive before World War II and in repairing the devastation that followed the war. Moreover, in areas where the political stakes were high, such as space technology, the planning system was able to concentrate skills and resources regardless of cost, which enabled the Soviet Union on more than one occasion to outperform similar undertakings in the West. Yet, charged with the orchestration of a civilian economy in normal peacetime conditions, the system of centralized planning failed seriously. Because of its failures, a far-reaching reorganization of the system was set into motion in 1985, by Mikhail Gorbachev, who coined the concept during 1975, under the banner of perestroika ("restructuring"), and glasnost (transparency). The extent of the restructuring can be judged by following changes proposed in the coordinative system:

(1) Scope and penetration of planning were to be greatly curtailed and directed mainly at general economic goals, such as rates of growth, consumption or investment targets, or regional development;
(2) Planning done for factory enterprises was to give way to planning by factories themselves, guided by considerations of profit and loss;
(3) Factory managers were no longer to be bound by instructions with respect to the sources of their inputs and the destination of their outputs but were to be free to buy from and to sell to whomever they pleased;

(4) Managers were also to be free to hire, and more importantly, to fire workers, who formerly could not be easily discharged; and

(5) Many kinds of small private enterprises were to be encouraged, especially in farming and the retail trades.

This programme obviously represented a dramatic retreat from the original idea of central planning. One cannot say, however, that it also represented a decisive turn from socialism to capitalism, for it was not clear to what extent the restructured planning system might embody other essential features of capitalism, such as private ownership of the means of production and exclusion of political power from the normal operations of economic life. Nor was it known to what extent economic *perestroika* was to be accompanied by its political counterpart, *glasnost* (openness). Thus, the degree of change in both the economic structure and the underlying political order remained indeterminate. The record of *perestroika* over the rest of the 1980s was disappointing. After an initial flush of enthusiasm, the task of abandoning the centralized planning system proved to be far more difficult than anticipated, to no small degree because the achievement of such a change would have necessitated creation of a new structure of economic (managerial) power, independent of, and to some extent in continuous tension with, that of political power, much as under capitalism. Also, the operation of the centralized planning system, freed from some of the coercive pressures of the past, but not yet infused with the energies of the market, rapidly deteriorated. Despite bumper crops, for example, it was impossible to move potatoes from the fields to retail outlets, so that rations decreased and rumours of acute food shortages raced through Moscow. By the end of the decade, the Soviet system was facing an economic breakdown, more severe and far-reaching than the worst capitalist crisis of the 1930s. Not surprisingly, the unrest aroused ancient nationalist rivalries and ambitions, threatening the dismemberment of the Soviet economic and political empire. As the Soviet central government gradually lost control over the economy at the republic and local levels, the system of central planning eroded without adequate free-market mechanisms to replace it. By 1990, the Soviet economy had slid into near paralysis, and this condition foreshadowed the fall from power of the Soviet Communist Party and the breakup of the Soviet Union itself into a group of independent republics in 1991.

POLITICAL SYSTEM, THE NEED FOR PSU

The Functions of Government

Whether government would function as an umpire and play the role of a facilitator, or enter into the functions of a development agency has been debated for quite some time. Though there has not been any clear demarcation of role, and functions can not be segregated into water-tight compartment, apart from functioning as an umpire, government have to play an active role to bring about improvement in the quality of life of common man. In all modern States, governmental functions have greatly expanded with the emergence of government as an active force in guiding social and economic development. In Socialist countries, government has a vast range of responsibilities for many types of economic behaviour. Even in the United States, where there remains a much greater attachment than in most societies to the idea that government should be only an umpire, adjudicating the rules by which other forces in society compete, such governmental activities as the Tennessee Valley Authority or the use of credit controls to prevent economic fluctuations are now accepted with relatively little questioning. Government has, thus, become the major or even the dominant organizing power in all contemporary societies. The historical stages by which governments have come to exercise their contemporary functions make an interesting study in themselves. The scope of government in the ancient polis involved comprehensive regulation of the ends of human existence. As Aristotle expressed it, "what did government not command, was forbidden". Christianity and its insistence on a division of those things that belong separately to Caesar and to God challenged the extent of the functions of government in the ancient world. When the feudal world succeeded the Roman Empire, however, the enforcement of the sanctions of religion became one of the first objects of political authority. In feudal India, the Brahminical culture was so rampant that the kings were entirely dependent on the divine grace and dictum emanating from the religious gurus, i.e., the teachers. The pronouncements of the saints, and palace religious teachers were absolute and final. Gradually, the concept of religious absolutism came under attack. It all started in the second century B.C, when Gautam Buddha challenged the Brahminical monopoly and propounded a new religion called Buddhism. Similarly, in Western countries, the tendencies that began in the 18th century separated church from State, and State from society, and the modern concept of government came into being. The first aim of government is to secure the right to life; this comprehends the safety of fellow citizens as regards one another and self-preservation of the nation as regards foreign powers. Life exists for the exercise of liberty, in terms of both natural and civil rights, and these, along with other specific functions of government, provide those conditions upon which men may pursue happiness, an end that is finally entirely private and beyond the competence of government. With the advent of the Marxist conception of the State, the ends of human existence once again became the objects of comprehensive government regulation. Marxism sees the State as a product of class warfare that will pass out of existence in the future age of perfect freedom. Aristotle believed human perfection to be possible only within political society. Marx believed that perfection of man would follow abolition of political society.

Before the final disposal of the State, however, many Marxists believe that forceful use of governmental power is justified in order to hasten mankind's progress toward the last stage of history.

State's tasks; Self-preservation

The State has numerous functions to perform. Human development, upward movement in quality of life, protection of life and property are some of such solemn duties. It is a complex one. The first right of men and nations is self-preservation. The task of maintaining the nation, however, is more complex than the individual's duty of self-preservation, for the nation must seek to command the attachment of a community of citizens as well as to preserve itself from external violence. As Thomas Hobbes insisted, civil war constitutes the greatest threat to governments, for it represents the dissolution of the "sovereign power". In modern terms, civil war signifies that the government has lost one of the basic attributes of political authority: its monopoly of force and its control over the use of violence. In a fundamental sense, political authority may be preserved from the threat of civil war only when there exists in the political community an agreement on the basic principles of the regime. Such a consensus is the result, among other things, of a shared "ideology" that gives fellow citizens a sense of communal belonging and recognizes interlocking values, interests, and beliefs. Ideology, in this sense, may be the product of many different forces. Sometimes it is associated with ancient customs, sometimes with religion, sometimes with severe dislocations or the sort of common need that has led to formation of many nation-States, and sometimes with the fear of a common enemy. The ideological commitment that people call patriotism is typically the product of several of these forces. Governments neglect at their peril the task of strengthening the ideological attachment of their citizens to the regime. In this sense, civic education should be counted among the essential functions of the State, for it is primarily through systems of education that citizens learn their duties. Indeed, as a number of sociological studies have shown, the process of political socialization that transforms people into citizens begins in kindergarten and grade school. Even more than this, education is the instrument by which governments further the cohesion of their societies and build the fundamental kinds of consensus that support their authority. It is not surprising, therefore, that national systems of education are often linked to central elements of the regimes. In France, public education was traditionally mixed with the teachings of the Roman Catholic Church; in Great Britain a private system of education supported the class divisions of society; and in the United States a primarily secular form of public education traditionally used constitutional documents as the starting point of children's training in patriotism. The preservation of the authority of the State also requires a governmental organization capable of imposing its jurisdiction on every part of the national territory. This involves maintenance of means of communication, use of administrative systems, and employment of police forces capable of controlling domestic violence. The police function, like education, is often a key to the character of a regime. In Nazi Germany, Hitler's Brown shirts took over the operation of local and regional police systems and often supervised administration of law in the streets. In the Soviet Union, the security police acted to check any deviation from the policy of the Party or State. In the United States, the police powers are left in the hands of the 50 states and local agencies of government. With the exception of certain offenses created by the McCarran Act and some parallel statutes, political crimes as such are unknown. In addition, there are state militias that act, under the control of the governors of the various states, in moments of local emergency, such as riots or natural catastrophes. The Federal Bureau of Investigation (FBI), the only equivalent of a national police force, is an agency established to carry out specific assignments dealing with a limited but important class of crimes. Since there is no comprehensive federal criminal code, there is, strictly speaking, no federal police. In India, there has been a clear division of powers between the Central government and the provincial government as per *Constitution of India*. There is a Central List, which endows to Government of India an exclusive domain to perform its duties. Similarly, state governments also do perform their functions within the State List. The Concurrent List is for both Central as well as state governments. Maintenance of law and order has been the exclusive function of a state government. But education comes within the Concurrent List. Similarly, criminal codes and penal codes have been framed by Central Government but state government may tune them to the local needs and aspirations. Judiciary acts as an arbiter between the citizens on one hand and the state on the other. Judiciary has been a fully independent body. The executive has no control over the judiciary in the constitutional framework. Parliamentary system of government has taken its root in India and the process of decentralizing the democratic functions to the grass root is on. Governments must preserve themselves against external as well as domestic threats. For this purpose, they maintain armed forces and carry on intelligence activities. They also try to prevent entry of aliens, who may be spies or saboteurs; imprison or expel the agents of foreign powers; and put an embargo on export of materials that may aid a potential enemy. The ultimate means of preserving the State against external threats, of course, is war. In war, governments usually enlarge the scope of their domestic authority; they may raise conscript forces, imprison conscientious objectors, subject aliens to internment, sentence traitors to death, impose extraordinary controls on the economy, censor the press, compel settlement of labour disputes, impose internal-travel limitations, withhold passports, and provide for summary forms of arrest and trials. Many forces generate clashes between nations, including economic rivalry and disputes over trade, the desire to dominate strategic land or sea areas, religious or ideological conflict, and imperialistic ambition. All national governments develop organizations and policies to meet these and other situations. They have foreign ministries for the conduct of diplomatic relations with other states, for representing them in international organizations, and for negotiating treaties. Some governments conduct programmes such as foreign aid, cultural exchange, and other activities designed to win goodwill abroad. In the 20th century, relationships among governments have been affected by a developing awareness that world peace and prosperity depend on multinational and international cooperation. The League of Nations and the United Nations, together with their associated agencies, have represented major efforts to establish substitutes for traditional forms of di lomacy. Regional alliances and joint efforts, such as the Organization of American States, the North Atlantic Treaty Organization, the European Economic Community, and the Organization of African Unity, represent another type of cooperation among nations.

Functions of Government

Protection of Political and Social Rights

To some extent, all modern governments assume responsibility for protecting the political and social rights of their citizens. The protection of individual rights has taken two principal forms. Firstly, it is the protection of liberty in the face of governmental oppression and, secondly, it is the protection of individual rights against hostile majorities and minorities. From the 1960s to the mid-1980s the sphere of public discussion in the Soviet Union was gradually, though erratically, widened. While this widening never extended to the purely political, some of the sociological discussion allowed served to set the intellectual stage for the Gorbachev period of radical reform. Although the Soviet Union suppressed most expression of political opinion until the late 1980s, domination by a central authority protected the basic human rights of some groups from violent rival minorities. On a larger scale, this is also what suppressed many long-standing rivalries in Eastern Europe during the Cold War. The degree of repression in the former Communist states varied from country to country and changed with time after the death of Stalin. In the United States, the Supreme Court expanded the rights of the criminally accused; and after 1954 the national government acted to bar legal discrimination against ethnic minorities. Indeed, almost all the freedoms detailed in the first 10 amendments to the Constitution have been extended since World War II. Constitution of India guarantees human dignity, liberty, freedom of expression and speech, in various forms, irrespective of caste, creed, religion, race, faith, place of birth and colour. The Supreme Court of India has been given enormous powers to negate any violation of fundamental and human rights enshrined in the Constitution. Indeed, in the recent past the Supreme Court has expanded its jurisdiction by entertaining various public interest litigations, thereby protecting and upholding the right to life, and liberty, human dignity, equality before law, freedom of expression and speech. India has also a National Human Rights Commission headed by a retired Chief Justice of Supreme Court, which in the recent past has expanded its area of jurisdiction by incorporating human dignity, and quality of life in its ambit. Provincial Governments have also followed the suit and have set up Human Rights Commissions in their states.

Another type of government regulation, having bearing on the individuals, is the law of immigration and emigration. The great mass migrations of the 19th and early 20th centuries came to an abrupt halt after 1914 with the proliferation of government controls on the freedom of movement across national boundaries. After some later liberalization, immigration to the industrialized states again saw increased restrictions near the end of the 20th century. This law of immigration restricting the flow of men and women to the countries of their choice does act as a barrier to achieve the concept of a 'village world'.

Provision of Goods and Services

All modern governments participate directly in the economy, purchasing goods, operating industries, providing services, and promoting various economic activities. One of the indispensable functions of government like national defense has made governments the most important consumers of goods, and they have not hesitated to use their resulting pricing, purchasing, and contracting powers to achieve various economic aims. In efforts to avoid dependence on private sources of strategic goods and defense materials, some governments have taken a further step and established their own military production plants. In wartime, governments have assumed control over entire industries and have subjected the work force to military direction in addition to rationing goods and regulating prices. In nearly all political systems, certain functions are recognized as public, or belonging to the government. In addition to national defense, these include the maintenance of domestic peace, public education, public health, fire protection, traffic control, aid to the indigent, conservation of natural resources, disaster mitigation management, flow of currency, fixation of rate of interest, and postal services and so on. These are the sovereign functions of a government. But governments, even in non-socialist countries, have assumed responsibility for many other commercial operations. The sale of electric power, for example, is one of the established enterprising functions of national, state, and local governments in the United States and Canada. Municipally owned power utilities exist in about 2,000 cities in North America, 14 states of the U.S. have public power districts, and the U.S. government markets power through the Tennessee Valley Authority, the Bureau of Reclamation, and several other agencies. Another range of functions is performed by other national agencies, including the Rural Electrification Administration, which loans money to rural cooperatives to finance local power projects; the Export-Import Bank of Washington, which doles out loans to finance export and import trade; the Maritime Administration, which holds mortgages on ships; and the Veterans Administration, which gives loans for farm or home purchases to military veterans. The United States government, acting through agencies-such as the Social Security Board, the Federal Deposit Insurance Corporation, and the Federal Housing Administration-is also the largest insurer in the nation. Through other agencies, such as the Housing and Home Finance Agency, the Urban Renewal Administration, and the Public Works Administration, the national government has also developed a major role in the construction and rental of residential housing for low-income persons. Other miscellaneous enterprises in which governments are involved, include the provision of health care, the operation of public transport facilities, the development of public works, airport and port maintenance, and water-supply systems. In Great Britain, the government operates hospitals and provides medical care under the National Health Service. In the United States, many state and local governments operate hospitals on a commercial basis, although providing some charity care. At the local level, in the United States, the Port of New York Authority constructs and operates bridges, terminals, and airports. The states in the Delaware Basin have joined in a contract to establish an agency to control the use of water from the basin, institute programmes to prevent pollution, provide recreation facilities, transmit and sell hydroelectric power, and provide watershed management. Cities in the United States and Canada operate more than 70 urban transit systems, 600 municipal gas utilities, and more than 4,000 water-supply systems. Cities are also generally responsible for garbage disposal and sometimes operate commercial slaughterhouses, coal yards, laundries, ice plants, and golf courses. Finally, packaged liquor sales, either wholesale or retail or both, are often made by the state governments. In India, which follows a policy of mixed economy, all state Governments and Central Government run hospitals free of cost, carry out all kinds of construction activities, run public transport systems, milk booths, hotels, airports, shipping companies, electricity boards, and engage itself in production of all kinds of consumable articles. However, since 1991 there has been a perceptible change in the attitude of the political parties in this regard, and the process is being reversed.

5

Industrial Policy Resolutions

British Government always protected its domestic industries at the cost of industries in its colonies. Therefore, during its colonial rule, the British Government always spurned the idea of an industrial policy for India. Soon after India attained Independence in August 1947, the Government in its Industrial Policy Resolution in 1948 made enunciations of principles for industrial development. This resolution envisaged a progressively dominant role for the State in country's industrial development, within the context of planned development of the Indian economy. These policies sought to accelerate the rate of economic growth, develop basic industries and lay down a sound economic foundation, thereby increasing employment opportunities and improving the standard of living and the working conditions of the masses. The policy also sought to reduce the disparities in income and prevent the concentration of economic power. The new Government reposed faith in the industrial growth and had further undertaken to reduce bottlenecks of any kind and set up committees to minimise any bureaucratic hurdles.

Industrial Policy Resolution, 1948

This resolution was a document that sought to clarify the new Indian government's economic policies and objectives. The government recognized the need for a mixed economy and reserved national monopolies for only the munitions, atomic energy, and railroad industries. While extant industries held by private firms could continue, the government had the exclusive rights to initiate projects in six other industries namely, coal, iron, and steel, aircraft manufacturing, shipbuilding, telephone and telegraph, and minerals. If need be, it could seek the aid of the private sector in these areas. Besides, the government could regulate and license 18 other industries of national importance. This resolution reassured foreign investors and the domestic business community that their holdings would not be confiscated or nationalized. In 1956, the government expanded the list of public sector holdings to capital and intermediate goods. Some services, such as the insurance business, and banking, latter only partly, were gradually nationalized by 1973.

The Industrial Policy Resolution, 1948 approved by Parliament on April 6th, 1948 described for the first time, the role of State in industrial development of the country. The Resolution stressed "the State must play a progressively active role in the development of industries, but ability to achieve the main objective should determine the immediate extent of state responsibility and limits to private enterprise". Under the then conditions, the mechanism and the resources of the state did not permit it to function forth with in industry as widely as one may consider desirable. In this context it was felt necessary that "for some times to come, the state could contribute more quickly to the increase of national wealth by expanding its present activities wherever it is operating and concentrating on the new units of production in other fields, rather than on acquiring and running existing units." This Resolution, for the first time paved the way for strengthening mixed economy in the country in which the State and private agencies were visualized to participate in the industrial development of the nation as direct entrepreneur and work together to achieve the national objective. In this policy resolution it was also decided "that the manufacture of arms and ammunitions, the production and control of atomic energy, and the ownership and management of railway transport should be the exclusive monopoly of the Central Government. Further in any emergency the government would always have the powers to take over any industry for national defence".

It was also enunciated in this policy resolution that State would be responsible for establishment of new industrial units, like iron and steel, coal, and aircraft manufacturing, ship building, manufacture of telephone and telegraph with wireless ingredients and so on, except where, in the national interest, the State found it necessary to secure the cooperation of private enterprise subject to control and regulation as the Central Government might prescribe. The rest of the industrial field would normally be open to private enterprise, individual as well as cooperative. Besides, "the state in addition to participating in these fields, would not hesitate to intervene whenever the progress of an industry under private enterprise was unsatisfactory."

Government of India set out the details of Industrial Resolution Policy, 1948 as follows:

1. "No. 1(3)-44(13)/48- The Government of India have given careful thought to the economic problems facing the country. The nation has now set itself to establish a social order where justice and equality of opportunity shall be secured to all the people. The immediate objective is to provide educational facilities and health services on a much wider scale, and to promote a rapid rise in the standard of living of the people by exploiting the latent resources of the country, increasing production and offering opportunities to all for employment in the service of the community. For this purpose, careful planning and integrated effort over the whole field of national activity are necessary, and the Government of India proposes to establish a National Planning Commission to formulate programmes of development and to secure their execution. The present statement, however, confines itself to Government's policy in the industrial field.

2. Any improvement in the economic conditions of the country postulates an increase in national wealth. It is true that a mere redistribution of existing wealth would make no essential difference to the people and would merely mean the distribution of poverty. A dynamic national policy must, therefore, be directed to a continuous increase in production by all possible means, side by side with measures to secure its equitable distribution. In the present state of the nation's economy, when the mass of the people is below the subsistence level, the emphasis should be on the expansion of production. Both agricultural and industrial; and in particular on the production of capital equipment of goods satisfying the basic needs of the people and of commodities the export of which will increase earnings of foreign exchange.

3. The problem of State participation in Industry and the conditions in which private enterprises should be allowed to operate must be judged in this context. There can be no doubt that the State must play a progressively active role in the development of industries, but ability to achieve the main objectives should determine the immediate extent of State responsibility and the limits to private enterprise. Under present conditions, the mechanism and the resources of the State may not permit it to function forthwith in industry as widely as may be desirable. The Government of India are taking steps to remedy the situation; in particular, they are considering steps to create a body of men trained in business methods and management. They feel, however, that for some time to come, the State could contribute more quickly to the increase of national wealth by expanding its present activities wherever it is already operating and by concentrating on new units of production in other fields, rather than on acquiring and running existing units. Meanwhile, private enterprise, properly directed and regulated, has a valuable role to play.

4. On these considerations the Government have decided that the manufacture of arms and ammunition, the production and control of atomic energy, and ownership and management of railway transport should be the

exclusive monopoly of the Central Government. Further in any emergency, the Government would always have the power to take over any industry vital for national defence. In the case of the following industries, the state which in this context, includes Central, Provincial and State Governments and other Public Authorities like Municipal Corporations will be exclusively responsible for the establishment of new undertakings, except where, the national interest, the State itself finds it necessary to secure the co-operation of private enterprise subject to such control and regulation as the Central Government may prescribe:

1. Coal (the India Coalfields Committee's proposals will be generally followed);
2. Iron and Steel;
3. Aircraft manufacture;
4. Shipbuilding;
5. Manufacture of telephone, telegraph and wireless apparatus, excluding radio receiving sets; and
6. Mineral oils.

While the inherent right of the State to acquire any existing industrial undertaking will always remain, and will be exercised whenever the public interest requires it, Government have decided to let existing undertakings in these fields to develop for a period of ten years, during which they will be allowed all facilities for efficient working and reasonable expansion. At the end of this period, the whole matter will be reviewed and a decision taken in the light of circumstances obtaining at the time. If it is decided that the State should acquire any unit, the fundamental rights guarantec by the Constitution will be observed and compensation will be awarded on a fair and equitable basis.

Management of State enterprise will, as a rule, be through the medium of public corporations under the statutory control of the Central Government, who will assume such powers as may be necessary to ensure this.

5. The Government of India has recently promulgated a measure for the control by the State of generation and distribution of electric power. This industry will continue to be regulated in terms of measures.

6. The rest of the industrial field will normally be open to private enterprise, individual as well as co-operative. The State will not only progressively participate in this field; but will not also hesitate to intervene whenever the progress of an industry under private enterprise is unsatisfactory. The Central Government have already embarked on enterprises like large river valley developments, which are multipurpose projects of great magnitude, involving extensive generation of hydro-electric power and irrigation on a vast scale, and calculated in a comparatively short time to change the entire face of large areas in this country. Projects like the Damodar Valley Scheme, the Kosi Reservoir, the Hirakund Dam, etc., a class by themselves, can stand comparison with any of the major schemes in America or elsewhere. The Central Government have also undertaken the production of fertilizer on a very large scale, and have in view other enterprises like the manufacture of essential drugs, and of synthetic oil from coal; many Provincial and State Governments are also proceeding on similar lines.

7. There are certain basic industries of importance, apart from those mentioned in paragraph 4, the planning and regulation of which by the Central Government is necessary in the national interest. The following industries whose location must be governed by economic factors of All-India import, or which require considerable investment of a high degree of technical skill, will be the subject of Central regulation and control:

1. Salt;
2. Automobiles and tractors;
3. Prime movers;
4. Electric engineering;
5. Other heavy machinery;
6. Machine tools;

7. Heavy chemicals, fertilizers , pharmaceuticals and drugs;
8. Electro-chemical industries;
9. Non-ferrous metals;
10. Rubber manufactures;
11. Power and industrial alcohol;
12. Cotton and woolen textiles;
13. Cement;
14. Sugar;
15. Paper and Newsprint;
16. Air and Sea transport;
17. Minerals;
18. Industries related to defense.

The above list cannot obviously be of an exhaustive nature. The Government of India, while retaining the ultimate direction over this field of industry, will consult the Governments of the Provinces and States at all stages and fully associate them in the formulations and execution of plants. Besides these Governments, representatives of Industry and Labour will also be associated with the Central bodies, which they propose to establish, as recommended by the Industries Conference.

8. Cottage and small-scale industries have a very important role in the national economy. Offering as they do scope for individual, village or co-operative enterprise, and means for the rehabilitation of displaced persons. These industries are particularly suited for better utilisation of local resources and for the achievement of the local self-sufficiency in respect of certain types of essential consumer goods like food, cloth and agricultural implements. The healthy expansion of cottage and small scale industries depends upon a number of factors like the provision of raw materials, cheap power, technical advice, organised marketing of their produce, and where necessary, safeguards against intensive competition by large scale manufacture, as the education of the worker in the use of the best available technique. Most of these fall in the Provincial sphere and are receiving the attention of the

Governments of the Provinces and the States. The Resolution of Industries Conference has requested the Central Government to investigate how far and in what manner these industries can be co-ordinated and integrated with large scale industries. The Government of India accept this recommendation. It will be examined, for example, how the textile mill industry can be made complementary to, rather than competitive with the handloom industry, which is the country's largest and best organised cottage industry. In certain other lines of production, like agricultural implements, textile accessories, and parts of machine tools, it should be possible to produce components on a cottage industry scale and assemble these into their final product at a factory. It will also be investigated how far industries at present highly centralised could be decentralised with advantage.

The Resolution of the Industries Conference has recommended that Government should establish a Cottage Industries Board for the fostering of small scale industries. The Government of India accept this recommendation and propose to create suitable machinery to implement it. A Cottage and Small Scale Industries Directorate will also be set up within the Directorate General of Industries and Supplies.

One of the main objectives will be to give a distinctly co-operative bias to this field of industry. During and before the last war, even a predominantly agricultural country like China showed what could be done in this respect and her mobile industrial co-operative units were of outstanding assistance in her struggle against Japan. The present international situation is likely to lessen to a marked degree our chances of getting capital goods for large scale industry and the leeway must be made up by having recourse to small-size industrial co-operative throughout the country.

9. The Government, however, recognise that their objective, viz securing the maximum increase in production will not be realised merely by prescribing the respective

spheres of the State and of Private enterprise in Industry. It is equally essential to ensure the fullest co-operation between labour and management and the maintenance of stable and friendly relations between them. A resolution on this subject was unanimously passed by the Industries Conference, which was held in December last. Amongst other things, the resolution states:

'.... The system of remuneration to capital as well as labour must be so devised that, while in the interest of the consumers and the primary producers excessive profits should be prevented by suitable methods of taxation and otherwise, both will share the product of their common effort, after making provision for payment of fair wages to labour, a fair return on capital employed in the industry and reasonable reserves for the maintenance and expansion of the undertakings.'

Government accept this Resolution. They also consider that labour's share of the profits should be on sliding scale normally varying with production. They propose, in addition to the over all regulation of industry by the State, to establish machinery for advising on fair wages, fair remuneration for capital, and conditions of labour. They will also take steps to associate labour in all matters concerning industrial production.

The machinery, which Government propose to set up, will function at different levels, central regional and unit. At the Centre, there will be Central Advisory Council, which will cover the entire field of industry, and will have under it Committees for each major industry. These Committees may be split up into sub-committees dealing with specific questions relating to the industry, e.g. production, industrial relations, wage fixation and distribution of profits. The regional machinery under thc Provincial Governments will be Provincial Advisory Boards which like the Central Advisory Council, will cover the entire field of industry within the Province; they will have under them Provincial Committees for each major industry. The Provincial Committees may also be split up into various sub-committees dealing with specific questions relating to production, wage fixation and industrial relations. Below the Provincial Committees will come the Works Committees and the Production Committees attached to each major industrial establishment.

The Works Committees and the Production Committees will be bi-partite in character, consisting of representatives of employers and workers only, in equal numbers. All other Committees will be tri-partite, with representatives of Government, employers and workers.

Government hope that the machinery proposed will substantially reduce the volume of industrial disputes. In the case of unresolved conflicts, Government trust that management and labour will, in their own interests and in the larger interests of the country, agree to settle them through recognised channels of conciliation and arbitration, which will be provided by Government. The Industrial Relations Machinery, both at the Centre and in the Provinces, is being strengthened, and permanent industrial tribunals are being established for dealing with major disputes.

The Government of India are also taking special steps to improve industrial housing as quickly as possible. A scheme for the construction of one million workers' houses in ten years is under contemplation, and a Housing Board is being constituted for this purpose. The cost will be shared in suitable proportions between Government, employers and labour, the share of labour being recovered in the form of a reasonable rent.

In order to ensure quick decisions on the various matters arising out of Industrial Truce Resolution, Government are appointing a special officer.

10. The Government of India agree with the view of the Industries Conference that, while it should be recognised that participation of foreign capital and enterprise, particularly as regards industrial technique and knowledge, will be of value to the rapid industrialisation of the country, it is necessary that the conditions under which they may

participate in Indian industry should be carefully regulated in the national interest. Suitable legislation will be introduced for this purpose. Such Legislation will provide for the scrutiny and approval by the Central Government of every individual case of participation of foreign capital and management in industry. It will provide that, as a rule, the major interest in ownership, and effective control, should always be in Indian hands; but power will be taken to deal with exceptional cases in a manner calculated to serve the national interest. In all cases, however, the training of suitable Indian personnel for the purpose of eventually replacing foreign experts will be insisted upon.

11. The Government of India are fully alive to their direct responsibility for the development of these industries, which they have found necessary to reserve exclusively for State enterprise. They are equally ready to extend their assistance to private or cooperative enterprise in the rest of the industrial field, and in particular, by removing transport difficulties and by facilitating the import of essential raw-materials to the maximum possible extent. The tariff policy of Government will be designed to prevent unfair foreign competition and to promote the utilisation India's resources without imposing unjustifiable burden on the consumer. The system of taxation will be reviewed and readjusted where necessary to encourage saving and productive investment and to prevent undue concentration of wealth in a small section of the population.

12. The Government of India hope that this elucidation of their intentions on fundamental aspects of industrial policy will remove all misapprehensions, and they are confident that a joint and intensive effort will now be made by labour, capital and the general public, which will pave the way for the rapid industrialisation of thc country."

Aftermath of Industrial Policy Resolution 1948

India had an industrial policy for the first time after it achieved independence. The Government of India set out in the Resolution, the policy, which they proposed to pursue in the industrial field. The Resolution emphasised the importance of the economy of securing continuous increases in production and its equitable distribution, and pointed out that the State must play of progressively active role in the development of industries. It laid down that besides arms and ammunition, atomic energy and railway transport, which would be the monopoly of the Central Government, the State would be exclusively responsible for the establishment of new undertakings in six basic industries-except where, in the national interest, the State itself found it necessary to secure the cooperation of private enterprise. The rest of the industrial field was left open to private enterprise though it was made clear that the State would also progressively participate in this field.

In the eight years, after the first industrial policy, the country had witnessed many important changes and developments. The Constitution of India was enacted, guaranteeing certain Fundamental Rights and enunciating Directive Principles of State Policy. Contrary to the Fundamental Rights, Directive Principles of State Policy was not enforceable in a court of law. But Parliament had the authority to enact laws in consonance with the Directive Principles. Planning had proceeded on an organized basis, and the First Five Year Plan had recently been completed. Parliament had accepted the socialist pattern of society as the objective of social and economic policy. These important developments necessitated a fresh statement of industrial policy, more particularly as the Second Five Year Plan was about to be placed before the country. In the light of these, the industrial policy must be governed by the principles laid down in the Constitution, the objective of socialism, and the experience gained during these years.

The Constitution of India, in its preamble, has declared that it aims at securing for all its citizens:

> WE THE PEOPLE OF INDIA, having solemnly resolved to constitute India into a
> SOVEREIGN SOCIALISTIC SECULAR DEMOCRATIC REBUBLIC and to secure

To all its citizens:

> "JUSTICE, Social, economic and political;
> LIBERTY of thought, expression, belief, faith and worship;
> EQUALITY of status and opportunity; and to promote among them all;
> FRATERNITY assuring the dignity of the individual and the unity of the Nation".

In its Directive Principles of State Policy, it is stated that:

> "The State shall strive to promote the welfare of the people by securing and protecting as effectively as it may a social order in which justice, social economic and political, shall inform all the institutions of the national life."

Further that:

"The State shall, in particular, direct its policy towards securing-

(a) that the citizens, men and women equally, have the right to an adequate means of livelihood;

(b) that the ownership and control of the material resources of the community are so distributed as best to sub serve the common good;

(c) that the operation of economic system does not result in the concentration of wealth and means of production to the common detriment;

(d) that there is equal pay for equal work for both men and women;

(e) that the health and strength of workers, men and women, the tender age of children are not abused and that citizens are not forced by economic necessity to enter vocations unsuited to their age or strength;

(f) that children are given opportunities and facilities to develop in a healthy manner and in the conditions of freedom and dignity and that childhood and youth are protected against exploitation and against moral and material abandonment."

These basic and general principles were given a more precise direction when Parliament accepted in December 1954, the socialistic pattern of society as the objective of social and economic policy. Industrial policy, as other policies, must therefore, be governed by these principles and directions.

In order to realise this objective, it was essential to accelerate the rate of economic growth and to speed up industrialisation and, in particular, to develop heavy industries and machine-making industries, to expand the public sector, and to build up a large and growing cooperative sector. The objectives of equal distribution of material wealth to sub serve common good, prevention of concentration of wealth, and to prevent regional disparity were the main force behind expansion of public sector in India. Such objectives in the Directive Principles of State Policy were a result of centuries of social, economic, and political deprivations of a class or classes of people in the society. The independence as well as the new Constitution gave an ample opportunity to bring about an end to such discrimination. The government pursued its policy vigoursely with a conviction that such a disparity could be bridged only through an expansion of public sector.

Industrial Policy Resolution, of 30th April, 1956

Highlights of the Policy

> "These provide the economic foundations for increasing opportunities for gainful employment and improving living standards and working conditions for the mass of the people.
>
> Equally, it is urgent to reduce disparities in income and wealth, which exist today, to prevent private monopolies and concentration of economic power in different fields in the hands of small numbers of individuals.
>
> Accordingly, the State will progressively assume a predominant and direct responsibility for setting up new industrial undertakings and for developing transport facilities.

It will also undertake State trading on an increasing scale. At the same time, as an agency for planned national development, in the context of country's expanding economy, the private sector will have the opportunity to develop and expand.

The principle of cooperation should be applied whenever possible and a steadily increasing proportion of the activities of the private sector developed along cooperative lines."

The adoption of the socialist pattern of society as the national objective, as well as the need for 'planned and rapid development' required that all industries of basic and strategic importance', or in the nature of 'public utility services' should be in the public sector. Other industries, which were essential and required investment on a scale, which only the State, in those circumstances, could provide, had also to be in the public sector. The State had, therefore, to assume direct responsibility for the future development of industries over a wide area. Nevertheless, there were limiting factors, which made it necessary at that stage for the State to define the field in which it would undertake sole responsibility for further development, and to make a selection of industries in the development of which it would play a dominant role. After considering all aspects of the problem in consultation with the Planning Commission, the Government of India decided to classify industries into three categories, having regard to the part, which the State would play in each of them. "These categories would inevitably overlap to some extent and to great rigidity might defeat the purpose in view. But the basic principles and objectives had always to be kept in view and the general directions hereafter referred to be followed. It should also be remembered that it was always open to the State to undertake any type of industrial production".

In the first category would be the industries, the future development of which would be the exclusive responsibility of the State.

The second category would consist of industries, which would be progressively State-owned, and in which the State would, therefore, generally take the initiative in establishing new undertakings, but in which private enterprise would also be expected to supplement the efforts of the State.

The third category would include all the remaining industries, and their future development would, in general, be left to the initiative and enterprise of the private sector.

Industries in the first category were listed in Schedule-A of this Resolution. All new units in these industries, save where their establishment in the private sector had already been approved, would be sent only by the State. This did not preclude the expansion of the existing privately owned units, or the possibility of the State securing the cooperation of private enterprise in the establishment of new units when the national interests so required. Railways and air transport, arms and ammunition and atomic energy would, however, be developed as Central Government monopolies. Whenever cooperation with private enterprise was necessary, the State would ensure, either through majority participation in the capital or otherwise, that it has the requisite powers to guide the policy and control the operations of the undertakings.

Industries in the second category would be those listed in Schedule-B. With a view to accelerating their future development, the State would increasingly establish new undertakings in these industries. At the same time, private enterprise would also have the opportunity to develop in this field, either on its own or with State participation.

All the remaining industries would fall in the third category, and it was expected that their development would be undertaken ordinarily through the initiative and enterprise of the private sector, though it would be open to the State to start any industry even in this category. It would be the policy of the State to facilitate and encourage the development of these industries in the private sector, in accordance with the programmes formulated in successive Five Year Plans, by ensuring the development of transport, power and other services, and by appropriate fiscal and other measures. The State would continue to foster institutions to provide financial aid to these industries, and special assistance would be given to enterprises organised on cooperative lines for industrial and agricultural purposes. In suitable cases, the State might also grant financial assistance to the private sector. Such assistance, especially when the amount involved was substantial, would preferably be in the form of participation in equity capital, though it might also be in part, the form of debenture capital.

Industrial undertakings in the private sector had necessarily to fit into the framework of the social and economic policy of the State and would be subject to control and regulation in terms of the Industries (Development and Regulation) Act and other relevant legislation. The Government of India, however, recognised that it would, in general, be desirable to allow such undertakings to develop with as much freedom as possible, consistent with the targets and objectives of the national plan. When there existed in the same industry both privately and publicly owned units, it would continue to be the policy of the State to give fair and nondiscriminatory treatment to both of them.

The division of industries into separate categories did not imply that they were being placed in watertight compartments. Inevitably, there would not only be an area of overlapping but also a great deal of dovetailing between industries in the private and the public sectors. It would be open to the State to start any industry not included in Schedule-A and Schedule-B when the needs of planning so required or there were other important reasons for it. In appropriate cases, privately owned units might be permitted to produce an item falling within Schedule-A, for meeting their own requirements or as byproducts. There would ordinarily be no bar to small privately owned units undertaking production, such as the making of launches and other light craft, generation for power for local needs and small scale mining. Further, heavy industries in the public sector might obtain some of their requirements of lighter components from the private sector, while the private sector in turn would rely for many of its needs on the public sector. The same principle would apply with even greater force to the relationship between large scale and small scale industries.

The Government of India would, in this context, stress the role of cottage and village and small scale industries in the development of the national economy. In relation to some of the problems that needed urgent solutions, they offered some distinct advantages. They provided immediate large scale employment; addressed directly to the social sectors, which so far remained unattended to; they offered a method of ensuring a more equitable distribution of the national income; and they facilitated an effective mobilization of resources of capital and skill which might otherwise remained unutilized. Some of the problems that unplanned urbanisation tends to create would be avoided by the establishment of small centres of industrial production all over the country.

The State had been following a policy of supporting cottage and village and small scale industries by restricting the volume of production in the large scale sector, by differential taxation, or by direct subsidies. While such measures would continue to be taken, whenever necessary, the aim of the State Policy would be to ensure that the decentralized sector acquired sufficient vitality to be self supporting and its development was integrated with that of large-scale industry. The State would, therefore, concentrate on measures designed to improve the competitive strength of the small-scale producer. For this, it was essential that the technique of production should be constantly improved and modernised, the pace of transformation being regulated so as to avoid, as far as possible, technological unemployment. Lack of technical and financial assistance, of suitable working accommodation and inadequacy of facilities for repair and maintenance were among the serious handicaps of small scale producers. A start had been made with the establishment of industrial estates and rural community workshops to make good these deficiencies. The extension of rural electrification, and the availability of power at prices, which the workers could afford, would also be of considerable help. Many of the activities relating to small scale production would be greatly helped by the organisation of industrial cooperatives. Such cooperatives should be encouraged in every way and the State should give constant attention to the development of cottage and village and small scale industry.

In order that industrialisation might benefit the economy of the country as a whole, it was important that disparities in levels of development between different regions should be progressively reduced. The lack of industries in different parts of the country was very often determined by factors such as the availability of the necessary raw material and other natural resources. A concentration of industries in certain areas had also been due to the ready availability of power, water supply and transport facilities, which had been developed there. It was one of the aims of national planning to ensure that these facilities were steadily made available to areas which were at present lagging behind industrially or where there was greater need for providing opportunities for employment provided the location was otherwise suitable. Only by securing a balanced and coordinated development, of the industrial and the agricultural economy in each region, could the entire country attain higher standards of living.

This programme of industrial development would make large demand on the country's resources of technical and managerial personnel. To meet these rapidly growing needs for the expansion of the public sector and for the development of the village and small scale industries, proper managerial and technical cadres in the public services were to be established. Steps were also to be taken to meet shortages at supervisory levels, to organize apprenticeship schemes of training on a large scale both in public and in private enterprises, and to extend training facilities in business management in universities and other institutions.

It was necessary that proper amenities and incentives should be provided for all those engaged in industry. The living and working conditions of workers should be improved and their standards of efficiency raised. The maintenance of industrial peace was one of the prime requisites of industrial progress. In a socialist democracy, labour was a partner in the common task of development and should participate with enthusiasm. Some laws governing industrial relations had been enacted and a broad common approach had developed with growing recognition of the obligations of both management and labour. There should be joint consultation and workers and technicians should where ever possible, be associated progressively in management. Enterprises in the public sector had to set an example in this respect.

With the growing participation of the State in industry and trade, the manner in which these activities should be conducted and managed assumed considerable importance. Speedy decisions and a willingness to assume responsibility were essential if those enterprises were to succeed. For this wherever possible, there should be decentralisation of authority and their management should be along business lines. It was to be expected that public enterprises would augment the revenues of the State and provided resources for further development in fresh fields. But such enterprises might sometimes incur losses. Public enterprises had to be judged by their total results and in their working they should have the largest possible measure of freedom.

The Industrial Policy Resolution of 1948 dealt with a number of other subjects, which had since been covered by suitable legislation or by authoritative statement of policy. The division of responsibility between Central Government and the State Governments in regard to industries had been set out in the Industries (Development and Regulation) Act. The Prime Minister, in his statement in Parliament on 6 April 1949, had enunciated the policy of the State in regard to foreign capital.

The Government of India trusted that this statement of their Industrial Policy would receive the support of all sections of the people and promote the rapid industrialisation of the country.

SCHEDULE-A

Items included in Schedule -A of the Resolution were as follows:

1. Arms and ammunition and allied items of defence equipment;
2. Atomic energy;
3. Irons and Stee;
4. Heavy castings and forgings of iron and steel;
5. Heavy plant and machinery required for iron and steel production, for mining, for machine tool manufacture and for such other basic industries as may be specified by the Central Government;
6. Heavy electrical plant including large hydraulic and steam turbines;
7. Coal and lignite;
8. Mineral oils;
9. Mining of iron ore, manganese ore, chrome-ore, gypsum, sulphur, gold and diamond;
10. Mining and processing of copper, lead, zinc, tin, molybdenum and wolfram;
11. Minerals specified in the Schedule to the Atomic Energy (Control of Production and Use) Order, 1953;
12. Aircraft;
13. Air transport;
14. Railway Transport;
15. Ship Building;
16. Telephones and telephone cables telegraph and wireless apparatus (excluding radio receiving sets); and
17. Generation and distribution of electricity.

Industrial Policy Highlights

(Units involving investment in plant and machinery up to Rs.7.5 lakh and up to Rs.10 lakh for ancillary undertakings).

1. Preference would be given to small and medium entrepreneurs over the large industrial houses and foreign companies in the setting up of new capacity. Cooperatives, small and medium entrepreneurs would also be encouraged to participate in the production of mass consumption goods.

2. Exemption from licensing provisions for substantial expansion and new undertakings of up to Rs.1 crore by way of fixed assets in land, building and machinery was specified though for MRTPAct and foreign companies this exemption would not apply. Exemption from licensing would also not apply to existing licensed or registered undertakings having fixed assets exceeding Rs.5 crore.

3. The growth of public sector in India had been guided by the Industrial Policy Resolution, 1956 which gave the public sector a strategic role in the economy. At the time of India's independence in 1947, there were various problems confronting the country, which needed to be tackled in a planned and systematic manner. India basically had been an agrarian economy with a week industrial base, low level of savings and inadequate investment and near absence of infrastructural facilities. A vast population was extremely poor. There existed considerable inequalities in income, levels of employment as well as glaring regional imbalances in economic attainment and trained manpower in various fields of management. It was, thus, obvious that the country was to speed up its economic growth and maintain it in the long run at a steady level; a big push was required from the government. As such the state's intervention in all sectors of economy was inevitable because private sector had neither the necessary resources in terms of funds, managerial, and scientific skills nor the will to undertake risks involved in large long gestation investments. They were also not willing to take up social responsibility. Among the imperatives were

the removal of poverty, better distribution of income, expansion of employment opportunities, removal of regional imbalances, accelerated growth of agriculture and industrial production, better utilization of natural resources, and a wider ownership of economic power to prevent its concentration in a few hands. Given the type and range of problems faced by the country on its economic, social and strategic fronts and the various imperatives, it became a pragmatic compulsion to deploy public sector as an instrument of self reliant economic growth so as to develop a sound agriculture and industrial base, diversify the economy and overcome the economic backwardness. It emphasized the need for establishment of a socialistic pattern of society and the need for a planned and balanced industrial development of the nation. The state was, therefore, "to assume direct responsibility for the future development of industries over a wide area."

In this policy, all the industries were classified into three categories. *The first category* consists of seventeen industries, which were to be developed exclusively by the State. In *the second category* of twelve industries, the State would take initiative for the establishment of the same but private sector would also be involved wherever necessary. *The rest of the industries* were left to the private sectors but with an option to intervene in the interest of the State. This policy conceptualized the objective for establishing the "socialistic pattern of society". *However the public sector would not compete with the private sector, but would operate in a way complementing and supplementing to the later with a view to achieve the overall objective of the planned and balanced industrial development of the nation.*

This being main purpose behind the policy of 1956, massive investments have been made over the past about five decades to build a public sector. Many of these enterprises successfully expanded production, opened up new areas of technology and built up a reserve of technical competence in a number of areas. Nevertheless, after the initial concentration of public sector investment in key infrastructure areas, public sector enterprises began to spread into all areas of the economy including non infrastructure and non core areas.

Government enunciated Industrial policy during 1970, 1973, 1977, and in 1980, more or less reiterating and strengthening the earlier policy of 1956. Industrial policies have been outlined as below:

The Industrial Licensing Policy of February 18, 1970

It placed certain restrictions on undertakings belonging to the large industrial houses defined on the basis of assets exceeding to Rs.35 crores. In 1973, the definition of large industrial houses for industrial licensing restrictions was adopted in conformity with that in the Monopolies and Restrictive Trade Practices Act (MRTPA) 1969, on the basis of assets exceeding Rs.20 crores to provide more effective control on concentration of economic power. MRTP companies and foreign concerns were eligible to participate in industries that were not reserved for production in the public sector (Schedule A of IPR, 1956) or the small scale sector. It was these restrictions, which did not encourage foreign direct investment in India, as a result of which the country could not bring about rapid industrialization. There was no encouragement for foreign participation. Nationalistic concept and the concept of prevention of concentration of wealth in the hands of a few weighed very heavily in the minds of the planners. This resulted in less spending in crucial areas like infrastructure, and social sectors. Government evinced keen interest for investment in the areas which should have been left to private players.

Industrial Policy—Government decision of February 2, 1973: Key Provisions

In the 1973 Policy Statement it was noted that though some elements of the Industrial Policy Resolution of 1956 still remained valid, certain structural distortions had crept in the system. Hence new policies were directed towards removing these distortions. It provided for a closer interaction between the agricultural and industrial sectors, accorded the highest priority to generation and transmission of power. An exhaustive analysis of industrial products was made to identify products, capable of being produced in the small-scale sector. The list of industries exclusively reserved for the small-scale sector was expanded from 180 items to more than 500 items. It provided for an annual review of this list in view of new products and new processes of manufacture that emerge within the small-scale sector, a tiny sector was also defined with investment in machinery and equipment up to Rs. one lakh, situated in towns with a population of less than 50,000 according to 1971 census figures, and in villages. Special legislation to protect cottage and household industries was also proposed to be introduced. A District Industries Center would be set up to provide, under a single roof, all the services and support required by small and village entrepreneurs. In addition, the Khadi and Village Industries Commission would plan and develop the 22 village industries under its purview. The areas delineated for the large-scale industry were:

(a) basic industries that are essential for providing infrastructure and for the development for small and village industries, such as steel, non-ferrous metals, cement, and oil refineries;
(b) capital goods industries;
(c) high technology industries that require large-scale production and that are related to agricultural and small scale industrial development, such as fertilizers, pesticides and petro-chemicals; and
(d) other industries that are outside the list of reserved items for the small-scale sector, such as machine tools, and organic and inorganic chemicals. It was also clarified that foreign companies that diluted their foreign equity up to 40% under the Foreign Exchange Regulation Act (FERA), 1973 would be treated on par with Indian companies. A list of industries was issued where no foreign collaboration, financial or technical, was considered necessary

since indigenous technology was fully developed in the field. For all approved foreign investment, complete freedom for remittance of profits, royalties, dividends and repatriation of capital (subject to rules and regulations common to all) was provided. Only in highly export oriented and/or sophisticated technology areas, fully owned foreign companies were to be permitted. It was also decided that compulsory export obligations, merely for ensuring the foreign exchange balance of the project, would no longer be insisted upon while approving new industrial capacity. In cases, where a relaxation from industrial policy has been accorded specially on considerations of export alone, compulsory export obligations would continue to be imposed for sufficiently long periods. In order to secure balanced regional development, it was decided that industrial licenses would not be issued to new industrial units for location within certain limits of large metropolitan cities, having a population of more than one million and urban areas with a population of more than 5 lakhs as per the1971 census. In the areas of price control of agricultural and industrial products, the prices would be regulated to ensure an adequate return to the investor. The take over of the management of sick units by the Government would be resorted to only selectively in view of the fact that although large amounts of public funds have been pumped into sick units so taken over, yet these units continued to make losses which again have to be financed by the public exchequer.

Key Provisions of Industrial Policy— of December 23, 1977

Industrial Policy Highlights

A unique concept was designed to bring up the small industrial units. The nucleus plant would work for upgrading the technology of small units. The Government would promote the development of a system of linkages between nucleus large plants and the satellite ancillaries. To boost development of small-scale industries, the investment limit in the case of tiny units was enhanced to Rs.2 lakh, that of a small- scale unit to Rs.20 lakh and that of ancillaries to Rs.25 lakh. A scheme for building buffer stocks of essential raw materials for the Small Scale Industries was introduced for operation through the Small Industries Development Corporations in the States and the National Small Industries Corporation in the Center. In order to ensure fullest utilisation of existing industrial capacities, particularly in core industries and in industries with a long term export potential, the facility of automatic expansion of capacity of 5% per annum or 25% in a five year plan period to be taken in one or more stages was permitted to all industries. Requests for setting up 100% export-oriented units and for expansion of existing units for purposes of export would also be considered sympathetically. Industrial processes and technologies aimed at optimum utilisation of energy or exploitation of alternative sources of energy would be given special assistance, including finance on concessional terms. Similar benefits would be given to activities that contribute directly to improvement of the environment and reduce the deleterious effects on air and water.

Government of India pronounced its Industrial Policy Resolution of 1977, in the following words:

"For the past 20 years, Government Policy in the sphere of industry has been governed by the Industrial Policy Resolution of 1956. While some of the elements of that Resolution in regard to desirable pattern of industrial development still remain valid, the results of actual policies in the industrial field have not been up to the expectations or declared objectives. The growth of per capital national income during the last 10 years has been about 1.5 per cent per annum and is clearly inadequate to meet the needs of a developing economy. Unemployment has increased, rural-urban disparities have widened and the rate of real investment has stagnated. The growth of industrial output in the last decade has been no more than 3 to 4 per cent per annum on an average. The incidence of industrial sickness has become widespread and some of the major industries are the worst affected. The pattern of industrial costs and prices has tended to be distorted; and dispersal of industrial activity away from the larger urban concentration has been very slow.

The new Industrial Policy must, therefore, be directed towards removing the distortions of the past so that genuine aspirations of the people can be met within a time-bound programme of economic development.

The close interaction between the agricultural and industrial sectors of our economy cannot be over-emphasised. Much of our industrial production is based on agricultural raw materials. Similarly, in order to increase our agricultural productivity by adaptation of modern technology and agronomic practices to our own conditions, important inputs have to come from our industrial sector. The highest priority must be accorded to generation and transmission of power. Our recent experience demonstrates that lack of adequate power availability has become one of the most important constraints in the development of agriculture and industry. Similarly, cement and steel required to build our irrigation projects, the implements for ploughing and preparing the land, the equipment for processing high quality seeds, fertilizers and pesticides, oil and power, a wide range of industrial products are essential for increasing the level of our agricultural production. The prosperity and the distribution of income arising from a broad based growth of agriculture and related activities in the countryside have to provide the basic demand for a wide range of industries producing articles of consumption. It is only by such a process of reinforcing interaction of the agricultural and industrial sectors that employment can be found for the large number of the rural population who cannot be absorbed in the agricultural sector.

Today, our assets in terms of food grains and foreign exchange reserves are considerable. But much more importantly, our most valued asset is the willing hands of our rural manpower and the technicians who today form the third largest group of skilled manpower in the world. Great opportunities and great challenges are open to us now; but they cannot be seized by timid and half-hearted policies. A new approach is called for in several areas of our national life. This new approach should reflect not only our vast resources and special endowments but should show particular concern for the utilisation of these resources and endowments for the amelioration of the living conditions of the majority of our people, the new industrial policy should and will hereafter place man at the centre of planning and implementation of projects and schemes.

Small Scale Industries

The emphasis of industrial policy so far has been mainly on large industries, neglecting cottage industries and completely relegating small industries to a minor role. It is the firm policy of this Government to change this approach.

The main thrust of the new Industrial Policy will be on effective promotion of cottage and small industries widely dispersed in rural areas and small towns. It is the policy of the Government that whatever can be produced by small and cottage industries must only be so produced. For this purpose, an exhaustive analysis of industrial products has been made to identify those items, which are capable of being established or expanded in the small-scale sector. This list of industries, which would be exclusively reserved for the small- scale sector, has been significantly expanded and will now include more than 500 items as compared to about 180 items earlier. However, it must also be ensured that production in this sector is economic and of acceptable quality. The list of industries reserved for the Small Scale Sector has to be continually reviewed so that capacity creation does not lag behind the requirements of the economy. An annual review of reserved industries will be undertaken in order to ensure that reservation accorded to the small scale is efficient and is also continually expanded as new products and new processes capital of being manufactured in the small scale are identified.

Tiny Sector

While the existing definition of small- scale industries will remain, within the small- scale sector, special attention will be given to units in the tiny sector, namely those with investment in machinery and equipment up to Rs. One lakh and situated in towns with a population of less than 50,000 according to 1971 census figures, and villages. Schemes will be drawn up for making available margin money assistance, especially to tiny units in the small scale sector as well as to cottage and household industries.

Legislation for Cottage Industries

While there has been reservation for the small- scale sector, there has been no special protection for cottage and household industries sector. Government will consider introducing special legislation for protecting the interest of cottage and household industries with a view to ensuring that these activities, which provide self-employment, in large numbers get due recognition in our Industrial Development.

District Industries Centres

In the past, there has been a tendency to proliferate schemes, agencies and organisations which have tended more,to confuse the average small and rural entrepreneur than to encourage and help him. The focal point of development for small scale and cottage industries will be taken away from the big cities and State capitals to the district headquarters. In each district, there will be one agency to deal with all requirements of small and village industries. This will be called the District Industries Centre. Under the single roof of the District Industries Centre, all the services and support required by small and village entrepreneurs will be provided. These will include economic investigation of the district's raw materials and other resources, supply of machinery and equipment, provision or raw material, arrangements for credit facilities, and effective set-up for marketing and a cell for quality control, research and extension. The Centre will have a separate wing for looking after the special needs of cottage and household industries as distinct from small industries. The Centre will establish close linkages with the Development Blocks, on the one hand, and with specialised institutions, like Small Industries Service Institutes, on the other. It is the intention of the Government to extent this important organisational pattern to all the districts in the course of the next four years. Suitable financial and organisational support will be provided to the State Governments to achieve this objective. The financial assistance given to small and cottage industries under the Rural Industries Programme will also be extended to all the districts in the country within the next four years.

Effective Financial Support

In order to provide effective financial support for promotion of small village and cottage industries, the Industrial Development Bank of India has taken steps to set up a separate wing to deal exclusively with the credit requirements of this sector. It will coordinate, guide and monitor the entire range of credit facilities offered by other institutions for the small and cottage sector, for whom separate wings will be set up in these institutions, particularly nationalized banks. Banks will also be expected to earmark a specified proportion of their total advances for promotion of small, village and cottage industries. It is the policy of Government to see that no worthwhile scheme of small or village industry is given up for want of credit.

The growth of the scale and cottage industries sectors has been tardy mainly for want of satisfactory marketing arrangements for their products. The marketing of goods of these sectors with its concomitant of product standardisation, quality control, maximum support for these activities, is necessary on a priority basis. Measures such as purchase preference and reservation for exclusive purchase by Government Departments and Public Sector Undertakings will also be used to support the marketing of these products.

Khadi and Village Industries Commission

At present, 22 village industries are within the purview of the Khadi and Village Industries Commission. The promotional work in this area has, however, been haphazard and progress has been slow. The Khadi and Village Industries Commission will work out detailed plans for development of these village industries by adopting modern management techniques. Especially for the production of footwear and soaps, special programmes would be drawn up to increase progressively their share in the total production of these items in the country. The list of items currently under the purview of the Commission will be revamped so that it can more effectively fulfill the role assigned to it. In the programme for development of village industries, the promotion of Khadi has a special place. A breakthrough in the field of Khadi is in sight with prospects of spinning and weaving polyester fibre along with cotton fibre. The preliminary works done so far holds out the hope of developing a large market of polyester khadi spinners and weavers. The Khadi and Village Industries Act is being amended to permit the implementation of a large-scale programme in "Nai Khadi". The Government is committed to providing maximum financial and marketing support that is needed for promotion of the khadi programme.

Along with khadi, the clothing needs of the masses can be progressively met through development of the handloom sector, which provides employment to the bulk of people engaged in the production of textiles. Government will not permit any expansion in the weaving capacity in the organised mill and power loom sector. In order to provide adequate supply of yarn for the handloom sector, the Government will ensure that the handloom sector has priority in the allocation of yarn spun in the organised sector. In case there is any shortage, Government will ensure that steps are taken to increase spinning capacity. Further, in order to provide a ready market for handloom products, it will be ensured that the organised mill sector does not provide unfair competition to the handloom sector. Certain items of textiles are already reserved for production in the handloom sector. However, such reservation has not been very effective. The Government will enforce the existing reservation and further extend it to other items.

Appropriate Technology

The development and application of technology appropriate to our socio-economic conditions has so far not received adequate attention. It will henceforth be an integral part of policy and Government will ensure that this important area gets adequate attention. Special arrangements will be made to ensure an effective and coordinated approach for the development and widespread application of suitable small and simple machines and devices for improving the productivity and earning capacity of workers in small and village industries. It will further be Government's endeavor to fully integrate such appropriate techniques of production with the broader programme of all round rural development.

Role of Large Scale Industries

In addition to small and village industries, there is also a clear role for large-scale industry in India. However, the Government will not favour large-scale industry merely for demonstration of sophisticated skills or as monuments of irrelevant foreign technology. The role of large scale industry will be related to the programme for meeting the basic minimum needs of the population through wider dispersal of small scale and village industries and strengthening of the agricultural sector. In general, areas for large scale industry will be: (a) basic industries which are essential for providing infrastructure as well as for development of small and village industries, such as steel, non-ferrous metals, cement, oil refineries; (b) capital goods industries for meeting the machinery requirement of basic industries as well as small scale industries; (c) high technology industries which require large scale production, and which are related to agricultural and small scale industrial development, such as fertilizers, pesticides, and petro-chemicals etc; and (d) other industries which are outside the list of reserved items for the small sale sector, and which are considered essential for the development of the economy, such as machine tools, organic and inorganic chemicals.

Large Houses

Past experience shows that Government policies have not succeeded in restraining the disproportionate growth of large Houses. While a certain measures of growth of existing enterprises is inevitable and also necessary for continued health of these enterprises, the growth of large Houses has been disproportionate to the size of their internally generate resources and has been largely based on funds borrowed from public financial institutions and banks. This process must be reversed.

In future, expansion of Large House will be guided by the following principles:

- The expansion of existing undertakings and establishments of new undertakings will continue to be subject to the provisions of the Monopolies and Restrictive Trade Practices Act. The provisions of this Act, including those relating to dominant undertakings would be effectively implemented;

- Except in the case of industries eligible for automatic growth of capacity, the expansion of existing undertakings into new lines and establishments of new undertakings by large Houses, will require specific approval of Government; and
- Large Houses will have to rely on their own internally generated resources for financing new or expansion projects. While an appropriate debt equity ratio will be permitted in the case of industries, like fertilizers, paper, cement, shipping, petrochemicals, etc. which are relatively more capital intensive in nature, the debt equity ratio in the case of other less capital-intensive or less sophisticated industries will be so fixed as to reflect the greater use of their own internally generated resources by the large houses.

In its licensing policy, Government will regulate the activities of the large houses to bring them in line with the country's socio-economic goals, where large scale units, whether belonging to large houses or not are already engaged in the manufacture of items since reserved for the small scale sector, there will be no expansion in their capacity. On the other hand, the share of these units in the total capacity for these items will be steadily reduced and that of small scale and cottage Sector increased. In licensing other activities of large scale industry, particularly of units belonging to large houses, Government would pay due regard to the existing share of these units in the total domestic production of these items. It will be the policy of government to ensure that no unit or business group acquires a dominant or monopolistic position in the market. The present industrial activities of the large houses will be scrutinised so that unfair practices arising out of manufacturing inter-linkages are avoided.

In order to ensure social accountability, the financial institutions, whose support is vital for setting up and running of large scale enterprises, will be expected to assure a more active role in overseeing the activities of undertakings financed by them in order to ensure that management increasingly acquires professionalism and conforms to national priorities.

Public Sector

The public sector in India has today come of age. Apart from socialising the means of production in strategic areas, public sector provides a countervailing power to the growth of large houses and large enterprises in the private sector. There will be an expanding role for the public in several fields. Not only will it be the producer of important and strategic goods of basic nature, but it will also be used effectively as stabilising force by shouldering the responsibility essential supplies for the consumer. The public sector will be charged with the responsibility of encouraging the development of a wide range of ancillary industries, and contribute to the growth of decentralised production by making available its expertise in technology and management to small scale and cottage industry sectors. It will also be the endeavour of Government to operate public sector enterprises on profitable and efficient lines in order to ensure that investment in these industries pays an adequate return to society. The Government attaches high priority to the building up of a professional cadre of managers in the public sector who would be given the necessary autonomy and entrusted with the task of providing dynamic and efficient management to such enterprise.

Indigenous and Foreign Technology

The country has well-developed infrastructure of scientific establishments. Future development of industries in India must be based on indigenous technology as far as possible. Full scope will be given to the development of indigenous technology. It is also essential that development of indigenous technology is responsive to the objective of efficient production in increasing quantities of goods that society urgently needs. Science and technology must contribute to improvement in the living standards and the quality of life of the large mass of our people.

In order to promote technological self-reliance, the Government recognises the necessity for continued inflow of technology in sophisticated and high priority areas where Indian skills and technology are not adequately developed. In such areas, the Government's preference would be for outright purchase of the best available technology and then adapting such technology to the country's needs. Indian firms, which are permitted to import foreign technology, would be required in appropriate cases to set up adequate Research and Development facilities so that imported technology is properly adapted and assimilated. The Government will also set up a national registry of foreign collaboration in the Secretariat of the Foreign Investment Board so that there is continuous monitoring of these efforts.

Foreign Investment

The Government would also like to clarify its policy regarding participation of foreign investment and foreign companies in India's Industrial development. So far as existing foreign companies are concerned, the provisions of the Foreign Exchange Regulation Act would be strictly enforced. After the process of dilution under this Act has been completed, companies with direct non-resident investment not exceeding 40 per cent will be treated on par with Indian companies, except in cases specifically notified, and their future expansion will be guided by the same principles as those applicable to Indian companies.

Foreign investment and acquisition of technology necessary for Indian's industrial development would be allowed only on such terms as are determined by the Government of India to be in the national interest. In areas where foreign technological know-how is not needed, existing collaborations will not be renewed and foreign companies operating in such fiends will have to modify their character and activities in conformity with national priorities within the framework of the Foreign Exchanges Regulation Act. To guide entrepreneurs, Government will issue a revised illustrative list of industries where no foreign collaboration, financial or technical, is considered necessary since indigenous technology has fully developed in this field.

For all approved foreign investment, there will be complete freedom for remittance of profits, royalties, and dividends as well as repatriation of capital subject, of course, to rules and regulations common to all. As a rule, majority interest in ownership and effective control should be in Indian hands though Government may make exceptions in highly export-oriented and/or sophisticated technology areas. In hundred percent export-oriented cases, Government may consider even a fully owned foreign company.

Indian Joint Ventures Aboard

A number of units have been set up in joint ventures in many developing countries by Indian Entrepreneurs in collaboration with local associates. At the present stage of the country's industrial development, substantial export of capital from India will neither be feasible nor desirable. The contribution of the Indian entrepreneur to the joint ventures abroad shall, therefore, have to be mainly in the form of machinery and equipment, structurals and also technical know-how and management expertise. In cases where, in addition, some cash investment is found necessary, Government will be willing to consider such investment up to a maximum limit to be prescribed for this purpose.

Import Liberalisation

Self-reliance must continue to be a paramount objective of country's industrial and economic policy. Recent events in the international economy have demonstrated that the main burden of adjustment to external shocks and changing international environment has to be borne by the country itself. Our industrial strategy, therefore, must respond to the objective of creating an industrial base, which is sufficiently diversified and sufficiently strong to withstand the vagaries of international trade and aid relationship. The creation of a strong and diversified industrial economy does not mean that the country should not or need not participate in international trade, both as exporter and importer of industrial goods. This we must continue to do. In fact, the favorable changes that have taken place in our foreign exchange situation and the progress that we have made in the industrial field should now enable us to selectively dispense with import quotas and quantitative restrictions, while retaining the protection given through tariffs. Relaxation of quantitative import controls, must, however, be consistent with our overall Plan priorities. Such relaxation will be in areas where existing quantitative restrictions are hurting rather than helping the future development of high priority industries, for example by unduly delaying the future development of high priority industries, or unduly delaying the implementation of critical projects or where indigenous industry is taking advantage of such restrictions for raising costs and prices beyond tolerable limits. Indian industry would, of course, be given all assistance to improve their competitive position and their technology. Many Indian firms are even today in a position to compete successfully in international field and, therefore, no longer require the protection through quotas.

Exports of Manufactures

Exports of manufactures are an important and growing segment of our export trade. Government will consider favourable proposals for export-oriented manufacturing capacity in fields where such investment is likely to be internationally competitive after making allowance for the structure of indirect taxation in the form of customs and excise duties and other similar levels. In the case of wholly export-based activities, Government will also be willing to consider exemption from customs/excise duties on inputs, provided there is a substantial net value added in the export product and also such production is likely to generate additional direct and indirect employment.

Compulsory Exports

In many cases, compulsory export obligations have been imposed while approving new industrial capacity because of the need to ensure that import of raw materials and capital goods required by the project are paid for through future exports. Compulsory export obligations, merely for ensuring the foreign exchange balance of the project, would no longer be insisted upon. At the same time, in future, an export commitment for a limited period of five years will not be given the same weightage as before for relaxation of industrial policy. However, in case where a relaxation from industrial Policy has been accorded especially on consideration of export, compulsory export obligations would continue to be imposed and for sufficiently long period. In the past, while export obligations were imposed, equal attention was not paid to ensuring that compulsory export obligations are adhered to in actual practice.

Location of Industries

The Government attaches great importance to balanced regional development of the entire country so that disparities in levels of development between different regions are progressively reduced. Government have noted with concern that most of the industrial development that has taken place in our country since independence has been concentrated around the metropolitan areas and large cities. The result has been a rapid deterioration in the living conditions, especially for the working classes in the larger cities and attendant problems of slums and environmental pollution. The Government have decided that no more licences should be issued to new industrial units with in certain limits of large metropolitan cities having a population more than one million and urban areas with a population of more than 5 lakhs as per the 1971 census. State Government and financial institutions will be requested to deny support to new industries in these areas, such as those which do not require an industrial licence. The Government of India would also consider providing assistance to large existing industries, which want to shift from congested metropolitan cities to approved locations in backward areas.

Pricing Policy

A sound price policy has to aim at a reasonable degree of price stability and a fair parity between prices of agricultural and industrial products. There has been a tendency to regulate prices of industrial products, which are vital to the needs of development in a manner, which made their production less attractive than production catering to the needs of the elite. It will be the policy of Government to ensure that in cases where there is price control, the controlled price will include an adequate return to the investor provided that the industry is operating at a fairly high utilisation of capacity and is conforming to the technologically attainable norms. It will be permitted to earn a sufficient return to provide for a reasonable dividend to the shareholder and also adequate funds to plough back into business for modernisation and growth. By the same time, Government cannot permit exorbitant profits being made by industries, which are operating well below their capacity, or by units, which operate in a monopolistic environment.

Workers' Participation

The most important single resources of any country is the skill and hard work of its people. We, in India, have an abundant supply of labour, which is capable of acquiring new skills very quickly, and also an existing reservoir of technical and managerial personnel. These resources can be used effectively only in an environment in which the workers and managers develop a sense of personal involvement in the working of the enterprise. Family control of business, particularly in the field of large scale industry, is an anachronism, and it will be Government's policy to insist on professionalism in management. At the same time, ways and means have to be found to create amongst workers, both in public and private sector industries, a stake in the efficient working of their units. The Government are examining the possibilities of encouraging workers' participation in the equity of industrial units without, in any way, adversely affecting their interests. Such equity participation together with an active association of workers in decision making from the shop floor level to the Board level will provide the necessary environment for a meaningful participation by workers in the management of industry.

Sickness in Industry

One of the disturbing features of the industrial scene in recent years has been the growing incidence of sickness of both large and small units. In some cases, such as cotton and jute and textiles or sugar, a high proportion of the units in the industry have become sick with the result that in order to protect employment, Government has had to take over a number of such units. While Government cannot ignore the necessity of protecting existing employment, the cost of maintaining such employment has also to be taken into account. In a many case, very large amounts of public funds have been pumped into the sick units, which has been taken over, but they continue to make losses, which have to be financed by the public exchequer. This process cannot continue indefinitely.

In future, the take-over of management of units would be resorted to selectively and only after careful examination of the steps required to revive the units. It would also be the policy of the Government to take quick and effective steps for rehabilitation and reconstruction of the units and to ensure professional management of such units on a continuing basis. The cost of overcoming sickness in industry becomes much more manageable if such sickness can be diagnosed at an early date. For this purpose, Government in co-operation with the Reserve Bank of India, have instituted arrangements for monitoring incipient sickness in industrial units so that corrective action can be initiated as soon there is evidence of mismanagement of financial and technological weakness. The Government is also considering measures whereby managers or owners, who are responsible for mismanaging and turning their units sick are not permitted to play any further part in the management of other units.

Streamlining of Procedures

Government will continue its effort to remove irritants in the industrial approval procedures, which come in the way of accelerating industrial development. Since costs of delay are heavy and our country which is seeking to pull itself by its boost-straps can ill-afford them and swift progress should be our watch ward, every effort will made to improve administrative arrangements so as to result not only in further speedy and orderly approval procedures but also in enforcing an expeditious translation of letters of intent and industrial licences into productive capacity on ground. In order to streamline and simplify procedures and policies relating to industrial licensing as well as imports and exports, Government have set up high level committees which will submit their report shortly.

Conclusion

Industrial development is a complex process requiring the effective interaction and co-operation of all sections of society. If the objectives of the new Industrial Policy of accelerating the pace of industrial growth, rapid increase in levels of employment, productivity and income of industrial workers and a wide dispersal of small and village industries have to be achieved, the willing co-operation of industrial worker, trade unions, managers, entrepreneurs, financial institutions and various governmental authorities responsible for implementing schemes of assistance will be essential. The main brunt of the effort has, however, to be borne by our industrial workers and managers who are second to none in their skills and efficiency. The Government earnestly appeals to all these groups to work together in a spirit of dedication to the national cause. It is only by our own skills and efforts that we can hope to solve the numerous problems facing the country.

1977 has been a year of historical changes and people's expectations in the political and economic fields are high. It is hoped that the new direction that is being given to the industrial policy of the country will help in the creation of a just and equitable society in which, all the people will share the benefits of industrial development."

The Industrial Policy Statement of July 1980

It was based as the Industrial Policy Resolution of 1956, and spelt out the following socio-economic objectives:

1. Optimum utilisation of installed capacity;
2. Maximum production and achieving higher productivity;
3. Higher employment generation;
4. Correction of regional imbalances;
5. Strengthening of the agricultural base through agro based industries and promotion of optimum inter-sectoral relationship;
6. Promotion of export-oriented industries;
7. Promotion of economic federalism through equitable spread of investment and dispersal of returns; and
8. Consumer protection against high prices and bad quality.

The change in Industrial Policy in different Five Year Plans could not bring about any perceptible improvement in the industrial scenario of the country. Noting the erosion in people's faith in the public sector, it was decided to launch a drive to revive the efficiency of public sector undertakings through a time-bound programme of corrective action on a unit- by- unit basis. Effective steps would also be taken to develop the management cadres of public sector undertakings in functional fields, such as operations, finance, marketing and information system. In order to eliminate the artificial distinction of conflicting interests between small and large scale industry, the concept of economic federalism would be promoted through the setting up of a few nucleus plants in identified industrially backward districts.

Statement on Industrial Policy July 23, 1980—Key Provisions

The policy objectives had been set out in the 1980 policy statement in the following words:

"1. The first Prime Minister of India Pandit Jawaharlal Nehru laid the foundations of modern India. His vision and determination have left a lasting impression on every facet of national endeavour since Independence. It is due to his vision and initiative that India now has a strong and diversified industrial base and is a major industrial nation of the world. The goals and objectives set out for the nation by Pandit Nehru on the eve of Independence were namely,

i. the rapid agricultural and industrial development of our country,
ii. rapid expansion of opportunities for gainful employment, progressive reduction of social and economic disparities,
iii. removal of poverty and attainment of self-reliance remain as valid today as at the time.

Pandit Nehru first set them out before the nation. Any industrial policy must contribute to the realisation of these goals and objectives at an accelerated pace. The present statement of industrial policy is inspired by these very concerns, and represents a renewed initiative towards consolidating the gains of national reconstruction at this crucial stage.

2. In 1948, immediately after Independence, Government introduced the Industrial Policy Resolution. This outlined the approach to industrial growth and development. It emphasised the importance to the economy of securing a continuous increase in production and ensuring its equitable distribution. After the adoption of the Constitution and the socio-economic goals, the Industrial Policy was comprehensively revised and adopted in 1956. To meet new challenges, from time to time, it was modified through statements in 1973, 1977 and 1980.

3. The Industrial Policy Resolution of 1948 was followed by the Industrial Policy Resolution of 1956 which had as its objective the acceleration of the rate of economic growth and the speeding up of industrialisation as a means of achieving a socialist pattern of society. In 1956, capital was scarce and the base of entrepreneurship not strong enough. Hence, the 1956 Industrial Policy Resolution gave primacy to the role of the State to assume a predominant and direct responsibility for industrial development. It emphasized the need to eliminate the economic disparities, prevent concentration of wealth with the few, equal distribution of wealth, and remove regional disparities.

4. The Industrial Policy Statement of 1973, *inter alias*, identified high-priority industries where investment from large industrial houses and foreign companies would be permitted.

5. The Industrial Policy Statement of 1977 laid emphasis on decentralisation and on the role of small-scale, tiny and cottage industries. It took some measures to identify the discrepancies in small scale area and rectified them. It set up Village and Khadi Industries to help rapid industrialization in the identified areas.

6. The Industrial Policy Statement of 1980 focussed attention on the need for promoting competition in the

domestic market, technological upgradation and modernisation. The policy laid the foundation for an increasingly competitive export base and for encouraging foreign investment in high technology areas. This found expression in the Sixth Five Year Plan, which bore the distinct stamp of Smt. Indira Gandhi. It was Smt. Indira Gandhi who emphasised the need for productivity to be the central concern in all economic and production activities.

7. These policies created a climate for rapid industrial growth in the country. Thus, on the eve of the Seventh Five Year Plan, a broad-based infrastructure had been built up. Basic industries had been established. A high degree of self-reliance in a large number of items, raw materials, intermediates, and finished goods had been achieved. New growth centres of industrial activity had emerged, as had a new generation of entrepreneurs. A large number of engineers, technicians and skilled workers had also been trained.

8. The Seventh Plan recognised the need to consolidate on these strengths and to take initiatives to prepare Indian industry to respond effectively to the emerging challenges. A number of policies and procedural changes were introduced in 1985 and 1986 under the leadership of Shri Rajiv Gandhi aimed at increasing productivity, reducing costs and improving quality. The accent was on opening the domestic market to increased competition and readying our industry to stand on its own in the face of international competition. The public sector was freed from a number of constraints and given a larger measure of autonomy. The technological and managerial modernisation of industry was pursued as the key instrument for increasing productivity and improving our competitiveness in the world. For the first time the computerization of functions in the key areas, like railways was introduced. It gave a tremendous boost, and generated confidence in the areas having public interface. People could perceive the change. The net result of all these

changes was that Indian industry grew by an impressive average annual growth rate of 8.5% in the Seventh Plan period."

Industrial Policy of 1990

Policy measures for the promotion of Small Scale and Agro - based Industries and changes in the procedures for Industrial approvals

Government have been considering the need to take measures for promotion of small scale and agro-based industries and to change procedures for grant of industrial approvals.

In pursuance of policy to re-orient industrial growth to serve the objective of employment generation, dispersal of industry in the rural areas, and to enhance the contribution of small scale industries to exports, it was decided to take the measures enumerated below:

- The investment ceiling in plant and machinery for small-scale industries (fixed in 1985) would be raised from the present Rs. 35 lakhs to Rs. 60 lakhs and correspondingly, for ancillary units from Rs. 45 lakhs to Rs. 75 lakhs. In order to enable small scale industries to play an important role in the total export effort, such of the small scale units which could export at least 30 per cent of the annual production by the third year would be permitted to step up their investment in plant and machinery to Rs. 75 lakhs.
- Investment ceiling in respect of tiny units would also be increased from the present Rs. 2 lakhs to Rs. 5 lakhs. However, with regard to their location, the population limit of 50,000 as per the 1981 census would continue to apply. Steps would be taken to ensure better inflow of credit and other vital inputs and to improve the infrastructure support to the constituents of the Tiny Sector.

- 836 items had been reserved for exclusive manufacture in the small- scale sector. Efforts would be made to identify more items amenable to similar reservation. Encroachment and violation by large scale units into areas reserved for small- scale sector would be effectively dealt with.
- A new scheme of Central Investment Subsidy exclusively for the small- scale sector in rural and backward areas capable of generating higher level of employment at lower capital cost would be implemented.
- With a view to improving the competitiveness of the products manufactured in the small- scale sector, programmes for modernisation and upgradation of technology would be implemented. A number of technology centers, tool rooms, Process and Product Development Centers, testing centers, etc., would be set up under the umbrella of an apex Technology Development Center in Small Industries Development Organiasation.
- To ensure adequate and timely flow of credit to the small scale industries, a new apex bank known as SIDBI had already been established. One of the major tasks of SIDBI and other commercial banks / financial institutions would be to channelise need-based, higher flow of credit, both by way of term loan and working capital, to the tiny and rural industries. A targeted approach would be adopted to ensure implementation and to facilitate monitoring this objective.
- The existing regime of fiscal concessions would be reviewed, both to provide sustained support to the units in the small-scale sector and to remove the disincentives for their graduation and further growth.
- An exercise would be undertaken to identify locations in rural areas endowed with adequate power supply and intensive campaigns would be

launched to attract suitable entrepreneurs, provide all other inputs and foster small scale and tiny industries. Similarly, industries which were not energy-intensive would be identified for proliferation in rural areas where power supply was then a constraint.

- In order to widen the entrepreneurial bases, the Government would lay particular emphasis on training of women and youth under the Entrepreneurial Development Programme. A special cell would be established in SIDO and State Directorates of Industries to assist women entrepreneurs.
- One of the persistent complaints of the small-scale units was their being subjected to a large number of Acts / Laws, their being required to maintain a number of registers, submit plethora of returns and face an army of Inspectors, particularly in the field of labour legislations. These bureaucracy controls would be reduced so that unnecessary interference was eliminated. Further, procedure would be simplified and paper work cut down.
- In order to assist the large number of artisans engaged in the rural and cottage industries, the activities of the KVIC and KVI Boards would be expanded, and these organizations would be strengthened to discharge the responsibility more effectively. Special marketing organizations at the Center and State levels should be created to assist rural artisans in marketing their products and also in supply of raw materials. Besides, providing concessional credit, training facilities and free consultancy to groups of artisans would also be provided.
- In agro- processing industries, greater success had been achieved where growers and processors had been integrated, as in the case of sugar. For the

success of other agro-based industries also, close links must be forged between the growers and processor units. Industrial Policy would, therefore, especially promote projects, which were organized in close co-operation on the basis of joint ownership. Growers would be encouraged to set up processing units within the framework of co-operative societies or similar institutional framework. This would also ensure the transmission of better technology for enhanced agricultural production.

- In sectors where units required licensing, the policy would also encourage location of processing units in rural areas where growers were concentrated. Apart from economic benefits of proximity to raw materials, it would help in dispersal of industry and increasing employment in rural areas.
- Agro- processing industry would receive high priority in credit allocation from the Financial Institutions. In appointment of working capital, bank would give higher priority to such industries as compared to the rest of the industrial sector.
- In order to bring best technology available to these industries, technology approvals would be given 30 days of presentation to the secretariat for Industrial Approvals in the Department of Industrial Development. Government would actively promote the generation, adaptation and adoption of new technologies in the field.

Procedures for Industrial Approvals

Indian industry must be made more competitive internationally. It should also be released from unnecessary bureaucratic shackles by reducing the number of clearances required from the Government. While the Government would continue to examine large projects in view of resource constraints, decisions in respect of medium- sized investments would be left to the entrepreneurs. To achieve these objectives, the following decisions were taken.

Delicensing

- All new units up to an investment of Rs. 25 crores in fixed assets in non-backward areas and Rs. 75 crores in Centrally notified backward areas would be exempt from requirement of obtaining license / registration.
- For import of Capital Goods, the entrepreneur would have entitlement to import up to a landed value of 30% of the total value of plant and machinery required for the unit.

Raw materials and components

For imports of raw materials and components, imports would be permissible up to a landed value of 30% of the ex-factory value of annual production. The ex-factory value of production would exclude the excise duty on the item of production. Raw materials and components on OGL would not be included within this 30 percent limit. For all licensable items of raw materials and components, import licensing procedures would continue to operate.

Foreign collaboration

In respect of transfer of technology, if the entrepreneur considered import of technology necessary, he could conclude an agreement with the collaborator, without obtaining any clearance from the Government, provided that royalty payment did not exceed 5% on domestic sales and 8% on exports. If, however, lump sum payment was involved in the import of technology, the proposal would require Government clearance, but a decision would be communicated to the entrepreneur within a period of 30 days.

Foreign Investment

Keeping in view the need to attract effective inflow of technology, investment up to 40% of equity would be allowed on an automatic basis. In such proposals also, the landed value of imported C.G. should not exceed 30% of value of plant and machinery.

Minimum Economic Size

In order to ensure that investment would lead to production of goods that would attain international competitiveness and that maximum efficiency was ensured, the unit would have to conform to the minimum economic size in cases where such a size had been prescribed.

Expansion

The de-regulation suggested above would cover all cases of expansion and would not be restricted only to new units.

Broad-banding

The existing broad- banding scheme would continue to be in force. In addition, of no extra investment was required, no clearance from the Government would be necessary for production and sale of any new item by existing unit. This would not include those items, which were reserved for small scale industries.

Location Policy and Environmental Clearances

The Centre except for location in and around metropolitan cities, would not apply the location policy to such industries with population above 4 million. For these cities, location would not be permissible within 20 km calculated from the periphery of the metropolitan area except in prior designed industrial areas and for non-polluting industries, such as electronics, computer software and printing. It would be up to State Government to regulate industrial locations keeping in mind local conditions and requirements and their respective special development plans, and zoning and town planning laws. Similarly, environmental clearance would have to be obtained from the prescribed authority at the State level. In further, these industrial units would also be subject to central legislations introducing new provisions, if any, in future.

Export Oriented Units

100% export oriented units (EOUs) and units to be set up in export processing zones (EPZs) were also being delicensed under the scheme up to an investment limit of Rs. 75 crores.

Convertibility Clause

Such investment should be exempt from the "Convertibility Clause" applicable to financing the Indian Financial Institutions. It was clarified that in the application of the proposals listed above, 836 items, which were reserved for production the small- scale sector, would continue to be excluded.

The above proposals would be applicable to all manufacturing items in a specified list. The list should follow the nomenclature of the Indian Trade Classification based on the Harmonised System. In such section of the classification, apart from positive mention of approved items, those not permissible should be specifically excluded from the benefit of the proposals list above. Approval for excluded items would be as per the existing industrial policy regime and procedures.

Units set up by MRTP / FERA companies would be covered by the procedures set out above, but they would continue to need clearances under the provisions and regulations of these two Acts.

The existing De-licensed Industries Scheme, Exempted Industries Scheme and DGS&D Registration System stood abolished.

Industrial Policy Resolution of 1991

This policy completely changed the direction. The protectionist regime was replaced with that of a more open and transparent one. Indian economy opened up and tried to get more and more FDI in different sectors. Keeping pace with the international scenario, the situation revealed that the economy of the Eastern Europe and the erstwhile Soviet Russia have started collapsing. In order to improve the portfolio and performance of public enterprises in a liberalized economy, the Government of India announced on 24th July 1991 as a part of the 'Statement of Industrial Policy', a statement on Public Sector Policy also. The text of the statement on industrial policy objectives is as under:

Policy objectives

1. The industrial policy began with the vision of Pandit Jawaharlal Nehru, who laid the foundations of modern India. His vision and determination had left a lasting impression on every facet of national endeavour since Independence. It was due to his initiative that India could have a strong and diversified industrial base and could become a major industrial nation of the world. The goals and objectives set out for the nation by Pandit Nehru on the eve of Independence, namely, the rapid agricultural and industrial development of India, rapid expansion of opportunities for gainful employment, progressive reduction of social and economic disparities, removal of poverty and attainment of self-reliance are as valid as these were at the time when Pandit Nehru first set them out before the nation. Any industrial policy must contribute to the realisation of these goals and objectives at an accelerated pace. The Statement of Industrial Policy of 1991 was inspired by these very concerns, and represented a renewed initiative towards consolidating the gains of national reconstruction at that crucial stage.

2. In 1948, immediately after Independence, Government introduced the Industrial Policy Resolution. This outlined the approach to industrial growth and development. It emphasised the importance to the economy of securing a continuous increase in production and ensuring its equitable distribution. After the adoption of the Constitution and the socio-economic goals, the Industrial Policy was

comprehensively revised and adopted in 1956. To meet new challenges, from time to time, it was modified through statements in 1973, 1977 and 1980.

3. The Industrial Policy Resolution of 1948 was followed by the Industrial Policy Resolution of 1956 which had as its objective the acceleration of the rate of economic growth and the speeding up of industrialisation as a means of achieving a socialist pattern of society. In 1956, capital was scarce and the base of entrepreneurship not strong enough. Hence, the 1956 Industrial Policy Resolution gave primacy to the role of the State to assume a predominant and direct responsibility for industrial development.

4. The Industrial Policy statement of 1973, *inter alia*, identified high-priority industries where investment from large industrial houses and foreign companies would be permitted.

5. The Industrial Policy Statement of 1977 laid emphasis on decentralisation and on the role of small-scale, tiny and cottage industries.

6. The Industrial Policy Statement of 1980 focussed attention on the need for promoting competition in the domestic market, technological upgradation and modernisation. The policy laid the foundation for an increasingly competitive export base and for encouraging foreign investment in high-technology areas. This found expression in the Sixth Five Year Plan, which bore the distinct stamp of Smt. Indira Gandhi. It was Smt. Indira Gandhi who emphasised the need for productivity to be the central concern in all economic and production activities.

7. These policies created a climate for rapid industrial growth in the country. Thus, on the eve of the Seventh Five Year Plan, a broad-based infrastructure had been built up. Basic industries had been established. A high degree of self-reliance in a large number of items - raw materials, intermediates, and finished goods - had been achieved. New growth centres of industrial activity had emerged, as had a new generation of entrepreneurs. A

large number of engineers, technicians and skilled workers had also been trained.

8. The Seventh Plan recognised the need to consolidate on these strengths and to take initiatives to prepare Indian industry to respond effectively to the emerging challenges. A number of policy and procedural changes were introduced in 1985 and 1986 under the leadership of Shri Rajiv Gandhi aimed at increasing productivity, reducing costs and improving quality. The accent was on opening the domestic market to increased competition and readying our industry to stand on its own in the face of international competition. The public sector was freed from a number of constraints and given a larger measure of autonomy. The technological and managerial modernisation of industry was pursued as the key instrument for increasing productivity and improving our competitiveness in the world. The net result of all these changes was that Indian industry grew by an impressive average annual growth rate of 8.5% in the Seventh Plan period.

9. Government, through this policy resolution, pledged to launch a renewed struggle for social and economic justice, to end poverty and unemployment and to build a modern, democratic, socialist, prosperous and forward-looking India. It was felt that such a society could be built if India would grow as part of the world economy and not in isolation.

10. While Government would continue to follow the policy of self-reliance, there would be greater emphasis placed on building up our ability to pay for imports through our own foreign exchange earnings. Government was also committed to development and utilisation of indigenous capabilities in technology and manufacturing as well as its upgradation to world standards.

11. Government would continue to pursue a sound policy framework encompassing encouragement of entrepreneurship, development of indigenous technology through investment in research and development, bringing

in new technology, dismantling of the regulatory system, development of the capital markets and increasing competitiveness for the benefit of the common man. The spread of industrialisation to backward areas of the country would be actively promoted through appropriate incentives, institutions and infrastructure investments.

12. Government would provide enhanced support to the small-scale sector so that it would flourish in an environment of economic efficiency and continuous technological upgradation.

13. Foreign investment and technology collaboration would be welcomed to obtain higher technology, to increase exports and to expand the production base.

14. Government would endeavour to abolish the monopoly of any sector or any individual enterprise in any field of manufacture, except on strategic or military considerations and open all manufacturing activity to competition.

15. The Government would ensure that the public sector plays its rightful role in the evolving socio-economic scenario of the country. Government would ensure that the public sector would run on business lines as envisaged in the Industrial Policy Resolution of 1956 and would continue to innovate and lead in strategic areas of national importance. In the 1950s and 1960s, the principal instrument for controlling the commanding heights of the economy was investment in the capital of key industries. Later, the State had other instruments of intervention, particularly fiscal and monetary instruments. The State also had the bulk of the nation's savings. Banks and financial institutions were under State control. Wherever State intervention would be necessary, these instruments would prove more effective and decisive.

16. Government would fully protect the interests of labour, enhance their welfare and equip them in all respects to deal with the inevitability of technological change. Government believed that no small section of society could corner the gains of growth, leaving workers to bear its pains.

Labour would be made an equal partner in progress and prosperity. Workers' participation in management would be promoted. Workers cooperatives would be encouraged to participate in packages designed to turn around sick companies. Intensive training, skill development and upgradation programmes would be launched.

17. Government would continue to visualise new horizons. The major objectives of the new industrial policy package would be to build on the gains already made, correct the distortions or weaknesses that might have crept in, maintain a sustained growth in productivity and gainful employment and attain international competitiveness. The pursuit of these objectives would be tempered by the need to preserve the environment and ensure the efficient use of available resources. All sector of industry, whether small, medium or large, belonging to the public, private or cooperative sector, would be encouraged to grow and improve on their past performance.

18. Government's policy would be continuity with change.

19. In pursuit of the above objectives, Government decided to take a series of initiatives in respect of the policies relating to the following areas:

A. Industrial Licensing.
B. Foreign Investment
C. Foreign Technology Agreements.
D. Public Sector Policy
E. MRTP Act.

A package for the Small and Tiny Sectors of industry were announced separately.

Industrial Licensing Policy

20. Industrial Licensing was governed by the Industries (Development & Regulation) Act, 1951. The Industrial Policy Resolution of 1956 identified the following three categories of industries:

i. that would be reserved for development in public sector,

ii. that would be permitted for development through private enterprise with or without State participation, and

iii. in which investment initiatives would ordinarily emanate from private entrepreneurs.

No nation, which would contemplate progress through industrial development, can ever have a rigid policy. The policy ought to be dynamic, and tuned to the international scenario. Over the years, keeping in view the changing industrial scene in the country and in the international arena, the policy had undergone modifications. Industrial licensing policy and procedures had also been liberalised from time to time. A full realisation of the industrial potential of the country called for a continuation of such process of change.

21. It was decided to achieve the objectives of the strategy for the industrial sector for the 1990s and beyond for which it was necessary to make a number of changes in the system of industrial approvals. Major policy initiatives and procedural reforms were called for in order to actively encourage and assist Indian entrepreneurs to exploit and meet the emerging domestic and global opportunities and challenges. The bedrock of any such package of measures must be to let the entrepreneurs make investment decisions on the basis of their own commercial judgments. The attainment of technological dynamism and international competitiveness required that enterprises must be enabled to swiftly respond to fast changing external conditions that had become characteristic of the industrial world. Government policy and procedures must be geared to assisting entrepreneurs in their efforts. Government should play a proactive role and act as a facilitator instead of creating roadblocks in the shape of rigid licensing policy. This could be done only if the role played by the government were to be changed from that of only exercising control to one of providing help and guidance by making essential procedures fully transparent and by eliminating delays. That would only be possible with a change in the politico-

bureaucratic mind set and proper tuning of judicial concept. Dead wood in all sectors had to be removed, with proper modernization and series of enactments in the old and obsolete laws.

22. There were perceptible changes everywhere. The industrial licensing system had been gradually moving away from the concept of capacity licensing. The system of reservations for public sector undertakings had been evolving towards an ethos of greater flexibility and private sector enterprises were being gradually allowed to enter into many of these areas on a case by case basis. Further impetus to these changes was necessary, which alone could push this country towards the attainment of its entrepreneurial and industrial potential. This called for bold dynamic and imaginative decisions designed to remove restraints on capacity creation, while at the same, ensuring that over riding national interests were not jeopardized and putting regulatory bodies in place, so as to ensure that the consumers are not duped. Mindless change may lead to chaos. Gradual but constant change would be in the interest of the business class and would benefit Indian economy. This could be a reality, if there is political consensus.

23. Keeping in view the above, it was decided that industrial licensing would henceforth be abolished for all industries, except those specified, irrespective of levels of investment. These specified industries (Annex-II), would continue to be subject to compulsory licensing for reasons related to security and strategic concerns, social reasons, problems related to safety and over-riding environmental issues, manufacture of products of hazardous nature and articles of elitist consumption. The exemption from licensing would be particularly helpful to the many dynamic small and medium entrepreneurs who had been unnecessarily hampered by the licensing system. As a whole, the Indian economy would benefit by becoming more competitive, more efficient and modern and would take its rightful place in the world of industrial progress. Though shift in the

attitude in bureaucratic and political circles was noticeable, the mandate for change must be loud and clear. It must also be visible so that the fruit percolates to the grass root and the deprived sections of the society perceive the change.

Foreign Investment

24. While freeing Indian industry from official controls, opportunities for promoting foreign investments in India should also be fully exploited. In view of the significant development of India's industrial economy in the last 40 years, the general resilience, size and level of sophistication achieved, and the significant changes that have also taken place in the world industrial economy, and the relationship between domestic and foreign industry needed to be much more dynamic than it had been in the past in terms of both technology and investment. Foreign investment would bring attendant advantages of technology transfer, production of quality products, and confidence in the minds of the consumers, marketing expertise, introduction of modern managerial techniques and new possibilities for promotion of exports. This was particularly necessary in the changing global scenario of industrial and economic cooperation marked by mobility of capital. Industrial economy was changing and changing fast. The East European countries were dismantling their protectionist policies and opening up their economy to the outer world. Such mobility of capital would not only boost economy but also generate more employment opportunities. The government would therefore welcome foreign investment, which was in the interest of the country's industrial development.

25. In order to invite foreign investment in high priority industries, requiring large investments and advanced technology, it was decided to provide approval for direct foreign investment up to 51% foreign equity in such industries. There should be no bottlenecks of any kind in this process. This group of industries had generally been

known as the "Appendix I Industries" and was areas in which FERA companies had already been allowed to invest on a discretionary basis. This change would go a long way in making Indian policy on foreign investment transparent. Such a framework would make it attractive for companies abroad to invest in India.

26. Promotion of exports of Indian products called for a systematic exploration of world markets possible only through intensive and highly professional marketing activities. To the extent that expertise of this nature was not well developed so far in India, Government would encourage foreign trading companies to assist us in our export activities. Attraction of substantial investment and access to high technology, often closely held, and to world markets, involves interaction with some of the world's largest international manufacturing and marketing firms. The Government would appoint a special board to negotiate with such firms so that one could engage in purposive negotiation with such large firms, and provide the avenues for large investments in the development of industries and technology in the national interest.

Foreign Technology Agreement

27. There was a great need for promoting an industrial environment where the acquisition of technological capability would receive priority. In the fast changing world of technology, the relationship between the suppliers and users of technology must be a continuous one. Such a relationship would become difficult to achieve when the approval process includes unnecessary governmental interference on a case to case basis involving endemic delays and fostering uncertainty. The Indian entrepreneur has now come of age so that he no longer needs such bureaucratic clearances of his commercial technology relationships with foreign technology suppliers. Indian industry could scarcely be competitive with the rest of the world if it is to operate within such a regulatory environment.

28. With a view to injecting the desired level of technological dynamism, Government would provide the following facilities in Indian industry:

i. Automatic approval for technology agreement related to high priority industries within specified parameters.
ii. Similar facilities would be available for other industries as well, if such agreements did not require the expenditure of free exchange.
iii. Indian companies would be free to negotiate the terms of technology transfer with their foreign counterparts according to their own commercial judgment. The predictability and independence of action that this measure in providing to Indian industry would induce them to develop indigenous competence for the efficient absorption of foreign technology. Greater competitive pressure would also induce our industry to invest much more in research and development and they have been doing in the past.
iv. In order to help this process, the hiring of foreign technicians and foreign testing of indigenously developed technologies, would also not require prior clearance as prescribed so far, individually or as a part of industrial or investment approvals.

Public Sector Policy

29. The public sector has been central to our philosophy of development. In the pursuit of our development objectives, public ownership and control in critical sector of the economy has played an important role in preventing the concentration of economic power, reducing regional disparities and ensuring that planned development serves the common good.

30. The Industrial Policy Resolution of 1956 gave the public sector a strategic role in the economy. Massive investments have been made over the past four decades to build a public sector, which assumed a commanding role in

the economy. Today key sectors of the economy are dominated by mature public enterprises that have successfully expanded production, opened up new areas of technology and built up a reserve of technical competence in a number of areas. They have also been able to some how arrest the regional imbalance, created employment opportunities, developed infrastructure, played pivotal role in essential infrastructure, as well as social sectors, and defense sectors.

31. But in the recent past, a number of problems have begun to manifest themselves in many of the public enterprises. Serious problems are observed in the insufficient growth in productivity, poor project management, over-manning, and lack of continuous technological upgradation, and inadequate attention to R&D and human resource development. In addition, there was lots of inbuilt institutional lacunae for which public enterprises have shown a very low rate of return on the capital invested. This has inhibited their ability to re-generate themselves in terms of new investments as well as in technology development. The result is that many of the public enterprises have become a burden rather than being an asset to the Government. The original concept of the public sector has also undergone considerable dilution. The most striking example is the take over of sick units from the private sector. This category of public sector units accounts for almost one-third of the total losses of central public enterprises. Another category of public enterprises, which does not fit into the original idea of the public sector being at the commanding heights of the economy, is the plethora of public enterprises, which are in the consumer goods and services sectors. This was against the original concept that the public sector would limit itself to infrastructure building as the private players had limited resources at that time, and in the areas of defence production as it involves national security.

32. It was under this backdrop that the Government contemplated to adopt a new approach to public enterprises. It was considered necessary that there must be a greater commitment to the support of public enterprises, which were

essential for the operation of the industrial economy. Measures must be taken to make these enterprises more growth oriented and technically dynamic. Units, which might be faltering but were potentially viable must be restructured and given a new lease of life. The priority areas for growth of public enterprises in the future would be the following:

- Essential infrastructure goods and services.
- Exploration and exploitation of oil and mineral resources.
- Technology development and building of manufacturing capabilities in areas, which were crucial in the long term development of the economy and where private sector investment was inadequate.
- Manufacture of products where strategic considerations predominate such as defence equipment.

At the same time the public sector would not be barred from entering areas not specifically reserved for it.

33. In view of these considerations, Government would review the existing portfolio of public investments with greater realism. This review would be in respect of industries based on low technology, small scale and non-strategic areas, inefficient and unproductive areas, areas with low or nil social considerations or public purpose, and areas where the private sector had developed sufficient expertise and resources.

34. It was also considered necessary that Government would strengthen those public enterprises, which did fall in the reserved areas of operation or were in high priority areas or were generating good or reasonable profits. Such enterprises would be provided a much greater degree of management autonomy through the system of Memoranda of Understanding. Competition would also be induced in these areas by inviting private sector participation. In the case of selected enterprises, part of Government holdings in

the equity share capital of these enterprises would be disinvested in order to provide further market discipline to the performance of public enterprises. There were a large number of chronically sick public enterprises incurring heavy losses, operating in a competitive market and serve little or no public purpose. These needed to be attended to. The country must be proud of the public sector that it owns and it must operate in the public interest.

Monopolies and Restrictive Trade Practices Act (MRTP ACT)

35. The principal objectives sought to be achieved through the MRTP Act are as follows:

i. Prevention of concentration of economic power to the common detriment, control of monopolies, and
ii. Prohibition of monopolistic and restrictive and unfair trade practices.

36. The MRTP Act became effective in June 1970. With the emphasis placed on productivity in the Sixth Plan, major amendments to the MRTP Act were carried out in 1982 and 1984 in order to remove impediments to industrial growth and expansion. This process of change was given a new momentum in 1985 by an increase of threshold limit of assets.

37. With the growing complexity of industrial structure and the need for achieving economies of scale for ensuring high productivity and competitive advantage in the international market, the interference of the Government through the MRTP Act in investment decisions of large companies had become deleterious in its effects on Indian industrial growth. The pre-entry scrutiny of investment decisions by so-called MRTP companies would no longer be required. Instead, emphasis would be on controlling and regulating monopolistic, restrictive and unfair trade practices rather than making it necessary for the monopoly house to obtain prior approval of Central Government for expansion,

establishment of new undertakings, merger, amalgamation and takeover and appointment of certain directors. The thrust of policy would be more on controlling unfair or restrictive business practices. The MRTP Act would be restructured by eliminating the legal requirement for prior governmental approval for expansion of present undertakings and establishment of new undertakings. The provisions relating to merger, amalgamation, and takeover would also be repealed. Similarly, the provisions regarding restrictions on acquisition of and transfer of shares would be appropriately incorporated in the Companies Act.

38. Simultaneously, provisions of the MRTP Act would have to be strengthened in order to enable the MRTP Commission to take appropriate action in respect of the monopolistic, restrictive and unfair trade practices. The newly empowered MRTP Commission would be encouraged to require investigation *suo moto* or on complaints received from individual consumers or classes of consumers.

Decisions of Government

39. In view of the considerations outlined above, Government decided to take a series of measures to unshackle the Indian industrial economy from the cobwebs of unnecessary bureaucratic control. These measures complement the other series of measures being taken by Government in the areas of trade policy, exchange rate management, fiscal policy, financial sector reform and overall macro economic management.

Industrial Licensing Policy

i. Industrial licensing would be abolished for all projects except for a short list of industries related to security and strategic concerns, social reasons, hazardous chemicals and overriding environmental reasons, and items of elitist consumption (list attached as Annexure II). Industries reserved for the small scale sector would continue to be so reserved.

ii. Areas where security and strategic concerns predominate would continue to be reserved for the public sector (list attached as Annex 1).

iii. In projects where imported capital goods were required, automatic clearance would be given in cases where foreign exchange availability was ensured through foreign equity or if the CIF value of imported capital goods required was less than 25% of total value (net of taxes) of plant and equipment, up to a maximum value of Rs. 2 crore. In view of the existing difficult foreign exchange situation, this scheme (i.e. (iii) b) would come into force from April 1992. In other cases, imports of capital goods would require clearance from the Secretariat for Industrial Approvals (SIA) in the Department of Industrial Development according to availability of foreign exchange resources.

iv. In locations other than cities of more than one million populations, there would be no requirement of obtaining industrial approvals from the Central Government, except for industries subject to compulsory licensing. In respect of cities with population greater than one million, industries other than those of a non-polluting nature, such as electronics, computer software and printing, would be located outside 25 kms of the periphery, except in prior designated industrial areas. A flexible location policy would be adopted in respect of such cities (with population greater than one million), which require industrial re-generation. Zoning and Land Use Regulation and Environmental Legislation would continuc to regulate industrial locations. Appropriate incentives and the design of investments in infrastructure development would be used to promote the dispersal of industry, particularly to rural and backward areas and to reduce congestion in cities.

v. The system of phased manufacturing programmes, run on an administrative case by case basis, would be applicable to new projects. Existing projects with such programmes would continue to be governed by them. Existing units would be provided a new broad-banding facility to enable them to produce any article without additional investment.

vi. The exemption from licensing would apply to all substantial expansions of existing units.

vii. The mandatory convertibility clause would no longer be applicable for term loans from the financial institutions for new projects.

Procedural Consequences

viii. All existing registration schemes (Delicensed Registration, Exempted Industries Registration, DGTD registration) would be abolished. Entrepreneurs would henceforth only be required to file an information memorandum on new projects and substantial expansions.

ix. The lists at Annex II and Annex III would be notified in the Indian Trade Classification (Harmonised System).

Foreign Investment

i. Approval would be given for direct foreign investment up to 51 percent foreign equity in high priority industries (Annex III). There should be no bottlenecks of any kind in this process. Such clearance would be available if foreign equity covers the foreign exchange requirement for imported capital goods. Consequential amendments to the Foreign Exchange Regulation Act (1973) should be carried out.

ii. While the import of components, raw materials and intermediate goods, and payment of know how fees and royalties would be governed by the general policy applicable to other domestic units, the payment of dividends would be monitored through the Reserve Bank of India so as to ensure that outflows on account of dividend payments were balanced by export earnings over a period of time.

iii. Other foreign equity proposals, including proposals involving 51% foreign equity, which did not meet the criteria under (I) above, would continue to need prior clearance. Foreign equity proposals did not need to be accompanied by foreign technology agreements.

iv. To provide access to international markets, majority foreign equity holding up to 51% equity would be allowed for trading companies primarily engaged in export activities. While the thrust would be on export activities, such trading houses should be at par with domestic trading and export houses in accordance with the Import Export Policy.

v. A special Empowered Board would be constituted to negotiate with a number of large international firms and approve direct foreign investment in select areas. This would be a special programme to attract substantial investment that would provide access to high technology and world markets. The investment programmes of such firms would be considered in totality, free from pre-determined parameters or procedures.

Foreign Technology Agreements

vi. Automatic permission would be given for foreign technology agreements in high priority industries (Annex III) up to a lump sum payment of Rs. 1 crore, 5% royalty for domestic sales and 8% for exports, subject to total payment of 8% of sales over a 10-year period from date of agreement or 7 years from commencement of production. The prescribed royalty rates were net of taxes and would be calculated according to standard procedures.

vii. In respect of industries other than those in Annex III, automatic permission would be given subject to the same guidelines as above, if no free foreign exchange were required for any payments.

viii. All other proposals would need specific approval under the general procedures in force.

ix. No permission would be necessary for hiring of foreign technicians, foreign testing of indigenously developed technologies. Payment might be made from blanket permits or free foreign exchange according to RBI guidelines.

Public Sector

i. Portfolio of public sector investments would be on strategic, high-tech and essential infrastructure. Whereas some reservation for the public sector was being retained, there would be no bar for areas of exclusivity to be opened up to the private sector selectively. Similarly, the public sector would also be allowed entry in areas not reserved for it.

ii. Units which were chronically sick and which were unlikely to be turned around would, for the formulation of revival/rehabilitation schemes, be referred to the Board for Industrial and Financial Reconstruction (BIFR), or other similar high level institutions created for the purpose. A social security mechanism would be created to protect the interests of workers likely to be affected by such rehabilitation packages.

iii. In order to raise resources and encourage wider public participation, a part of the government's shareholding in the public sector would be offered to mutual funds, financial institutions, general public and workers.

iv. Boards of public sector companies would be made more professional and given greater powers.

v. There would be a greater thrust on performance improvement through the Memoranda of Understanding (MOU) systems through which managements would be granted greater autonomy and would be held accountable. Technical expertise on the part of the Government would be upgraded to make the MOU negotiations and implementation more effective.

vi. To facilitate a fuller discussion on performance, the MOU signed between Government and the public enterprise would be placed in Parliament. While focusing on major management issues, this would also help place matters on day to day operations of public enterprises in their correct perspective.

MRTP Act

vii. The MRTP Act would be amended to remove the threshold limits of assets in respect of MRTP companies and dominant undertakings. This eliminates the requirement of prior approval of Central Government for establishment of new undertakings, expansion of undertakings, merger, amalgamation and takeover and appointment of Directors under certain circumstances.

viii. Emphasis would be placed on controlling and regulating monopolistic, restrictive and unfair trade practices. Simultaneously, the newly empowered MRTP Commission would be authorised to initiative investigations suo motu, or on complaints received from individual consumers or classes of consumers in regard to monopolistic, restrictive and unfair trade practices.

ix. Necessary comprehensive amendments would be made in the MRTP Act in this regard and for enabling the MRTP Commission to exercise punitive and compensatory powers.

ANNEXURE I

Proposed List of Industries to be reserved for the Public Sector;

Arms and ammunition and allied items of defence equipment, Defence aircraft and warships.

1. Atomic Energy.
2. Coal and lignite.
3. Mineral oils.
4. Mining if iron ore, manganese ore, chrome ore, gypsum, sulphur, gold and diamond.
5. Mining of copper, lead, zinc, tin, molybdenum and wolfram.
6. Minerals specified in the Schedule to the Atomic Energy (Control of Production and Use) Order, 1953.
7. Railway transport.

ANNEXURE II

LIST OF INDUSTRIES IN RESPECT OF WHICH INDUSTRIAL LICENSING WILL BE COMPULSORY

1. Coal and Lignite.
2. Petroleum (other than crude) and its distillation products.
3. Distillation and brewing of alcoholic drinks.
4. Sugar.
5. Animal fats and oils.
6. Cigars and cigarettes of tobacco and manufactured tobacco substitutes.
7. Asbestos and asbestos-based products.
8. Plywood, decorative veneers, and other wood based products such as particleboard, medium density fiber board, block board.
9. Raw hides and skins, leather, chamois leather and patent leather.
10. Tanned or dressed fur skins.
11. Motorcars.

12. Paper and Newsprint except biogases-based units.
13. Electronic aerospace and defense equipment; all types.
14. Industrial explosives, including detonating fuse, safety fuse, gunpowder, nitrocellulose and matches.
15. Hazardous chemicals.
16. Drugs and Pharmaceuticals (according to Drug Policy).
17. Entertainment electronics (VCRs, color TVs, C.D. Players, Tape Recorders).
18. White Goods (Domestic Refrigerators, Domestic Dishwashing machines, Programmable Domestic Washing Machines, Microwave ovens, Air conditioners).

Note : The compulsory licensing provisions would not apply in respect of the small-scale units taking up the manufacture of any of the above items reserved for exclusive manufacture in small-scale sector.

ANNEXURE I

LIST OF INDUSTRIES FOR AUTOMATIC APPROVAL OF FOREIGN TECHNOLOGY AGREEMENTS AND FOR 51% FOREIGN EQUITY APPROVALS

1. Metallurgical Industries

a. Ferro alloys.
b. Castings and forgings.
c. Non-ferrous metals and their alloys.
d. Sponge iron and pelletisation.
e. Large diameter steel welded pipes of over 300 mm diametcr and stainless steel pipes.
f. Pig iron.

2. Boilers and Steam Generating Plants

3. Prime Movers (other than electrical generators)

a. Industrial turbines.
b. Internal combustion engines.

c. Alternate energy systems like solar wind etc. and equipment there for
d. Gas/hydro/steam turbines up to 60 MW.

4. **Electrical Equipment**
   a. Equipment for transmission and distribution of electricity including power and distribution transformers, power relays, HT-switch gear synchronous condensers.
   b. Electrical motors.
   c. Electrical furnaces, industrial furnaces and induction heating equipment.
   d. X-ray equipment.
   e. Electronic equipment, components including subscribers' end telecommunication equipments.
   f. Component wires for manufacture of lead-in wires.
   g. Hydro/steam/gas generators/generating sets up to 60 MW.
   h. Generating sets and pumping sets based on internal combustion engines.
   i. Jelly-filled telecommunication cables.
   j. Optic fibre.
   k. Energy efficient lamps, and
   l. Midget carbon electrodes.

5. **Transportation**
   m. Mechanised sailing vessels up to 10,000 DWT including fishing trawlers.
   n. Ship ancillaries.
   o. Commercial vehicles, public transport vehicles including automotive commercial three wheeler jeep type vehicles, industrial locomotives.
   p. Automotive two wheelers and three wheelers.
   q. Automotive components/spares and ancillaries.
   r. Shock absorbers for railway equipment, and
   s. Brake system for railway stock and locomotives.

6. Industrial Machinery

Industrial machinery and equipment.

7. i. Machine tools and industrial robots and their controls and accessories.

ii. Jigs, fixtures, tools and dies of specialised types and cross land tooling, and

iii. Engineering production aids such as cutting and forming tools, patterns and dies, and tools.

8. Agricultural Machinery

i. Tractors.

ii. Self-propelled Harvestor Combines.

iii. Rice transplanters.

9. Earth Moving Machinery

Earth moving machinery and construction machinery and components thereof.

10. Industrial Instruments

Indicating, recording and regulating devices for pressures, temperatures, rate of flow weights levels and the like.

11. Scientific and Electro medical Instruments and LaboratoryEquipment

12. Nitrogenous & Phosphatic Fertilizers falling under

Inorganic fertilizers under '18-Fertilizers' in the First Schedule to IDR Act, 1951.

13. Chemicals (other than fertilizers).

i. Heavy organic chemicals including petro-chemicals.

ii. Heavy inorganic chemicals.

iii. Organic finc chemicals.

iv. Synthetic resins and plastics.

v. Man made fibres.

vi. Synthetic rubber.

vii. Industrial explosives.

viii. Technical grade insecticides, fungicides, weedicides, and the like.

ix. Synthetic detergents

x. Miscellaneous chemicals (for industrial use only)

a. Catalyst and catalyst support,

b. Photographic chemicals,

c. Rubber chemicals,

d. Polyols,

e. Isocyanines, urethanes, etc.,

f. Speciality chemicals for enhanced oil recovery,

g. Heating fluids,

h. Coal tar distillation and product there from,

i. Tonnage plants for the manufacture of industrial gases,

j. High altitude breathing oxygen/medical oxygen,

k. Nitrous oxide,

l. Refrigerant gases like liquid nitrogen, carbon dioxide etc. in large volumes,

m. Argon and other rare gases,

n. Alkali/acid resisting cement compound,

o. Leather chemicals and auxiliaries.

14. Drugs and Pharmaceuticals

15. i) Paper and pulp, including paper products.

ii) Industrial laminates.

16. i) Automobile tyres and tubes.

ii) Rubberized heavy-duty industrial beltings of all types.

iii) Rubberized conveyor beltings.

iv) Rubber reinforced and lined fire-fighting hosepipes.

v) High pressure braided hoses.

vi) Engineering and industrial plastic products.

17. Plate Glass

- Glass shells for television tubes.
- Float glass and plate glass H.T.
- Insulators.
- Glass fibres of all types.

18. Ceramics

- Ceramics for industrial uses.

19. Cement Products

- Portland cement.
- Gypsum boards, wallboards and the like.

20. High Technology Reproductions and Multiplication Equipment.

21. Carbon and Carbon Products

- Graphite electrodes and anodes.
- Impervious graphite blocks and sheets.

22. Pretensioned High Pressure RCC Pipes.

23. Rubber Machinery

24. Printing Machinery.

- Web-fed high speed off-set rotary printing machine having output of 30,000 or more impressions per hour.
- Photo composing/type setting machines.
- Multi-colour sheet-fed off-set printing machines of sizes 18"x25" and above.
- High speed rotogravure printing machines having output of 30,000 or more impressions per hour.

25. Welding Electrodes other than those for Welding Mild Steel

26. Industrial Synthetic Diamonds.

- Photosynthesis improvers.
- Genetically modified free-living symbiotics nitrogen fixer.
- Pheromones.
- Bio-insecticides.

27. Extraction and Upgrading of Minor Oils

28. Pre-fabricated Building Material.

29. Soya Products

- Soya texture proteins.
- Soya protein isolates.

- Soya protein concentrates.
- Other specialised products of soybean.
- Winterised and deodourised refined soybean oil.

30. (a) Certified high yielding hybrid seeds and syntheticseeds and
    (b) Certified high yielding plantlets developed through plant tissue culture.
31. **All food processing industries other than milk food, malted foods, and flour, but excluding the items reserved for small-scale sector.**
32. **All items of packaging for food processing industries, excluding the items reserved for small-scale sector.**
33. **Hotels and Tourism-related Industry.**

In nutshell, the policy resolution of 1991 contained the following decisions:

i. Portfolio of public sector investment would be reviewed with a view to focus the public sector on strategic, high-tech and essential infrastructure. Whereas some reservation for public sector was being retained, there would be no bar for area of exclusivity to be opened up to the private sector selectively. Similarly, the public sector would also be allowed entry in areas not reserved for it.

ii. Public enterprises, which were chronically sick and unlikely to turnaround would, for formulation of revival/rehabilitation schemes, be referred to the Board for Industrial and Financial Reconstruction (BIFR) or other similar high- level institutions created for the purpose. A social security mechanism would be created to protect the interest of workers likely to be effected by such rehabilitation packages.

iii. In order to raise the resources and encourage wider public participation, a part of the

Government's share-holding in the public sector would be offered to mutual funds, financial institutions, general public and workers.

iv. Boards of public sector companies would be made more professional and given greater powers.

v. There would be a greater thrust on performance improvement through the Memorandum of Understanding (MOU) system by which management would be granted greater autonomy and will be held accountable. Technical expertise on the part of the Government would be upgraded to make the MOU negotiations and implementation more effective.

vi. To facilitate discussion on performance, the MOU signed between Government and the public enterprises would be tabled in parliament. While focusing on major management issues, this would place matters on day-to-day operations of public enterprises in their correct perspective.

vii. The main elements of the Government policy towards public sector enterprise were:
   - Bring down Government equity in all non-strategic PSES to 26 percent or lower, if necessary;
   - Restructure and review potentially viable PSEs;
   - Close down PSEs which could not be revived; and
   - Fully protect the interest of workers.

Government modifies, revises and upgrades the policy from time to time through policy guidelines or in the budget speech in the floor of Parliament. The Industrial Policy of 1991 had been a major and a bold shift in the policy of Government of India. Such a shift in the policy has been necessitated due to change in the international scenario as well as the change in the mindset of the policy-makers of the day. Government was also able to implement the policy to a major extent amidst endless criticism and opposition: The same policy was also followed by successive Governments was a different matter altogether. The policy change brought about by the Government was followed by the successive Governments and saved the country from brink of an economic disaster. Such a policy on economic and industrial front redeemed India's financial status in the international scenario. India have to open up more, especially in areas of labour, interest rate, tariffs, and public sector enterprise. Enough needed to be done to boost confidence among foreign investors. It enhanced the foreign exchange position, stabilized the dollar-rupee ratio, and the balance of payment. Similarly, Government pronounced some of the changes in the budget speech of 2000-01 in the following manner.

Industrial Policy initiatives announced in the Budget 2000-01

- **a.** Rationalisation of excise duty by introduction of Central Value Added Tax (CENVAT) and reducing the number of rates of excise duty.
- **b.** Extension of Maximum Retail Price (MRP) based excise duty to an increasing number of items, which would lead to simplification of the excise procedure.
- **c.** The Security and Exchange Board of India (SEBI) was made sole regulator of Venture Capital Funds (VCF).
- **d.** Permission to raise FII equity limit to 40 per cent through a special resolution by shareholders.

e. Limit for providing collateral to obtain finance raised from Rs. 1 lakh to Rs. 5 lakh for SSI Units in the tiny sector.

f. Reduction of import duty on cinematic camera and other related equipment for use in the entertainment industry and grant of 100 per cent exemption on export profits extended to non corporate assesses.

g. Reduction in custom duty on several items of the IT & Telecommunication Sector.

h. Enhancing of corpus of Rural Infrastructure Development Fund (RIDF) VI and reducing the interest charged on this by half a percent.

Industrial Policy

- In order to consolidate the recovery in industrial growth during 1999-2000 and to push further the industrial policy reforms, major policy initiatives were announced in the Budget of 2000-01.
- The Union Budget 2000-2001 also announced a number of fiscal incentives and other measures for strengthening the capital markets and the banking system. These included:
  i) 100 per cent exemption on income from Investor Protection Funds of Stock Exchanges, exemption of income distributed under the US - 64 and other open-ended equity oriented schemes of UTI and mutual funds, and abolition of interest tax paid by banks and financial institutions.
  ii) Special thrust for the housing sector was continued by announcing measures like extending the benefits already available to this sector for two more years, raising the level of rebate on repayment of housing loans to Rs.20,000 per year under Section 88 of the Income Tax Act and removing the ceiling of ownership of one house for granting

exemption from tax on long term capital gains, if the capital gain from transfer of capital assets is invested in a house.

iii) Reforms, intending to restructure the public sector, were carried forward by making liberal tax exemption on voluntary retirement benefits of employees.

iv) The benefit for the infrastructure sector extended to essential sectors of urban infrastructure, viz. water treatment and solid based management.

v) In pursuance of Government's commitment to facilitate industrial growth through foreign participation, Foreign Direct Investment (FDI) was permitted through the automatic route for all industries except a small negative list. The time-frame for consideration of FDI proposals was reduced from 6 weeks to 30 days for communicating Government decisions.

More decisions were taken to further liberalise the FDI policy, which included:

- 100 per cent FDI permitted for Business-to-Business, e-commerce.
- Removal of cap on investment in the power sector.
- 100 per cent FDI permitted in oil refining.
- 100 per cent FDI allowed in Special Economic Zones (SEZs) for all manufacturing activities.
- Condition of Dividend Balancing on 22 consumer items removed forthwith.
- 100 per cent FDI allowed in Telecom Sector for certain activities with some conditions.
- Payment of royalty up to 2 per cent for exports and one per cent for domestic sales allowed under automatic route on use of trademarks and brand names of foreign collaborator without technology transfer.

- Payment of royalty up to 8 per cent on exports and 5 per cent on domestic sales by wholly owned subsidiaries to offshore parent companies allowed under the automatic route without any restriction on the duration of royalty payments.
- Offshore Venture Capital Funds/ Companies allowed to invest in domestic venture capital undertakings as well as other companies through the automatic route, subject only to SEBI regulations and sector specific caps on FDI.
- Existing companies with FDI were eligible for automatic route to undertake additional activities covered under automatic route.
- FDI up to 26 per cent made eligible under automatic route in the Insurance sector, as prescribed in the Insurance Act, 1999, subject to obtaining a license from the Insurance Regulatory & Development Authority.(IRDA).
- Automatic route was made available to proposals in the Information Technology Sector, even when the applicant Company has a previous joint venture or technology transfer agreement in the same field.
- In the process of review of laws, regulations and simplification of procedures, an Expert Group constituted by Government in its recommendations, has proposed enactment of a new Industry Act, which would focus on promotion and development of industry instead of regulation. The Government has initiated the process of examining the feasibility of framing a new enactment in this regard.

The predominant considerations for continued large investments in public sector enterprises were to accelerate the growth of core sectors of economy, to serve the equipment needs of strategically important sectors- like Railways,

Telecommunications, Nuclear power, Defence etc.- to enable the government to exert a countervailing power on operation of private monopolies and multinationals in selected area; and to provide a spring board for the economy to achieve a significant degree of self-sufficiency in the critical sectors. Another category of large number of public enterprises concerns essentially to consumer oriented industries, such as drugs, hotels and food industries, etc. The rationale to set up such enterprises was to ensure easier availability of vital articles of mass consumption, to introduce check on prices of important products and services or help promote emerging areas, like tourism etc. Further, a large number of enterprises, which were sick units, have been taken over from the private sector in order to sustain production and protect employment. A large number of public enterprises are also operating in national and international trade, consultancy contract and construction services, inland and overseas communications, etc. The overall profile of public sector in India is, thus, a heterogenous conglomerate of basic and infrastructure industries, industries producing consumer goods and engaged in trade and services, etc.

In the changing scenario, it would be prudent that instead of expanding the public sector more and more, these are modernized, and made competitive through cutting down the cost of production, and restructuring of different functions. The functions of the public sector should also be limited to areas, like infrastructure building, and social sectors, like health care, primary education, drinking water, human resources development, and so on.

6

Recommendations of Five Year Planson Industry and Public Sector

Scope of Planning Commission

The Planning Commission was set up in March 1950 by a Resolution of Government of India, which defined the scope of its work in the following terms:

"The Constitution of India has guaranteed certain Fundamental Rights to the citizens of India and enunciated certain Directive Principles of State Policy, in particular, that the State shall strive to promote the welfare of the people by securing and protecting as effectively as it may a social order in which justice, social, economic and political, shall inform all the institutions of the national life, and shall direct its policy towards securing, among other things -

a. that the citizens, men and women equally, have the right to an adequate means of livelihood;
b. that the ownership and control of the material resources of the community are so distributed as best to sub-serve the common good; and
c. that the operation of the economic system does not result in the concentration of wealth and means of production to the common detriment.

Having regard to these rights and in furtherance of these principles as well as of the declared objective of the Government to promote a rapid rise in the standard of living of the people by efficient exploitation of the resources of the country, increasing production, and offering opportunities to all for employment in the service of the community.

The Planning Commission will-

1. make an assessment of the material, capital and human resources of the country, including technical personnel, and investigate the possibilities of augmenting such of these resources as are found to be deficient in relation to the nation's requirements;
2. formulate a Plan for the most effective and balanced utilisation of the country's resources;
3. on a determination of priorities, define the stages in which the Plan should be carried out and propose the allocation of resources for due completion of each stage;
4. indicate the factors which are tending to retard economic development, and determine the conditions which, in view of the current social and political situation, should be established for the successful execution of the Plan;
5. determine the nature of the machinery which will be necessary for securing the successful implementation of each stage of the Plan in all its aspects;
6. appraise from time to time the progress achieved in the execution of each stage of the Plan and recommend the adjustments of policy and measures that such appraisal may show to be necessary; and
7. make such interim or ancillary recommendations as appear to it to be appropriate either for facilitating the discharge of the duties assigned to it; or, on a consideration of the prevailing economic conditions, current policies, measures and development programmes; or on an examination of such specific problems as may be referred to it for advice by Central or State Governments."

FIRST FIVE YEAR PLAN (1951 -1956)

The Planning Commission presented it in December 1952. In this plans importance was laid on expansion of economic activities of the State. It was made clear that public sector and private sector must function as complementary to each other and as a part of single organism. The First Plan envisaged that the public sector would develop and start those industries in which private entrepreneurs were unwilling or unable to put their resources. In the first Five Year Plan's outlay on development by public authorities involved an amount of Rs.2069 crores over the period 1951-56. In determining the targets of expenditure, one of the main considerations taken into account were "the close relationship between the rate of development and requirement of resources in the public and in the private sectors". The Commission, while outlining the roles to be played by public as well as private sector, emphasized the need for industrial development as per Industrial Policy Resolution 1948 as below:

> The essentials of government policy in the sphere of industrial development had been stated in the Industrial Policy Resolution of April 1948. The Resolution listed certain industries, like the manufacture of arms and ammunition, the production and control of atomic energy and the ownership and management of railway transport as being reserved exclusively for the Central Government. In cases of certain other industries also, such as coal, iron and steel, aircraft manufacture, ship-building, manufacture of telephone, telegraph, wireless apparatus and mineral oils, the State, including the Central and State Governments and other public authorities, would be responsible for further development except to the extent that it envisaged the co operation of private enterprise necessary for the purpose. The rest of the industrial field was to be open to private enterprise, individual as well as cooperative, but the State would intervene whenever the progress of any industry under private enterprise was found to be unsatisfactory. Central regulation and control was

envisaged for 18 specified industries of special importance from the points of view of the investment and technical skill involved. It was believed that within the framework of this policy, it was possible to have a programme of industrial development, which would meet the country's the then needs.

The distinction between the public and the private sector related to the mode of operation rather than to the ultimate objective. Private enterprise operating in terms of legitimate profit expectations and efficient use of available resources had an important part to play in developing the economy. The scope and need for development were so great that it was always preferable that the public sector develops those industries in which private enterprise was unable or unwilling to put up the resources required and run the risks involved, leaving the rest of the field free for private enterprise. In this matter of investment of the limited resources available to the public sector, there should be complete coordination between the Plans of the State Governments and of the Central Government. The nationalisation of the existing enterprises, which meant acquisition by Government of the existing productive assets, should have only a low priority, especially as most of the purposes of such a transfer of ownership could be served by judicious regulation. In a planned economy, justification of private enterprise was that, within the framework of national policy, it was capable of contributing to the fulfillment of the objectives defined in the Plan. This meant inevitably that it had to accept new obligations towards the worker, the investor and the consumer and had to maintain a high standard of integrity and efficiency. The large volume of resources needed for all-round development of the economy could be secured only if the public and the private sectors co-operated closely. Such co-operation was also necessary from the point of view of utilising to the best advantage the limited resources of initiative, technical skill and business experience available in the country. The economy could only grow, and achieve the desired objective, if both public and private sectors would work in tandem. One can only complement the other. Social obligations should not only be defined and limited to setting up of some schools, colleges or hospitals. It should be viewed in a larger perspective.

Mention was made in the Draft Outline Report of the Industries (Development and Control) Bill, 1949 that was then under Government's consideration. The Industries (Development and Regulation) Act, 1951 incorporated some of the suggestions made by the Commission in the Draft Outline Report. The principal object of this Act was to enable the Government to implement its policy for development and regulation of industries along the lines stated above. The Act was to apply to 37 industries listed in the first schedule. These included:

(a) consumer goods industries, like cotton and woolen textiles, vanaspati and vegetable oils, sugar and salt, pharmaceuticals and drugs, etc.;

(b) capital goods and producer goods industries like iron and steel, locomotives and rolling stock, non-ferrous metals and alloys, heavy machinery for industry, including ball and roller bearings, gear wheels, etc., and machine tools;

(c) industries producing fuel, such as coal, power and industrial alcohol, motor and aviation fuel, and other oils ;

(d) industries producing machinery and equipment for generation, transmission and distribution of electric energy, electric motors, batteries and electrical goods;

(e) heavy chemicals, including fertilizers;

(f) automobiles, including tractors, aircraft, ship-building and telephones, telegraph and wireless communication apparatus; and

(g) various others, such as arms and ammunition, agricultural implements, mathematical and scientific instruments, small and hand tools, sewing and knitting machines, bicycles, hurricane lanterns, glass and ceramics.

The important provisions of the Act were that all the existing industrial undertakings in the scheduled industries had to be registered with the Government within a prescribed period. The other provisions were as follows:

1. no new industrial unit could be established or substantial extensions to existing plants made without a licence from the Central Government;
2. the Government could order an investigation in respect of any scheduled industry or undertaking if, in its opinion, there had been or was likely to be an unjustifiable fall in the volume of production in the industry or undertaking or if there was a marked deterioration in quality or an increase in price for which there was no justification;
3. a similar investigation could also be ordered in respect of any industrial undertaking being managed in a manner likely to cause serious injury or damage to consumers;
4. in the event of an industry or undertaking not carrying out the directions issued after conducting an investigation, the Government could take over its management.

The Commission, while outlaying the details of Plan expenditure, also emphasized the need for the greater role to be played by private sector in rest of the areas. The relevant observations of the Commission were here under;

Development in Private Sector

Over the five year period, the total expenditure on the projects included in the Plans for the Central Government and for the States amounted to Rs. 94 crores. The bulk of this expenditure about Rs. 83 crores was in respect of projects directly under the Central Government. The projects under implementation by the State Governments were estimated to involve an expenditure of about Rs. 9 crores, of which Rs. 4-8 crores, would be advanced by the Central Government as loans. The industrial plan in the public sector envisaged in respect of certain projects participation of private capital, indigenous as well as external. The estimated contribution of such private capital was about Rs. 20 crores.

Major new industrial projects included in the Plan was the one for iron and steel, estimated to cost Rs. 80 crores in all over a period of six years from the date of commencement. The expenditure projected up to 1955-56 was Rs. 30 crores, of which the Government would provide Rs. 15 crores and the remainder was to be secured through participation of indigenous and external capital. The estimated capacity of this project would be about 800,000 tons of pig iron, while the steel capacity (in regard to which a firm decision would be taken later) would be a minimum of 350,000 tons, with further additions, if necessary, in the light of the availability of pig iron supplies from the expanded capacity in the private sector in the next few years. By 1955-56, this project, it was expected, would be producing about 350,000 tons of pig iron. The completion of this project by 1958 as well as the projects for expansion in the private sector would raise the availability of pig iron and steel from domestic sources by about 100 per cent. The Sindri plant, completed in October 1951, was capable of producing 350,000 tons of ammonium sulphate a year, and it was hoped that the corresponding monthly rate of output would be attained shortly. Another project, under consideration, was the expansion of the Sindri factory for the production of urea and ammonium nitrate. The all-steel coach factory, which was a part of the plan for railways, was expected to cost Rs. 4 crores. It would produce 350 units per annum by 1957 on single shift operation as against 50 units by 1955-56.

The Plan provided for completion within the five-year period of all the industrial projects in hand in the public sector. In fact, the concept was that most of these projects would be completed by 1953-54. The Chittaranjan Locomotive Factory, the total cost of which on completion would approximate to Rs. 15.0 crores (cost within the Plan period Rs. 4.73 crores) had already commenced manufacturing some of the necessary components and it was expected that by 1957 the factory would be able to produce 120 locomotives a year.

This was exclusive of the finance that might be allotted for industries out of the lump sum provision of Rs. 50 crores for basic industries and transport referred to in Chapter IV of the Plan. In the previous years of the period of the Plan, it was proposed to provide for a project for the manufacture of heavy electrical plant and equipment out of the lump sum provision. This figure of Rs. 94 crores differed from the estimates of expenditure on industry in the public sector given in Chapter IV of the Plan, since it had been prepared on a different basis and certain items, *e.g.*, expenditure on small scale and cottage industries, and finance for the establishment of Industrial Finance Corporations and trading estates, had not been included on imported components. This together with the output of 50 locomotives at TELCO would more or less meet the normal annual requirements of the railways. Work on the construction of the machine tool factory at Jalahalli in Mysore State had already commenced. The factory was estimated to cost Rs. 9.78 crores, and by 1955-56 it would produce 1,600 machine tools of the value of over Rs. 4 crores per annum. This factory would specialise in production of high precision machine tools and would thus provide the basis for the subsequent expansion of heavy as well as light engineering industries. The provision of over Rs. 14 crores for shipbuilding included the expenditure for the acquisition of the Vishakhapatnam Yard and its development besides the loans and subsidy was to be given to shipping companies for purchase of ships built in the Yard. The Plan provided for the manufacture of engines and boilers in the workshop at the Yard and also for expansion of berths for the building of ships so as to enable the Hindustan Shipyard Limited to bring down the cost of ships constructed to the level of those built in the U.K. The operation of the Yard would enable coastal shipping in India to meet the bulk of its replacement requirements.

It would be seen that most of the projects in this sector related to manufacture of capital goods or of intermediate products, which were of vital importance not only from the point of view of immediate needs but also in terms of future economic development. Their completion would correct to some extent the present lopsidedness of the industrial structure. The penicillin and D.D.T. factories, which did not fall in the category mentioned above, had a special importance at that juncture from the point of view of improvement in public health. Among the projects of the State Governments, mention must be made of the Madhya Pradesh newsprint project and expansion of the Mysore Iron and Steel Works. The former would produce about one-third of the country's requirement of newsprint, while the latter introduced for the first time the technique of electric smelting of iron ores.

With increasing participation of the Government in industrial development was conceived the idea of bench-marking the appropriate organisation for enterprises in the public sector. The criteria of successful operation for private or public enterprises were basically the same; the public must get the service of requisite quality at minimum cost, and the interests of the worker and the shareholder or the taxpayer must be adequately safeguarded. Indeed, the standards of performance expected of public enterprises had to be more rigorous. It was, therefore, of paramount importance that industrial units in the public sector should be so organised as to secure the advantages of flexibility in operation generally characteristic of private enterprise with technical efficiency and responsiveness to public need, short-term as well as long-term, which could form the core reason of government initiative and management in this field.

The drawbacks of departmental management of public enterprises were well known. Successful conduct of such enterprises required a great deal of initiative and the power to take quick decisions on the part of the executives in charge, and these could hardly be secured if the enterprise was directly under a government department. On the other hand, the extent of autonomy, which could be insisted upon for such enterprises was a matter on which a definite judgment could not be conceived except in the light of further experience. Several of the industrial undertakings directly under the Central Government had already been organised as joint stock companies with boards of directors vested with powers of management in the same manner as in any undertaking in the private sector. Enquiries into the working of industrial enterprises in some of the States reinforced the desirability of organising these enterprises as entities independent of day-to-day governmental control. The Planning Commission, therefore, recommended that industrial undertakings under the State Governments should also be organised as joint stock companies and operated on business lines with internal management entirely under the control of the board of directors. The main principle to be followed was that such enterprises should not be subject to governmental control in their day-to-day administration but should, nevertheless, be accountable to the public, which were their ultimate owner as well as beneficiary. What organisational structure and administrative procedures would answer these requirements best had to be determined in the light of experience. For the immediate present, the problem was to be seen that the right conventions in these matters were evolved. To a great extent, this was a matter of securing the right personnel for the boards of directors, the top executives and the technicians.

Expansion in the Private Sector

While the emphasis of industrial expansion in the public sector during first five-year period was on initiating and promoting investment in certain basic lines and on completing the projects in hand, the initiative and responsibility for securing the necessary expansion over the bulk of the field of industry was with private enterprise. The Planning Commission also set out the expansion programme in the private sector. For convenience of reference, a table summarising the more important expansion programmes is as under.

1. Expansion Programme in Certain Major Lines in the Private Sector

S.No.	Particulars	Unit	1950-51 Rated	1950-51 Production Capacity	1955-56 Rated	1955-56 Capacity
(1)						
	(a) Pumps, powe -d iven	Numbe s	33,460	34,310	69,400	80,000 to 85,000
	(b) Diesel engines	Numbe s	6,320	5,540	39,725	50,000
(2)	Aluminium	Tons	4,000	3,677	20,000	12,000
(3)	Automobiles (manufactu ing only).	Numbe s	30,000	4,077	30,000	30,000
(4)	Bicycles Ag icultu al Machine y:	Numbe s '000	120	99	530	530
(5)	Cement	Tons '000	3,194	2,692	5,016	4,550
(6)	Elect ic T ansfo me s	KVA '000	370	179	485	450
(7)	Fe tilize :					
	(i') Ammonium sulphate	Tons	78,670	46,528	131,270	120,000
	(ii) Supe phosphate	Tons	123,460	55.089	192,855	164,000
(8)	Glass Indust y :					
	Sheet glass	Tons	11,700	5,850	52,200	26,000
(9)	Heavy Chemicals :					
	(i) Caustic soda	Tons 'ooo	19	11	37	33
	(ii) Soda ash	Tons 'ooo	54	45	86	78
	(iii) Sulphu ic acid .	Tons 'ooo	150	99	213	192

(Table Contd....)

(10) I on and Steel :					
(i) Pig i on	Tons 'ooo	1,850	1,572	2,700	1,950
(ii) Steel(main p oduce s)	Tons 'ooo	975	976	1.550	1,280
(11) Pape and Boa d	Tons 'ooo	137	114	198	188
(12) Pet oleum Refining :					
(i) Liquid pet oleum p oducts	Gals. Million	N. A.	N. A.	N. A.	403
(ii) Bitumen	Tons	N. A.	N. A.	N. A.	37,500
(13) Powe Alcohol	Gals. Million	13	5	21	18
(14) Locomotives	Numbe s			50	50
.(15) Rayon :					
(i) Rayon filament	Lbs. Million	4	...	18	18
(ii) Staple fib e	Bales 'ooo	...	...	28	28

N. A. = Not available.

The total capital investment necessary for industrial expansion in the private sector was estimated at Rs. 233 crores. Some 80 per cent of this investment would be in respect of capital goods and producer goods industries. The major ones among those were iron and steel, which was estimated to take up about Rs. 43 crores; petroleum refineries, which would involve an expenditure of Rs. 64 crores; cement, estimated to cost Rs. 15 crores; aluminum, expected to take up Rs. 9 crores; fertilizers, heavy chemicals and power alcohol, estimated to cost about Rs. 12 crores. Additional electric power generation in the private sector would involve an expenditure of Rs. 16 crores in the five year period. In the consumer goods industries, although the emphasis was mainly on achieving increases in production through fuller utilisation of capacity already established, considerable investment was envisaged in certain new lines, such as rayon, paper and drugs and pharmaceuticals. In the programme for the textile industry, moderate expansion of capacity for yarn, both cotton and woollen, was included. The development programme for vegetable oils related mainly to the establishment of solvent extraction plants and the crushing of cottonseed.

In the formulation and assessment of the programmes in the private sector, it was necessary to keep in mind the fact that in an economy, which was not completely centralised, government could influence but not determine the actual course of investment. Nevertheless, the programmes of development as was presented were in the nature of best judgments as to what was feasible and desirable. The Commission had worked out these programmes in close consultation with representatives of the industries concerned and of the Central Ministries as also with independent experts and technicians, and had tried to assess carefully the need and scope for expansion in various fields in conformity with the order of priorities. The results of this detailed examination, which covered 42 organised industries, were also published separately in a special volume devoted to this subject by the Commission. The field of industry covered a wide variety of undertakings with large differences in financial resources, organisational set up, and scale of operations and background of experience. In many cases, the data necessary for arriving at an appropriate judgment of needs and possibilities were not satisfactory, and in some cases, the full facts regarding even the present position of the industry could not easily be ascertained. Nevertheless, it had been possible, to survey briefly the growth and present position of major industries in the country and to work out broadly the lines along which expansions might be expected to take place in the five-year period. The industries, thus studied, covered between them about 80 per cent of the investment in the large and medium scale industries in the country. The studies brought together in that volume might have certain lacunae but it was hoped that those would be made good in the near future. In this connection, it was pointed out that with the coming into force of the registration and licensing procedures laid down under the Industries (Development & Regulation) Act, a mass of valuable information pertaining to scheduled industries would become available and it was necessary that arrangements would be made for systematic and expeditious analysis of the same.

The First Five year plan set out an agenda for the growth of public sector in India which hitherto was not a priority area during the pre-independence era. The former rulers were more concerned for maintenance of law and order than for the overall development. The detailed analysis of the functional areas as well as the earmarking of funds for the different sectors set the tone for the upward trend of the public sector in India.

SECOND FIVE YEAR PLAN (1956-61)

Dominant Role of Public Sector

Soon after declaration of Industrial Policy Resolution of 1956, the second Five year Plan (1956-61) was finalized. It emphasized the need for the rapid growth of public sector in the country. While finalizing the Plan outlay, the dominant role of public sector enterprise was reiterated. Simultaneously, the private sector was also allowed investment in basic industries, like Iron and Steel, production of machinery, etc. The relevant paragraphs as laid down by the Commission are as follows:

a. "The Major point of departure in the second plan was the precedence that was accorded to the public sector in industrial and mineral development. Governmental initiative in the development of agriculture, power, transport and social services was already an established feature of economic planning in India. But projects of industrial and mineral development had hitherto not figured prominently in the investment plans of the public sector. Thus, in the first plan a total provision of Rs. 94 crores was made for the establishment of large-scale industries in the public sector as against an estimated programme of new investment in the private sector of Rs. 233 crores. In the second plan, the provision of Rs. 690 crores for large-scale industries and mining (including scientific research) in the public sector compared favourably with the estimated new investment of Rs. 575 crores for industries and mining in the private sector. While the private sector was expected to play an important part in the process of industrialisation, there was a pronounced shift in emphasis in favour of the projects in the public sector.

b. Practically the whole of the proposed outlay of Rs. 690 crores for large-scale industry and mining was for development of basic industries, such as iron and steel, coal, fertilizers, heavy engineering and heavy electrical equipment. During the second plan, three steel plants of one million tons ingot capacity each was to be established in the public sector at Rourkela, Bhilai and Durgapur. In addition, at one of these plants, 350,000 tons of pig iron would be produced for sale. Steel production at the Mysore Iron and Steel Works was to be expanded to 100,000 tons. The combined output of finished steel from all the projects in the public sector was expected to be of the order of two million tons by the end of the second plan.

c. The programme for the establishment of heavy engineering industries included a heavy steel foundry at the Chittaranjan Locomotive factory for meeting the requirements of railways for heavy castings and the establishment of heavy foundries, forges shops and structural shops, under the auspices of the N.I.D.C. Arrangements were being made for manufacture of heavy electrical equipment in the public sector. The Chittaranjan Locomotive factory was to be expanded to increase its output of locomotives to 300 per annum as against 125 per year. The Integral Coach Factory, which went into production in 1955, would produce 350 coaches per annum by 1959. Provision had also been made for a new meter gauge coach factory.

d. The output of minerals in the country was expected to increase by 58 per cent over the second plan period. Mention might be made particularly of coal in view of the large increase in requirements that was implied in the programmes of industrial and transport development. The existing production of coal in the country was of the order of 38 million tons. The bulk of this production was in the private sector, the share of the public sector being only 4.5 million tons; it was proposed to increase the production of coal by some 22 million tons in the next five years, some 12 million tons in the public sector and the remaining 10 million tons in the private sector.

e. In view of the paucity of coal deposits in Southern India, high priority was given to the multi-purpose Lignite Project at Neiveli in South Arcot district. Under this project, 3.5 million tons of lignite ore were to be produced and used for: (1) generation of power in a station of 211,000 kW capacity, (2) production of carbonised briquettes in a carbonisation plant of about 700,000 tons annual capacity, and (3) production of 70,000 tons of fixed nitrogen in the form of urea and sulphate/nitrate. In addition, two more fertilizer factories were to be set up. One of these, to be located at Nangal, was expected to produce nitro-limestone corresponding to 70,000 tons of fixed nitrogen per annum. The other fertilizer factory was to be established at

Rourkela. It would produce nitro-limestone equivalent to 80,000 tons of fixed nitrogen per annum. Further, the Sindri Fertilizer Factory would be expanded so as to increase its outputs from 66,000 tons of nitrogen to 117,000 tons.

f. Several of the projects completed during the first plan such as D.D.T. plant, Hindustan Cables, Hindustan Antibiotics and the Indian Telephone Industries had to be expanded. It was also proposed to establish a second D.D.T. plant in Travancore-Cochin. Among the projects included in the plans of States, mention might be made of the Durgapur coke-oven plant in West Bengal and the manufacture of electric porcelain insulators and transformers in Mysore.

g. The bulk of the investment in the private sector was also for the development of basic industries. Substantial programmes of expansion were envisaged for the iron and steel industry in the private sector and the capacity of the industry was expected to increase from 1.25 million tons of finished steel to 2.3 million tons by 1958. It was proposed to increase the production of cement from 4.3 million tons to 13 million tons-the capacity of the industry being raised to 16 million tons-by the end of the plan. Similarly, capacity for aluminium, ferro-manganese and refractories were proposed to be substantially stepped up.

h. The programmes of development in the private sector provided for a substantial increase in production of machinery in the country, including machinery for cotton textiles, jute, sugar, paper, cement, agriculture and road making. The chemical industry, which had already registered a sizeable advance in the first plan period, was to achieve significant diversification and growth in output. The production of soda ash, for example, was to be increased to three times and of caustic soda to four times of the present level. The third oil refinery at Visakhapatnam was proposed to be completed by 1957 and an increase in the production capacity for power and industrial alcohol from 27 to 36 million gallons was envisaged."

Approach to the Second Five Year Plan (1956 -1961)

Thus there had been a paradigm shift in the concept of industry and industrial development in the country in the second Industrial Resolution Policy of the Government of India as well as that of the Planning Commission. Both the Industrial Policy as well as the Planning Commission reflected the views of the Government. The Planning Commission in its approach paper for the Second Five Year plan put forth the objectives and techniques significant for the Plan. It did not set any specific target but desired to set an economic dynamism, which would lift continually not only the material well being but also cultural and intellectual achievements. While designing the approach paper, the Commission had in its mind the current levels of living conditions, low levels of production and so on. The Commission in its paper, had emphasized that to achieve the objective of continuous growth in the material, intellectual as well as in cultural field, India should have a socialistic pattern of society, and in its own words the approach paper put forth as follows:

> "Objectives and techniques significant as the achievements of the first plan have been, it is apparent that they have to be regarded as no more than a beginning. The task is not merely one of reaching any fixed or static point, such as doubling of living standards, but of generating dynamism in the economy which will lift it to continually higher levels of material well-being and of intellectual and cultural achievements. The current levels of living in India are very low. Production is insufficient even for satisfying the minimum essential needs of the population, and a large leeway has to be made before the services and amenities required for healthy living can be brought within the reach of any significant proportion of the population. There are large areas or regions of the country, which are underdeveloped even in relation to the rest of the country, and there are classes of the population, which are almost untouched by modern progressive ideas and

techniques. It is necessary to proceed faster with development, and this, it must be emphasised, is possible only to the extent that a larger measure of effort, both financial and organisational is forthcoming. For several plan periods to come, it is on the mobilisation of the effort rather than on the gains and returns arising therefrom that attention has to be concentrated. These gains and returns are important, but more important is perhaps the satisfaction that a community gets from attempting a worthwhile task which gives it a chance to bend its energies to productive and socially useful purposes. The 'costs' of development, viewed in this light, are a reward in themselves. There is no doubt that given a right approach to problems of development, including social policy and institutional change, a community can draw upon the latent energies within itself to an extent which ensures development at rates much larger than nice calculations of costs and returns or inputs and outputs may sometimes suggest."

The Socialistic Pattern of Society

India suffered long colonial rule. It had vast population of poor, uneducated and socially and economically backward people at the time of independence. The unprivileged and the people, who were socially as well and economically backward, had to have a special consideration in the early days of independence. Since they constituted the bulk of the population, development of the underprivileged people and those below the poverty line were viewed in its totality and in a macro level instead of calculating the gains in a short term perspective. The material development of such people was no doubt linked to the microeconomics of the area, but a sustained development could be perceived only with improvement in the quality of life in general. The Planning Commission, therefore, while interpreting the development, had observed that such development was possible through a 'socialistic pattern of society' enunciated in the preamble of the Constitution of India. The Commission in their own words observed as follows:

a. "A rising standard of life, or material welfare as it is sometimes called, is of course not an end in itself. Essentially, it is a means to a better intellectual and cultural life. A society which has to devote the bulk of its working force or its working hours to the production of the bare where-withal of life is to that extent limited in its pursuit of higher ends. Economic development is intended to expand the community's productive power and to provide the environment in which there is scope for expression and application of diverse faculties and urges. It follows that the pattern of development and the lines along which economic activity is to be directed must from the start be related to the basic objectives which society has in view. The task before an underdeveloped country is not merely to get better results within the existing framework of economic and social institutions but to mould and refashion these so that they contribute effectively to the realisation of wider and deeper social values.

b. These values or basic objectives have recently been summed up in the phrase 'socialist pattern of society'. Essentially, this means that the basic criterion for determining the lines of advance must not be private profit but social gain, and that the pattern of development and the structure of socio-economic relations should be so planned that they result not only in appreciable increases in national income and employment but also in greater equality in incomes and wealth. Major decisions regarding production, distribution, consumption and investment-and in fact all significant socio-economic relationships-must be made by agencies informed by social purpose. The benefits of economic development must accrue more and more to the relatively less privileged classes of society, and there should be a progressive reduction of the concentration of incomes, wealth and economic power. The problem is to create a milieu in which the small man who has so far had little opportunity of perceiving and participating in the immense possibilities of growth through organised effort is enabled to put in his best in the interests of a higher standard of life for himself and increased prosperity for the country. In the process, there is rise in economic and social status. Vertical mobility of labour is thus no less important than horizontal mobility, for nothing is more destructive of hope and more inhibitive of effort than a feeling that the accident of birth or of a poor start in life is likely to come in the way of a capable person rising in life in terms of economic and social status. For creating the appropriate conditions, the State has to take on heavy responsibilities as the principal agency speaking for and acting on behalf of the community as a whole. The public sector has to expand rapidly. It has not only to initiate developments which the private sector is either unwilling or unable to undertake; it has to play the dominant role in shaping the entire pattern of investments in the economy, whether it makes the investments directly or whether these are made by the private sector. The private sector has to play its part within the framework of the comprehensive plan accepted by the community. The resources available for investment are thrown up in the last analysis by social processes. Private enterprise, free pricing, private management are all devices to further what are truly social ends; they can only be justified in terms of social results.

c. The use of modem technology requires large scale production and a unified control and allocation of resources in certain major lines of activity. These include exploitation, of minerals and basic and capital goods industries, which are major determinants of the rate of growth of the economy. The responsibility for new developments in these fields must be undertaken in the main by the State, and the existing units have also to fall in line with the emerging pattern. Public ownership, partial or complete, and public control or participation in management is specially required in those fields in which technological considerations tend towards a concentration of economic power and of wealth. In several fields, private enterprise can, under present day conditions, make little headway without assistance and support from Government, and in these cases the public or semi-public character of the resources drawn upon has to be recognised.

In the rest of the economy, conditions have to be created in which there is full scope for private initiative and enterprise either on an individual or on a cooperative basis. In a growing economy which gets increasingly diversified, there is scope for both the public and the private sectors to expand simultaneously, but it is inevitable, if development is to proceed at the pace envisaged and to contribute effectively to the attainment of the larger social ends in view, that the public sector must grow not only absolutely but also relatively to the private sector.

d. The socialist pattern of society is not to be regarded as some fixed or rigid pattern. It is not rooted in any doctrine or dogma. Each country has to develop according to it own genius and traditions. Economic and social policy has to be shaped from time to time in the light of historical circumstances. It is neither necessary nor desirable that the economy should become a monolithic type or organisation offering little play for experimentation either as to forms or as to modes of functioning. Nor should expansion of the public sector mean centralisation of decision-making and of exercise of authority. In fact, the aim should be to secure an appropriate devolution of functions and to ensure to public enterprises the fullest freedom to operate within a framework of broad directives or rules of the game. The organisation and management of public enterprises is a field in which considerable experimentation will be necessary, and this holds, in fact, for the entire socialist pattern. What is important is a clear sense of direction, a consistent regard for certain basic values and a readiness to adapt institutions and organisations and their rules of conduct in the light of experience. The accent of the socialist pattern is on the attainment of positive goals, the raising of living standards, the enlargement of opportunities for all, the promotion of enterprise among the disadvantaged classes and the creation of a sense of partnership among all sections of the community. These positive goals provide the criteria for basic decisions. The Directive Principles of State Policy in the Constitution had indicated the approach in broad terms; the socialist pattern of society is a more concretised expression of this approach. Economic policy and institutional changes have to be planned in a manner that would secure economic advance along democratic and egalitarian lines. Democracy, it has been said, is a way of life rather than a particular set of institutional arrangements. The same could well be said of the socialist pattern."

The Planning Commission went on to add further the objectives for the public sector in the following words:

e. "Objectives

Within its broad approach the Second Five Year Plan has been formulated with reference to the following principal objectives: -

a. a sizeable increase in national income so as to raise the level of living in the country;
b. rapid industrialisation with particular emphasis on the development of basic and heavy industries;
c. a large expansion of employment opportunities; and
d. reduction of inequalities in income and wealth and a more even distribution of economic power.

These objectives are interrelated. A significant increase in national income and a marked improvement in living standards cannot be secured without a substantial increase in production and investment. To this end, the building up of economic and social overheads, exploration and development of minerals and the promotion of basic industries like steel, machine building, coal and heavy chemicals are vital. For securing an advance simultaneously in all these directions, the available manpower and natural resources have to be used to the best advantage. In a country in which there is relative abundance of manpower, expansion of employment opportunities becomes an important objective in itself. Further, the process and pattern of development should reflect certain basic social values and purposes. Development should result in a diminution of economic and social inequalities and should be achieved through democratic means and processes. Economic objectives cannot be divorced from social objectives and means and objectives go together. It is only in the context of a plan, which satisfies the legitimate urges of the people that a democratic society can put forward its best effort.

f. These objectives have to be pursued in a balanced way, for excessive emphasis on any one of them may damage the economy and delay the realisation of the very objective, which is being stressed. Low or static standards of living, underemployment and unemployment, and to a certain extent even the gap between the average incomes and the highest incomes are all manifestations of the basic underdevelopment which characterises an economy depending mainly on agriculture. Rapid industrialisation and diversification of the economy is thus the core of development. But if industrialisation is to be rapid enough, the country must aim at developing basic industries and industries which make machines to make the machines needed for further development. This calls for substantial expansion in iron and steel, non-ferrous metals, coal, cement, heavy chemicals and other industries of basic importance. The limitation is, of course, the scarcity of resources and the many urgent claims on them. Nevertheless, the criterion is not merely immediate needs but the continuing and expanding needs in the coming years as development goes forward. India's known natural resources are relatively large, and in many of these fields, as in steel for instance, she is likely to have a comparative cost advantage. It is desirable to aim at proceeding farthest in the direction of developing heavy and capital goods industries, which conform to this criterion.

g. Investment in basic industries creates demands for consumer goods, but it does not enlarge the supply of consumer goods in the short run; nor does it directly absorb any large quantities of labour. A balanced pattern of industrialisation, therefore, requires a well-organised effort to utilise labour for increasing the supplies of much needed consumer goods in a manner which economise the use of capital. A society in which labour is plentiful in relation to capital has to develop the art and technique of using labour-intensive modes of production effectively-and too much social advantage-in diverse fields. Indeed, in the context of prevailing unemployment, the absorption of labour becomes an important objective in itself. In using labour-intensive methods, it may well be that the cost of the product is somewhat higher. This entails a sacrifice, which can be reduced through technical and organisational improvements. In any case, a measure of sacrifice in the matter of consumption is inevitable while the economy is being strengthened at base. The sacrifice diminishes as more power, more transport, and better tools, machinery and equipment become available for increasing the productivity of consumer goods industries, and in the long run the community gets increasingly large returns. Meanwhile, the stress on utilisation of unutilised or underutilised labour-power alleviates the immediate problem of unemployment. Another point that may need stressing in this connection is that the use of labour-intensive methods often implies that a smaller proportion of the incomes generated are available for saving and reinvestment. Steps must be taken to ensure that this does not happen on any significant scale. It has to be remembered that employment at rising levels of income can be created only to the extent that the saving potential of the economy is raised.

h. The second five year plan accords high priority to industrialisation, and especially to the development of basic and heavy industries. A large expansion of public enterprise in the sphere of industrial and mineral development is envisaged. It is, in fact, intended to strengthen further the programmes of development in respect of heavy industries, oil exploration and coal and to make a beginning with the development of atomic energy. The main responsibility for these programmes rests upon the Central Government. The carrying through of these new programmes will entail, besides the financial investment required, a great deal of strengthening of the organisational and administrative personnel available to Government. It will also necessitate adoption of expeditious procedures in the matter of taking decisions and executing them. It cannot be emphasized too strongly that unless steps are taken to augment rapidly the output of the means of production and to build up the fuel and energy resources, which are so vital to development, the scale and pace of advance in the coming years will be inhibited. The dynamism of the second plan lies to a considerable extent in these new programmes, on the fulfillment of which effort has to be concentrated. The results, which the second plan promises, are impressive, but correspondingly large is the effort that it calls forth by way of mobilisation and application of real and financial resources.

i. These developments in the public sector have to be viewed together with, those envisaged in the private sector. The increase in the output of goods and services to be secured over the plan period is the result of developments in both these sectors. The two sectors have to function in unison and are to be viewed as parts of a single mechanism. The Plan as a whole can go through only on the basis of simultaneous and balanced development in the two sectors. The Plan incorporates the investment decisions taken by the public authorities, and the corresponding outputs or benefits can easily be estimated. As to the private sector, Government policy can influence private decisions through fiscal measures, through licensing and, to the extent necessary, through direct physical allocations so as to promote and to facilitate realisation of the targets proposed. A large part of the private sector consists of millions of small producers scattered all over the country. Investment estimates and targets in these fields can only be in the nature of broad indications. Even in the field of organised industry and business for which more data are available and which are more amenable to incentives or curbs offered or introduced by Government, there cannot obviously be the same degree of closeness or integration between resources and performance as in the case of activities directly undertaken by Government. Various investments in the public sector, such as for irrigation, power and transport, for instance, increase the production potential of the private sector and the producers or enterprises concerned can be expected to take advantage of these facilities. Given an appropriate structure of relative prices, which Government can and has to control and influence, the desired allocation of resources in the private sector can be induced. In fact, it is appropriate to think more and more in terms of an interpenetration of the public and private sectors rather than of two separate sectors.

j. These are general considerations bearing on the formulation of industrial policy in the context of planning. The Government of India's industrial policy since Independence has been shaped broadly in terms of the Industrial Policy Resolution of 1948. That Resolution emphasised clearly the responsibility of Government in the matter of promoting, assisting and regulating the development of industry in the national interest. It envisaged for the public sector an increasingly active role. While it reiterated the inherent right of the State to acquire any industrial undertaking, whenever the public interest requires it, it laid down, in view of the circumstances then existing, a certain demarcation of fields for the public and private sectors. Important developments have taken place since the Resolution was adopted in 1948. There is now a clear appreciation of the goals and direction of development. Planning has proceeded on an organised basis, and it is essential to strengthen and accelerate this effort in the coming years. The 1948 Resolution has been reviewed in the light of these considerations and the experience gained so far, and the Prime Minister placed the new Industrial Policy Resolution before Parliament on the 30th April 1956.

k. As the Resolution puts it, "The adoption of the socialist pattern of society as the national objective, as well as the need for planned and rapid development, requires that all industries of basic and strategic importance, or in the nature of public utility services, should be in the public sector. Other industries, which are essential and require investment on a scale, which only the State, in present circumstances, could provide, have also to be in the public sector. The State has, therefore, to assume direct responsibility for the future development of industries over a wider area". The Resolution classifies industries into three categories, having regard to the part, which the State would play in each of them. The first category shown in Schedule A consists of industries the future development of which will be the exclusive responsibility of the State. In the second category, shown in Schedule B, are industries which will be progressively State-owned and in which, therefore, the State will generally take the initiative in establishing new undertakings, but in which private enterprise will also be expected to supplement the effort of the State. The third category comprises all the remaining industries, further development of which will, in general, be left to the initiative and enterprise of the private sector. These categories are not intended to be rigid or watertight. In the industries listed in Schedule A, for instance, the expansion of existing privately owned units is not precluded, and the State is free to secure the cooperation of private enterprise in the establishment of new units when the national interest so requires, subject to the proviso that while securing such cooperation, it will ensure, through majority participation in the capital of the undertaking or otherwise, that it has the requisite powers to guide the policy and control the operations of the undertaking. Schedule B relates to what may be called the mixed sector, a sector in which the State will enter progressively and enlarge its operations, but private enterprise will, at the same time, have the opportunity to develop, either on its own or with State participation. In the rest of the field, development will ordinarily be undertaken through the initiative and enterprise of the private sector, but it will be open to the State to start any industry even in this field. The prime consideration determining State policy over the whole industrial field is promotion of rapid development in keeping with the overall objectives defined. The public sector has to grow rapidly and the private sector has to conform to the requirements of the Plan. There has necessarily to be "a great deal of dovetailing" between the two sectors, and it is recognised that the private sector has to be given the opportunity and facilities to function effectively within the field allotted to it. It is within the framework of this new Industrial Policy Resolution that rapid industrialisation has to be carried through in the coming years."

The Planning Commission had to address to the needs and aspirations of the people living below the poverty line. The commission also had in their mind to fulfill the obligations mandated in the Constitution of India. It was a huge responsibility cast up on the Commission. The Commission in their wisdom, and keeping in tune with the wishes of the elected government considered it appropriate that in order to mitigate the suffering of the poorest of the poor, to bridge the regional imbalances, to bring down the rate of unemployment, to prevent concentration of wealth with a few, and to attain a socialistic pattern of society, the public sector should be given the dominant role to play. It was in this context that the views of the Planning Commission were also reflected in the Industrial Policy Resolution of 1956.

Programme of Industrial Development

The Planning Commission assessed the programme of industrial progress in the second plan, the levels of development of capacity and production, technological advances, development of raw material, export target, expansion of different sectors, regional development of industries, and set the programme for industrial development. The Commission set forth the programme of industrial development vide Chapter 19, para 60, as below:

> **Assessment of Industrial Progress in the Second Plan; Levels of development of capacity and production** - The statement below of some of the principal overall targets in both the public and the private sectors showed that the second plan would be a period of intensive and many-sided industrial effort.

National targets for some major Industries

S.No.	Industry	Unit	1955-56 Capacity (estimated)	1955-56 Production (estimated)	1960-61 Capacity	1960-61 Production
1.	I on & Steel					
	(a) finished steel (main p oduce s)	000 tons	1300	1300	4680	4300
	(b) Pig i on fo found ies	000 tons	380	380	980	750
2.	St uctu al Fab ication	Tons	2,26,000	1,80,000	5,00,000	5,00,000
3.	Heavy Found y-cum-Fo ge Shops					
	(a) Steel Found y	tons			15,000	15,000
	(b) Fo ging Shops	tons			12,000	12,000
	(c) Cast I on Found ies	tons			10,000	10,000
4.	Fe o Manganese	tons	28,000	N.A.	1,71,800	1,60,000
5.	Aluminum	Tons	7,500	7,500	30,000	25,000
6.	Locomotives	Nos.	170	175	400	400
7.	Automobiles	Nos.	38,000	25,000	38,000	57,000
8.	Heavy Chemicals					
	(a) Sulphu ic	000 tons	242	170	500	470
	(b) Soda ash	tons	90,000	80,000·	2,53,000	2,30,000
	(c) Caustic Soda	tons	44,300	36,000	1,50400	1,35,400

(Table Contd....)

9.	Fe tilize s					
	(a) Nit ogenous (fixed nit ogen)	Tons	85,000	77,000	3,82,000	2,90,000
	(b) Phosphate	tons	35,000	20,000	1,20,000	1,20,000
10	Ship-building	GRT	—	50,000 (51-56)	—	90,000 (56-61)
11.	Cement	000 tons	4,930	4,280	16,000	13,000
12.	Refacto ies	Tons	4,44,000	2,80,000	10,00,000	8,00,000
13.	Pet oleum Refining (in tons of c ude p ocessed)	Mil tons	3,625	3.6	4.31	4.3
14.	Pape & pape boa d	000 tons	210	200	450	350
15.	Newsp int	Tons	30,000	4,200	60,000	60,000
16.	Rayon					
	(a) Rayon Filament	Mil. Lbs	22.0	15.0	68.0	68.0
	(b) Staple fibe		16.0	13.2	32.0	32.0
	(c) Chemical pulp		—	—	30.0	30.0
17.	Diesel Engines (below 50 HP)	H.P.	2,00,000	1,00,000	2,20,000	2,05,000
18.	Bicycles	000Nos.	760	550	895	1000£
19.	Elect ic Moto s (below 200 HP)	H.P.	2,92,000	2,40,000	6,00,000	6,00,000
20.	ACSR conducto	Tons	15,370	9000	20,400	18,000

Plant capacities and production costs

With the high prices for plant and machinery which had prevailed since 1950, it would only be possible to secure reasonably low cost of production in different industries by spreading overheads over a larger output. In other words, plant capacities had to be planned on a larger scale than hitherto. A detailed examination of proposals for different industries revealed that the new units proposed to be established in many industries would be large enough to offset higher capitalization costs. The sizes of coke ovens and blast furnaces in the steel plant had the production capacity of 1 000 ton and above. The daily capacity of new sulphuric acid plants would be 25 tons and above. One of the new plants would in fact have a daily capacity of 150 tons as against 10 ton plants which were common in the past and the maximum capacity of 75 tons per day installed till then. Similarly, the Development Council for Heavy Chemicals (Alkalis) had recommended the minimum size of electrolytic caustic soda plants at 20 tons per day. In the case of paper mills a minimum capacity of 25 to 50 tons per day was expected to be the normal feature at the end of the second plan. Cement plants would have normally a minimum capacity of 200,000 tons per annum. In this industry, economies in distribution costs were expected to be secured through widespread usage of bulk handling methods wherever possible. For facilitating bulk handling in a larger measure, the railway plan provided for increase in tank wagons and particularly those of special types such as were needed for the transport of chlorine and ammonia.

Technological Advances

After introduction of newer techniques in the plants proposed to be established, considerable advance was noticed. The new techniques and designs were proposed. The recovery of sulphur from coke-oven gases at the Durgapur Coke-oven plant and of ammonium sulphate and other by-products from coke-oven gas by utilising the waste pickling liquor in place of sulphuric acid at TISCO's works would mark the development of modem techniques in by-product recovery operations. Fermentation techniques would be more widely practiced in the production of antibiotics at Pimpri.

Transition to Metric System and Standardization of processes and products

Different standards were practiced at different places of the country which led to dissimilarities in action and most of the times administrative inconveniences. Following the decision of the government to switch over to the metric system on the basis of a phased programme, action had been initiated through a Standing Committee under the Ministry of Commerce and Industry. It was expected that, wherever possible, the metric system would be adopted in the new plants to be set up.

In the field of standardization of processes and products, it was envisaged that the work on steel economy initiated in 1954 by the Indian Standards Institution, as part of its programme under the first plan, would be completed, resulting in a measure of rationalisation in the consumption of steel. With the large expansion of domestic production contemplated in the second plan, standardisation would promote greater understanding and confidence between buyers and suppliers of industrial products both within the country and in foreign markets. The second five year plan provided Rs. 60.6 lakhs for the Indian Standards Institution. Success in implementing standards would depend largely on the existence of adequate facilities for testing of products. In the case of capital goods and durable consumer goods, these facilities should provide for the evaluation of performance specifications also. With the expansion of the Government Test House during the second plan, additional facilities were expected to be brought into existence. A proposal to establish a research center to meet the requirements for testing and development facilities for heavy electrical plant and equipment was also considered.

Development of Raw Materials

Development, distribution and consumption of raw materials were indeed essential in upward growth of industrial production. The consumption of primary mineral and agricultural raw materials in organised industries would increase considerably during the second five year plan. As regards some of the imported minerals, like crude petroleum, sulphur and rock phosphate, and consumption levels were expected to be as per para 64 of Chapter 19 of Second Planning Commission report, as follows:

The economy would be greatly strengthened as iron and steel, machine would grow rapidly during the next five years as follows:

Particulars	1955-56	1960-61
Rock phosphate ('000 tons)	55	400
Sulphu COOO tons)	75	210
C ude pet oleum (million tons)	3.23	3.9

It was expected that industrial programmes would also draw substantially upon agricultural raw materials like raw jute, cotton, sugarcane, oil-seeds, timber, bamboos and sabai grass. Additional requirements of timber would arise largely from production targets envisaged for chemical pulp and newsprint in comparison with which the demands arising from additional production of matches and plywood would be comparatively small. Targets for the production of oils included the utilization of about 300,000 tons of cottonseed and 800,000 tons of oilcakes as against current consumption levels estimated at 100,000 and 60,000 tons respectively. The requirements of bamboo as well as sabai grass grew from the programme for the development of the paper industry and newsprint production. It was difficult to assess the demand for bamboo with precision since there was scope for drawing upon other cellulosic materials like sabai grass, bagasse and certain semi-hard timbers. The extent to which different cellulosic raw materials would be available during the second plan was examined by a Committee set up by the Ministry of Food and Agriculture. As per para 65 of this Chapter of the report, requirements of raw cotton and sugarcane were estimated to be as follows:

Particulars	1955-56	1960-61
Raw cotton (million bales)	5.0	5.9
Suga cane (million tons)	16.7	22.5

Export Targets

In certain fields production targets was framed with special reference to the need for increasing foreign exchange earnings and stepping up exports. For the achievement of these targets, standardization of manufactured products, export promotion policies by way of rebate of import duties and establishment of Export Promotion Councils for major industries were already been taken in hand. In the nature of things it was difficult to lay down a rigid and long-term policy in regard to exports and, according to circumstances, appropriate policies and measures had to be devised. The following were the main export targets, as per para 66 of the report, which had been formulated for achievement by 1960-61.

Particulars	Quantity
Cotton textiles: cloth	1,000 to 1,100 million ya ds.
Jute Manufactu es	900,000 tons.
All silk fab ics	10.0 million ya ds.
Saleable steel	200,000 to 300,000 tons,
Fe o-manganese	100,000 tons.
Bicycles (numbe s)	150,000.
Enginee ing goods othe than bicycles	Value-Rs. 3 to 5.0 c o es.
Titanium Dioxide	1,000 to 10,000 tons.
Coke	30,000 tons-
Salt	300,000 tons.
Vegetable oils	2, 14,000 tons.
Sta ch	10,000 tons
Vanaspati	20.000 to 25,000 tons.

Expansion in Different Sectors

Progress in basic industries was one of the principal indicators of industrial development. During the first plan, some progress was made in this field through the establishment of the Sindri Fertilizer Factory, the Chittaranjan Locomotive Factory, the Tata Locomotive and Engineering Works, petroleum refineries and textile machinery factories. As a result of the increased emphasis given to industries under the second plan, progress could be achieved much more in building and other basic industries. Broadly speaking, the capital and producer goods sector registered increases during the quinquennium, which were substantially in excess of the investments made so far in these fields. The statement below did provide an indication of the pattern of industrial growth, which would begin to emerge during the second plan. By the end of the second plan the overall index of industrial production (1951 = 100) was estimated to rise to 194 from 130 in 1955-56. Considering the expansion of production sector-wise, it was anticipated that by 1960-61, the index of production of producer goods, which stood at 132 in 1955-56, would rise by about 73 per cent, compared to 18 per cent increase in the factory produced consumer goods sector, which stood in 1955-56 at 128.

Regional Development of Industries

Through successive plans, it was necessary to try to achieve a considerable measure of balance in industrial development as between different regions in the country. The second plan did make a beginning in this direction. Major projects included in it opened relatively less advanced areas in Orissa and Madhya Pradesh. Measures of long- term importance for a wider diffusion of the expansion of industries had been included, such as the pilot scheme for the production of pig iron in low-shaft blast furnaces which, if successful, had considerable potentialities for developing the iron and steel industry in relatively small units on the basis of low-grade coals occurring in different parts of the country. Surveys for mineral deposits in new areas were also calculated to achieve the same result. Intensification of research on the use of new materials and processes and development of substitutes was envisaged under the plan in the national laboratories and private institutions. Though the second plan could not provide a solution to the problem of the existing unbalanced growth of industries as between different regions, the problem had been kept in view and, through stress on research, mineral surveys and decentralisation of production, particularly in regard to agricultural processing industries the correct trends of development were being set in motion. Para 68 of Chapter 19 of the report gives the break-up as below:

Break-up of anticipated investment in the large-scale industries during 1956-61 (Rs in crores)

	Public-sector including new investments of NIDC	Private sector	Total
P oduce goods	463	296	759
Indust ial machine y and capital goods	84	72	156
Consume goods	12	167	179
Total	559	535	1094

No doubt, from the outset, the Planning Commission made it clear that the public sector would play a dominant role to achieve the mandate of the Preamble as well as that of the Directive Principles of State Policy enshrined in the Constitution of India. The Second Five year plan laid stress on ever-expanding role of public sector in the industrial development of the country. As per the words of the Commission

> "The public sector has to expand rapidly. It has not only to initiate development, which the private sector is either unwilling or unable to undertake; it has to play a dominant role in shaping the entire pattern of investment in the economy. In a growing economy, which gets increasingly diversified, there is scope for both public and private sector to expand simultaneously, but it is inevitable, if development is to proceed at the pace envisaged and to contribute effectively to the attainment of the larger social ends in view, that the public sector must grow not only absolutely but also relatively to the private sector."

ANNEXURE I SECOND FIVE YEAR PLAN

(A) Industrial Projects in the Public Sector (Central Government exclusive a/Schemes of NIDC)

Sl. No.	Name of the Scheme	Ministry Responsible	As at the end of March 1956			Second Five Year Plan (1960-61)	
			Investment (Rs. crores)	Capacity (1955-56)	Estimated production (1955-56)	Investment (Rs. crores)	Capacity (1960-61)
1	Three Steel Plants (Rourkela, Bhilai & Durgapur)	Iron & Steel	7.75	—	—	350	Finished Steel 23 million tons and Pig Iron 680,000 tons for foundries
2	South Arcot Lignite Project	Production	OS	—	—	52.0 (a)	3.5 million tons of lignite
							714,000 tons lignite briquettes, 211,000 KW. of Power 70,000 tons of nitrogen
3	Sindri Fertiliser Factory		28	70,000 tons of nitrogen	66,000 tons of nitrogen	7	117,000 tons of nitrogen
4	Nangal Fertiliser-cum-Heavy Water Factory	"	—	—	—	22	70,000 tons of nitrogen
5	Hindustan Shipyard	"	6.0 (1951-56)	—	50,000 GRT (1951-56)	9.8	—
6	Rourkela Fertiliser Factory	"	—	—	—	8	80,000 tons of nitrogen
7	Heavy Electrical Plant		02	—		20.0	
8	Hindustan Machine Tools		4.4	N.A	Lathes and Components worth Rs.025 crores.	2.0	400 lathes, milling & drilling machines
9	D. D. T. Factories	"	08	700 tons	284 tons	1.0	2,800 tons
10	Hindustan Antibiotics	"	2.1	4.8 mill. mega units	6.64 mill. mega units	1.0	24 mill. mega units, and 15,000 to 20,000 kg. of streptomycin

11	Hindustan Cables		1.6	470 miles of cables.(Singl e shift)	525 miles of cables	0,5	1000 miles of cables and 300 miles of coaxial cables
12.	National Instruments Factory (including optical glass project)		0.6	Instruments worth Rs. 40 lakhs	Instruments worth Rs. 14.2 lakhs	0.65	NA
13	Salt Development		0.3		84.6 Million Maunds (public and Private sectors)	2.0	
14	Chittaranjan Locomotive	Railways	14.6	120 locomotives	125 Locomotives .	5.0	300 locomotive
15	Integral Coach Factory	,,	52	—	20 coaches		350 coaches
16	New M. G. Coach Factory	"	Nil	—	Nil	10.0	N.A
17	Engineering Shops for spare parts	"	Nil	—	Nil	7.0	N.A
18	Indian Telephone Industries	Communic ations.	4.109		Telephones 50,000 Exchange lines 35,000	0.5	
19	Teleprinter Factory		—	—	—	0.75	N.A
20	Security Paper Mill	Finance	—		—	2.5	1,500
			75.8			501.7	

THIRD FIVE YEAR PLAN (1961-1966)

Before finalisation of Third Plan, the Government of India laid an added emphasis on checking and containing the concentration of wealth and economic power in fewer hands and as such government regarded that, if an increasingly important role is assigned to public sector, it would be an important instrument to curb concentration of wealth and economic power in a few hands. The Commission laid special emphasis on machine building, development of managerial skills, and technical know-how, as has been visualised from the words that, "In this programme, the public sector has been assigned a key role, but the private sector is also expected to have an important part to play within the framework of the plan. The share of the public sector in the net output of organised manufacturing industries is expected to increase from less than one-tenth in 1960-61 to about one-fourth in 1965-66, and the bulk of this will comprise capital and producer goods. For the development of industries and minerals, the Plan includes a programme costing Rs. 1882 crores but makes for the present a financial provision of Rs. 1520 crores in the public sector. In addition, the private sector is expected to provide about Rs. 1050 crores. The private sector is also expected to provide about Rs. 150 crores to meet the arrears of replacement and modernisation in certain pre-war industries." The Commission further went on to add:

"The expansion of industry will continue to be governed by the Industrial Policy Resolution of April, 1956. As in the Second Plan, the roles of the public and private sectors are conceived of as supplementary and complementary to one another. For example, in the case of nitrogenous fertilizers, where the public sector has already assumed a dominant role, it is envisaged that during the Third Plan, the private sector will enter this field in a bigger way than in the past and supplement the efforts of the public sector. In the case of pig iron, the policy has been relaxed to allow the establishment of plants in the private sector with a maximum capacity of 100,000 tons per year as compared to units of 15,000 tons permitted so far. Programmes for the manufacture of dyestuffs, plastics and drugs in the private sector will be largely complementary to the programme for the manufacture of primary aromatic compounds as by-products at the steel works and of organic intermediates to be undertaken in the public sector. Similarly, whereas the manufacture of bulk drugs will be organised in a big way in the public sector, the further processing of bulk drugs will also he undertaken in the private sector.

Against the background of the goal of a socialist pattern of society, it is necessary in encouraging and approving programmes in the private sector to guard against industrial development being concentrated in the hands of a few entrepreneurs and leading to complete or partial monopolies."

The central government grouped the projects into three categories as under:

1. Projects under execution and carried over from the Second Plan;
2. New projects for which external credits are already assured wholly or partly; and
3. New projects for which external credits have yet to be arranged.

The Commission desired that the projects falling under the category (1) would be completed within the Third plan and this would also apply to most of the projects in category (2). The Commission apprehended that some of the projects of category (2) would spill over to Fourth plan and there was uncertainty in respect of the projects of category (3). The overall desire of the Commission as well as that of the government was to have a rapid industrial development with public sector playing a dominant role and simultaneously preventing concentration of economic power and monopolistic tendencies.

FOURTH FIVE YEAR PLAN (1969-1974)

It has been till now the practice to emphasize the dominant role of public sector in the Planning Commission reports. As usual the government put emphasis on the increasing role of the public sector for ensuring a sound and balanced industrial development of the country in this Plan period also. The Planning Commission had an in-depth discussion regarding the investment in the public sector, the role played by it in industrial development and the future plans. The Commission outlined the diversified elements of public sector in its own words as below:

"Over the last decade, massive investments have been made by the Central Government in industrial and mineral projects. On a broad estimate, the total Central investments in public sector projects in mining and manufacturing sectors would amount approximately to Rs. 3400 crores at the beginning of the Fourth Plan. A substantial proportion of this has been in the development of heavy industries, such as steel, coal, lignite, heavy engineering including electrical equipment, petroleum and fertilisers. While these investments have contributed significantly to strengthening of the industrial structure; the overall performance has hot been uniformly satisfactory. Delays in completion schedules and large increases in original investment estimates have been the experience with several projects and the output has remained substantially below installed capacity. Expectations of a significant contribution to Plan resources from the internal resources of these enterprises have not been realised; on the other hand, several of them have to rely on budgetary support to meet their cash losses. Productivity and profitability of these enterprises are a matter of urgent importance. The bulk of the investments in the public sector are in basic and heavy industries with long gestation periods. These enterprises are not expected to achieve full rated capacity or production in a short time and show large profits. At the same time, there is considerable scope for improvement in efficiency and performance. The Administrative Reforms Commission has examined the operation of public enterprises and made recommendations. The problems involved are those relating to the development of appropriate relationship between the enterprises on the one hand and Government and Parliament on the other, which would leave adequate initiative and operational autonomy to the management. While Parliament must oversee and review the performance of public undertakings with a view to promoting and safeguarding public interest, the manner of achieving this purpose be such that it does not weaken initiative in the management and thus affect its efficiency. Similarly,

Government should be primarily concerned with reserving for itself only such powers as are required to determine questions of policy and to ensure that the programmes of the public enterprises conform to the accepted plans and that the enterprises are run on commercial lines. Subject to these considerations the management must have adequate powers to carry on the day-to-day administration on business and commercial principles. Equally important is the delegation of powers between the various tiers of management within the enterprise from the board of directors to the managing director and to the heads of departments.

Another matter requiring consideration is the recruitment, promotion and related personnel policies of public undertakings, particularly with reference to the selection and retention of top management personnel. The system of deputing officers from the administrative services for short periods with frequent transfers at the top level detracts from continuity and consistency in management policy. It does not provide for a commitment of the top management to the success of the public enterprises. There is need to develop a cadre of professional managers with adequate expertise in the fields of financial, production, personnel and marketing management. Adequate opportunities should exist for suitable persons from within the enterprise to rise to top management positions.

Each public sector enterprise must set down its objectives and targets and prepare an appropriate budget covering production, sales, cost of production, capital expenditure, cash flow and profit and loss estimates. The comparison of performance data with budget estimates should be undertaken periodically during the currency of the budget itself.

In several instances, the sales from one public enterprise would be to other public enterprises or to Governmental agencies. There is need in such cases for close coordination between the manufacturing plants and the user Ministries and Governmental agencies, so as to ensure dovetailing of supply and production. Questions relating to deliveries and prices within inter-enterprise transactions involved are matters of vital importance. They affect the formulation of detailed and long-term production programmes of public enterprises. There are several other directions in which the public sector units have to act in concert. In order to bring about effective coordination and integration of public sector enterprises, it is necessary to create appropriate machinery at a sufficiently high level."

The role of banks in nation building has been very important. But they were kept outside the purview of public sector for which their contribution in the upliftment of the downtrodden of the society was very marginal. The Commission observed that the nationalization of 14 big banks heralded an era that would go a long way to meet the requirement of common man and would bring huge resources in the social sector. It would also restrict the monopolistic operations of the privileged few. The public sector would be endowed with further responsibility and would grow in range and volume, being a product of mixed economy, without diluting the responsibilities of private sector. While defining the role of public sector in socialism, the Commission observed: "Socialism involves a reordering of society on a rational and equitable basis and this can only be achieved by assigning an expanding role to the public sector. Following the reorganisation of credit policies resulting from the nationalisation of major banks, the public sector can be expected more and more to occupy the commanding heights of the economy. It alone would be in a position to undertake investments of the requisite magnitude in such industries of vital importance to us as steel, machinery, machine tools, power generation, ship-building, petrochemicals, fuels and drugs. Naturally, the administration of public enterprises poses some problems of its own (here as in other countries) but they are not insuperable and will be overcome as we gain experience." It is indeed true that with the nationalization of banks in India, it heralded an era of public sector dominance *vis-a-vis* private sector in the country and gave a big jolt to private sector participation, but it also opened up a scope for bringing up the social sector to the fore front which had been neglected for long. These statements would further reveal that the government of the day, in order to bring about socialism, and to cater to the needs of the have-nots of the society devolved onerous responsibilities on the public sector, and desired that it should occupy the commanding heights of the economy.

Outlays

The Fourth Plan envisaged an investment of approximately Rs. 5298 crores in organised industry and mining, Rs. 30-18 crores in the public sector and Rs. 2250 crores in the private and cooperative sectors. The outlay in the public sector would be Rs. 3337.7 crores, since it included a sum of Rs. 250 crores for transfer to private and cooperative sectors through financial institutions and an amount of Rs. 40 crores for supporting plantation programmes which would have a bearing on export earnings and for State Industrial Development Corporations. Of the total outlay of Rs. 3337.7 crores in the public sector, Rs. 3150.9 crores would be in the Central Sector and Rs. 186.8 crores in States and Union Territories. Within the organised sector, it was thus contemplated that the public sector would continue to occupy a predominant role in new investments. Of the total investments envisaged in the Fourth Plan, the public sector would account for about 60 per cent, which was broadly in line with the proportion of investment between the public sector and the private sector envisaged in the Third Plan.

The major proportion of the outlay in the public sector was intended for completion of projects already under implementation and projects on which investment decisions had been taken. New projects were envisaged in high priority fields, like fertilisers, pesticides, petro-chemicals, non-ferrous metals and development of iron ore, and rock-phosphate resources. New investment in the engineering industries was limited to a few comparatively small projects for filling critical gaps. Among other schemes, mention may be made of the Textile Corporation for which a provision of Rs. 17.5 crores had been made primarily for the purpose of reconstruction and modernisation of viable mills taken over by Government. In view of the importance attached to the newsprint industry and the need for expanding production of paper, a provision of Rs. 60 crores was made for the Paper Corporation. The activities of the Cement Corporation were limited for the present to the completion of the two projects already under way and the establishment of three more projects during the Fourth Plan period in regions where there were shortages. The public sector programme included provision for the continuing activities of the Geological Survey of India, Indian Bureau of Mines, National Productivity Council (NPC) and Indian Standards Institution (ISI). The proposals for GSI included systematic mapping, detailed geological mapping as well as exploration of mineral deposits utilising sophisticated equipment. Its programme included airborne geo-physical operations and ground water explorations. The Indian Bureau of Mines did not only propose, to expand its mineral conservation activities but also take up consultancy services with a view to advising small mine owners. In petroleum, provision had been made for exploration of oil and expansion of refinery capacity in line with the projected growth in the consumption of petroleum products. The provision for the Atomic Energy Department took into account the need for surveying and prospecting of atomic minerals and the requirements of supporting programme in mining and industries in accordance with the nuclear power development envisaged in the Fourth Plan. Projects fostering the rapid growth of the electronics industry were also included.

In order to maintain continuity of growth, advance action would need to be taken during the Fourth Plan in some directions so as to bring additional capacity into being in the early years of the Fifth Plan. It was difficult at that stage to work out the investment requirements for that purpose and to identify the projects likely to be taken up.

However, certain provisions had been made for this purpose in the public sector programmes, particularly in industries with long gestation periods such as steel.

The allocations for programmes in the Central sector and the projects and schemes were included in the Fourth Plan. The provisions were based on the information then available. In several cases, the investments estimates would have to be firmed up. To this extent, adjustment in the provisions would be required. This was proposed to be done through the Annual Plans. The provision of Rs. 186.8 crores in the States and Union Territories was intended for completion of continuing projects and for supporting the operations of the development institutions in the States. Thus, provision had been made for the activities of the Industrial and Mineral Development Corporations, Industrial Areas Schemes and State Financial Corporations. As a part of the joint activities of the Centre and States in rehabilitating textile mills, State Textile Corporations would be set up in some of the States.

Taken as a whole, the public sector investments would strengthen the control of Government over the commanding heights of the economy. Thus, the public sector would account for a little over three-fourths of the investments envisaged in the 'core' sector during the Fourth Plan period, the balance being the share of the private sector. Looked at from another angle, 'core' industries would represent approximately 80 per cent of the total investment of around Rs. 3000 crores in large industries and minerals in the public sector. Thus, both in terms of the proportionate magnitude of investments and the nature of the investments, the public' sector had to occupy a pre-eminent position in the industrial field by the end of the Fourth Plan. At the same time, the public sector had to enter the field of consumer goods industries, particularly in fields in which adequate private investment was not forthcoming. Apart from the activities of the public sector through cooperatives in sugar and textiles, specific provision had been made for other consumer goods industries, like pharmaceuticals, cement, paper, scooters and watches.

Earlier in the approach and policy, while broadly outlining the aims and objectives of the Fourth Plan, the Commission delved into the Directive Principles of State Policy and the concept of 'socialistic pattern of society' enshrined in the Preamble of the Constitution and defined the role of public sector that the emergence of public sector would be a matter of crucial significance as the dominant and effective area of the economy and that it would enable to take charge more and more of the commanding heights in the production and distribution of basic and consumer goods.

FIFTH FIVE YEAR PLAN (1974-79)

The government did not make any special announcement regarding the role of public sector in the national economy during this Five Year Plan period. However, on February 2,1973, in the Industrial Policy press note, the Government of India reiterated the role of public sector in the following words:

> "In the context of the approach of the Fifth Five Year plan, the State will have to take direct responsibility for the future development of industries over a wide field in order to promote the cardinal objectives of growth, social justice, self reliance, and satisfaction of basic minimum needs."

There was an upward revision in the total plan outlay from Rs.37250 crore to Rs.39303 crore. Similarly, the outlay for the next two years was also revised to Rs.19902 crores as against the estimate for the next three years of the Plan, which aggregated to Rs.19401 crores.

SIXTH FIVE YEAR PLAN (1980-85)

There was no clear policy shift from that of the previous one. The existing importance to the public sector in the national economy would continue to be assigned as usual and it was stressed that "the commanding heights of national economy must continue and remain with public sector." In the Policy framework of the Plan, for the first time, it was conceded that the public sector enterprises had failed to generate adequate resources for expansion of public sector investment, and the measures for improving the performance of the public sector was considered a key area. Similarly, it was further noted that the State Electricity Boards were incurring huge losses, in the cases of irrigation the gross receipts were not sufficient to cover even the working expenses, and most of the State Road Transport Corporations were also making losses. It was suggested by the Commission that these undertakings, in order to improve their financial performance, should revise the tariffs, water charges, and taxes and other suitable measures. The Commission further went on to add:

"The principle of fair return is relevant to public enterprises as well. However, these enterprises are generally engaged in the provision of infrastructural services or in the manufacture and supply of basic industrial materials, such as coal, steel and (Petrol, Oil and Lubricants) POL, or agricultural inputs, such as fertilisers and the increase in their prices generally have a cascading effect. Hence, an attempt has been made to keep down their prices. This, together with managerial deficiencies and other factors, has resulted in inadequate resource generation by public enterprises, losses in some of them and a heavy draft on the public exchequer. It has also meant supply of goods and services produced in the public sector at subsidised prices even for non-priority uses, and, consequently, accentuated the imbalances between demand and supply. Further, a delay in the revision of prices results in the subsequent revisions having to be of a substantial order. In the interest of making public enterprises viable, enabling them to play their assigned role and raising additional resources for development, there is need for rationalising their pricing policies in a phased manner. While doing so, due weight will also have to be given to considerations of social costs and benefits.

It may be noted that in a number of public enterprises, there is sub-optimal utilisation of the existing capacities due to various factors, particularly infrastructural constraints and managerial deficiencies. Besides, delay in the implementation of projects has resulted in costs over-runs. Substantial improvement in the working of public enterprises as well as in the execution of projects is, therefore, necessary to increase production, reduce costs and improve the rate of return. Enterprises in both the public and private sectors have, therefore, to strive to achieve greater efficiency and reduce costs through the adoption of modern management techniques, better inventory control, etc. Wherever economies of scale exercise an important influence on the cost of production, the expansion of existing enterprises has to be preferred to setting up of new plants. Tariff policies may also be reviewed to avoid excessive protection to indigenous industries and induce them to improve their competitiveness."

The Commission, in the Plan period, provided for a total outlay in the public sector of Rs.13500 crores, which was mainly for maintenance of services created during the Plan period and did not create assets. Thus, the public sector outlay in the plan was to the tune of Rs.84000 crores. The Commission assessed the performance of the public sector and found the same to be satisfactory. It further observed that it should not be judged on the basis of the yardstick normally applied to the private sector, as the public sector had its broader socio-economic objectives, and devoted comparatively greater attention to research and development.

SEVENTH FIVE YEAR PLAN (1985-90)

The Commission felt that there was again a need for the public sector to play a dominant role to ensure rapid industrialization and sound economic development keeping an eye for balanced regional growth. In the chapter entitled "Planned Development: Retrospect and Prospect", it has been stated, "The public sector has initiated and sustained the industrial transformation of India. It shall continue to play its pivotal role in modernising Indian industry and in reducing the concentration of economic power. To perform its historic task, the public sector has to undergo basic structural changes to conform to the Plan priorities of efficiency and productivity. Only in the measure that the public sector generates investible surpluses can it play its indispensable social role of providing an adequate infrastructural base for the economy, being a vehicle for the introduction and absorption of new technology in critical sectors of the economy, and for achieving balanced regional growth." In the chapter "Development Perspective: Towards the Year 2000", while discussing the industrial perspective, it stated "the public sector will continue to play an important role in the core sector of the economy. It will also be a pacesetter and encourage emerging new high technology industries. Besides, contributing in no small measure to industrial growth, it will generate sizeable resources for investment. A major employer of the country's engineering manpower, the public sector will play a leading role in stimulating development of efficient ancillary manufacturing; and will strengthen the sinews of industry." Though the Commission desired that public sector would play a dominant role in shaping the economy of the country, and would be pivotal in bringing about a balanced regional growth, it perceived the problems that was endemic in the public sector in the areas like cost and time overruns, lack of creative productivity activity, lack of concern for improving the efficiency, lack of technological upgradation and so on. While reviewing the industrial development, the Commission observed that, "in the public sector, problems began with cost and time overruns in a large number of projects. After commissioning, inefficiency tended to persist at the operational stages of the projects. The functioning of the private sector had its own shortcomings. Very often the emphasis was on short-term maximisation of output rather than creative productive activity. As capacities remained under-utilised in many industries, the shortages in production, quite apart from eroding the economic viability of the units, had a chain effect within the industrial sector. Lack of concern for improving efficiency in factor use was reflected in increasing material intensity of production and increasing capital output ratios. In yet another dimension, economy in energy consumption, the performance of Indian industry has been well below the international norms. To some extent, this was due to inadequate attention paid by industry to technological upgradation. The widening technological gap between India and the rest of the world also had the wider effect of increasing obsolescence, raising costs, and inadequately upgrading quality. It may also be added that in the first phase of industrialisation, emphasis was laid on steel-based industries. The high cost of steel in later years affected competitiveness of such industries. In the next phase of industrialisation, we will be depending on other basic materials, such as petro-chemical intermediates, electronic components and materials. It must be ensured that these will be available at competitive prices." This was the first candid admission of the Planning Commission with regard to the performances of the public sector in India. It had also tried to analyse the reasons of various lacunae and the shortcomings prevailing in the public sector. The Commission also discussed about the industrial policy changes, and finally introduced a liberalized policy in the manufacture of computers and electronic items along with a package of incentives. They also allowed the private sector to manufacture telecommunication equipments hitherto reserved for development exclusively in the public sector. The Commission reviewed the industrial development and chalked out the strategies for the Seventh Plan. The main elements of the strategy for the industrial sector were restructuring of industry, efficient use of capital, improving infrastructural facilities, and modernise, productivity in thrust areas for exports and up-gradation of technology. Another area of far-reaching significance for industrial planning was that of product development. The Commission desired that all major public sector organisations should have time-bound goals for new product development and in this task they should associate research establishments and academic institutions.

The Commission did however; feel that the public sector had to improve its performance in order to gain the confidence of general population. However, against the perception that gained ground in a section of the share-holders, policy makers, and bureaucracy, that soon the public sector would have to give way to the private sector, was proved wrong. The Commission again emphasized that the public sector should be given a dominant role in the society in order to achieve the historical objective.

EIGHTH PLANNING COMMISSION, 1991

During this Plan period, the country witnessed a major policy shift with regard to the Industrial Policy Resolution as well as strategies by the Planning Commission. While defining the role of public sector enterprise, it was stated that "The public sector has played a pioneering role in the development of the Indian economy and has a number of achievements to its credit. It deserves a major share of the credit for the self-reliant growth of the economy so far. However, there are some notable weaknesses too, the most important being the inability of the public sector to generate adequate resources for sustaining the growth process. Besides, the private sector has now come of age and has developed considerable entrepreneurial, managerial, technological, financial and marketing strengths. In this background, a review of the role of the public and private sectors is called for in order to enable them to jointly shoulder the responsibility for further development of the economy. The commission worked out the profitability profile of public sector enterprise and found that a large number of industries were making losses and the overall profits were not in consonance with the volume of investment made. The profitability profile in the chapter on "Industry and Minerals" in statement- 5.1 has been indicated as under:

Profitability Profile of Public Sector Enterprises (Rs. in Crores)

SL.No	Details	1980-81	1985-86	1986-87	1987-88	1988-89	1989-90	1990-91
1.	No. of ope ating Ente p ises	168	211	214	220	226	233	236
2.	Capital Employed	18207	42965	51835	55617	67629	84760	101702
3.	G oss Ma gin	2401	8270	9897	11082	13438	16412	18510
4.	% of g oss ma gin to capital employed	13.19	19.25	19.09	19.93	19.87	19.36	18.02
5.	Dep eciation & Defe ed Revenue Expenditu e	983	2983	3376	4142	4866	579C	7151
6.	G oss P ofit	1418	5287	6521	6940	8572	10623	11358
7.	% of G oss P ofit to Capital Employed	7.79	12.31	12.58	12.48	12.68	12.53	11.17
8.	Inte est	1399	3115	3420	3587	4167	5329	7539
9.	P e-Tax P ofit/Loss	19	2172	3101	3353	4405	5293	3820
10.	Tax	222	1000	1329	1323	1411	1504	1452

(Table Contd....)

11.	Net P ofit/Loss	203	1172	1772	2030	2994	3789	2368
	(a) P ofit of p ofit-making ente p ises	557	2857	3478	3775	4917	5651	5432
	(no. of ente p ises)	(94)	(119)	(108)	(114)	(117)	(131)	(124)
	(b) Loss ofloss-making ente p ises	760	1685	1706	1745	1923	1962	3064
	(no. of ente p ises)	(74)	(90)	(100)	(103)	(106)	(98)	(109)
	(c) No. of ente p ises making neithe p ofit no loss		2	6	3	3	4	3
12.	% of Net P ofit/Loss to Capitals Employed	1.11	2.73	3.42	3.65	4.43	4.47	2.33
13.	Dividends	83	191	297	320	353	323	365
14.	Retained P ofit	286	981	1475	1710	2641	3466	2003

The new Industrial Policy of July 1991 brought down the number of areas reserved for public sector from 29 earlier to 17 areas. Now only 17 areas were reserved exclusively for public sector while twelve other areas were to be progressively State owned with State generally taking the initiative in establishing new undertakings in the following eight areas, namely, "arms and ammunition and allied items of defence equipment; defence aircraft and warships; atomic energy; coal and lignite; mineral oils; mining of iron ore, manganese ore, chrome ore, gypsum, sulphur, gold and diamond; mining of copper, lead, zinc, tin, molybdenum and wolform; minerals specified in the Schedule to the Atomic Energy (Control of Production and Use) Order, 1953; and railway transport." Thus, it would be seen that government decided to reduce the area of operation of public sector enterprise and desired the private sector to play an increasing role in the industrial activities where security, strategic or social considerations were not very important. It was further decided that the public sector would concentrate increasingly on basic and core sectors and the emphasis would be on financing industrial and mineral projects primarily through internal and other extra budgetary resources instead of depending on budgetary allocations. While recognizing the importance of public sector in the economic and industrial resurgence of the country, to make it more competitive and efficient, the Commission desired to undertake reforms in its own words as stated below:

> "Public Enterprises embody a major national capability in terms of physical, financial, institutional and human resources. Their effective utilisation can lead to significant economic growth. In the framework of the new Economic Policy, Public Sector industry has an important role as an autonomous, competitive and efficient sector, to provide essential infrastructure goods and services, development of natural resources and areas of strategic concern. A positive and productive future awaits public sector industry. To reach that goal, considerable restructuring is involved. The Eighth Plan recognises this and proposes a major

public sector reform initiative. This initiative will consist of the following integrated strategies:

1. Restructuring involving modernisation, rationalisation of capacity, product-mix changes, selective exit and privatisation is needed on a massive scale, to make public enterprises viable, efficient and competitive.
2. Increase in autonomy and performance accountability of public enterprises is critical to make them a dynamic force. The system of Memoranda of Understanding between administrative ministries and Central public enterprises, which has been launched in the Seventh Plan, has these objectives in its design. However, its effectiveness needs to be improved.
3. Changes in management practices at specific enterprise level to promote efficiency, dynamic leadership, resourcefulness and innovation are needed.
4. State level public enterprises have serious problems. Interference, lack of professionalism and ad-hoc investment and employment decisions has resulted in chronic sickness of many of them. A major effort is called for, in collaboration with the State Governments, to promote reforms in them.
5. In the changing economic environment, technology will be a major tool to improve competitiveness and efficiency of public enterprises. Their capability to develop import and use technology effectively or, to integrate technology in their corporate strategies (expansion, diversification, marketing etc.) is weak now. The new reform initiative needs to address this through building active linkages among R & D laboratories educational institutions and public enterprises. This is vital in the emerging inter-dependent and globalising.
6. The organisation of Government (Ministries and agencies) for public sector has historically grown

in a certain manner. Presently many regulations (price, distribution, investment and import controls) are being dismantled. This liberalisation not only calls for re-structuring of enterprises but also of the Government in the governance of industrial growth and management inter-face with the enterprises. A new institutional capability is needed in Government that is responsive to environmental change, professional and can facilitate operation of market forces, through orchestrisation of the efforts of various (R&D, education, engineering, manufacturing, trade, etc.) organisations towards priority targets in select areas, by building a consensus and partnership among the different stakeholders. The above call for a positive public sector reforms, by designed, selective and targeted interventions. The reform initiative needs to include: creating a knowledge base for reform, generating an institutional capability and developing a consensus among the stakeholders about policy goals and implementation strategies.

A network of institutions (academic, government, industry, consulting firms, financial institutions and international organisations) needs to be organised to design and implement the reforms. A coordinated strategy through a high-powered task force is needed to mobilize the resources for achieving the objectives reforms in the Eighth Plan period."

The Industrial Policy Resolution of 1991 had been similar to that of 1956 in many respects with a major exception that there had been reduction of industrial activity exclusively reserved for public sector from 17 to 8 industries and the new policy emphasized efficiency and surplus-generating capability in the public sector, a larger entrepreneurial and managerial freedom for both domestic private sector and foreign investment, a more open access to technology and greater reliance on the capital market for raising resources, while reiterating its commitment to a policy of mixed economy under which both the public sector and private sector enterprises coexist and function.

The performance of the Central public sector enterprises was also reviewed. As on March 31, 1991, there were 246 Central Public Sector Enterprises (PSEs) owned by the Government of India with a total investment of Rs. 113,234 crores. Out of these, 236 were operational enterprises with an employed capital of Rs. 101,702 crores and employee strength of 23.01 lakhs. Of these, 131 enterprises earned an overall net profit of Rs.5731 crores during 1990-91 and 109 suffered a net loss ofRs.3064 crores. The performance was also intensely debated by various groups, academicians and committees and government had to take some hard decisions to streamline the working of the public sector to make it more competitive and viable, as follows:

(i) Portfolio of public sector investments would be reviewed with a view to focusing the public sector on strategic, high-tech and essential infrastructure. Whereas some reservation for the public sector was retained, there would be no bar on areas of exclusivity being opened up to the private sector selectively. Similarly, the public sector would also be allowed entry in areas not reserved for it.

(ii) Public enterprises, which were chronically sick and which were unlikely to turn around, would, for the formulation of revival/rehabilitation schemes, be referred to the Board for Industrial and Financial Reconstruction (BIFR), or other similar high level institutions created for the purpose. A social security mechanism was created to protect the interests of workers likely to be affected by such rehabilitation packages.

(iii) In order to raise resources and encourage wider public participation, a part of the Government's share-holding in the public sector would be offered to mutual funds, financial institutions, general public and workers. This was contemplated to bring in greater public accountability and help create a new culture in the working of PSEs and improve their operational efficiency.

(iv) Boards of public sector companies would be made more professional and given greater powers.

(v) There would be a greater thrust on performance improvement through the Memoranda of Understanding (MOU) system through which managements would be granted greater autonomy and held accountable. Technical expertise on the part of the Government would be upgraded to make the MOU negotiations and implementation more effective.

(vi) To facilitate a fuller discussion on performance, the MOUs between the Government and the public enterprises would be placed in Parliament. While focusing on major management issues, this would also help place matters on day-to-day operations of public enterprises in their correct perspective.

The overall stress in the Eighth Plan was to have a quantitative upgradation and elimination of weaknesses. The upgradation would have to be in the areas like technology, efficiency, productivity, and human resources development; where as elimination of weaknesses would be in shedding the extra manpower, refurbishing old and outdated technology, restructuring the organization and so on.

NINTH PLAN (1996-2001)

In these fifty years since the independence, India could emerge as a strong, secular and souvereign country and that democratic institutions had taken firm root was quite visible in the areas like, Industry, Agriculture, Science and Technology, Urban and Rural Development etc., though there had been setbacks in quite a few areas, like social sectors and infrastructure development. The Eighth Five Year Plan was formulated with an approved public sector outlay of Rs. 434,100 crore. The anticipated Eighth Plan expenditure was of the order of Rs. 391,000 crore. The lower

Plan expenditure was the result of the shortfall of about 10 per cent in the resource mobilisation undertaken during the Plan period. The projected public sector plan outlay for the Ninth Plan, consistent with envisaged accelerated GDP growth of 6.5 percent per annum, was placed at Rs.859200 crore at 1996-97 prices. This represented a step up of about 48 per cent and 33 per cent in real terms over the anticipated Eighth Plan expenditure and the approved Eighth Plan outlay respectively. Though the Commission, in its objectives, prioritised agriculture, accelerating growth rate of economy, nutrition, drinking water, primary health care, housing, connectivity, containing population growth, empowerment of women, etc., in its development strategy, indicated that there was an urgent need for change of its strategy from excessive reliance on public sector enterprises to a more liberalized atmosphere for the growth of private sectors in the country. The Commission, in its own words, signified the urgent necessity of such a change as " India's development strategy, like that of most other developing countries, has evolved over successive Plan periods, reflecting the growing strength of our economy, structural transformations taking place in the domestic economy and also developments in the world economy. In the early stages of development planning, government was viewed as the principal actor in development exercising strict control over private investment, ensuring a dominant role for the public sector in all important industries. Trade policy tended to be inward oriented, focusing on industrial development through import substitution, which was encouraged through a tight control over imports and maintenance of high tariffs. The limitations of this strategy became evident by the end of the 1970s and early 1980s when it became clear that these policies reduced efficiency and competitiveness and growth was much lower than targeted. While government was over-active in industry, it was under-active in many areas, especially relating to social development and this was reflected in a very slow pace of improvement in critical social indicators. Some efforts were made to reform the system in the second half of the 1980s to address the shortcomings in our development strategy. However it was not until 1991 that a wide ranging programme of economic reforms aimed at decontrolling and debureaucratising the economy was initiated. These reforms have been pursued by successive governments since 1991 and enjoy a broad base of support. They have also yielded good results thus far. There is no doubt that the Indian economy has responded well to the change in policy direction and the growth rate increased from 5.8% in the Seventh Plan (1985 to 1990) to 6.8% in the Eighth Plan. And yet there are many dimensions in which performance has lagged behind expectations. Faster growth has not reduced poverty as much as it should have, nor has it created the number of high-quality jobs we need to satisfy the aspirations of our increasingly educated youths. Growth has not been as regionally balanced, as it should have been. The deficiencies in social development indicators have also continued and our low level of social development is today a major constraint on reaching a growth rate of 8 per cent, which should be our medium term target. The Ninth Plan is being implemented at a time when we are about to enter the new millennium. The international environment is also full of uncertainties in the aftermath of the East Asian crisis. It is appropriate at this critical period to articulate a development strategy which reaffirms and builds upon what has worked well, initiates corrective steps where needed, and take new initiatives to meet the new challenges which face the economy in the years ahead." There were also times during Fourth and Fifth Plan periods when the growth slumped to 1.5%. However, the present economic policy has been able to reverse the trend and put the economy in the right track. The Commission further stressed that the State instead of being a pervasive controller of private sector activity, and also a direct producer in many areas through its public sector enterprises should play a different role, and encourage growth of private sector enterprises in a big way. The private sector must be allowed to realise its full potential for raising production, which would ultimately lead to creation of jobs, raising income levels in the society. It was further emphasised that the State, instead of playing the role of a controller and licensor of private enterprise, should increase its involvement in the area of social development especially in the rural areas and improve basic services, such as health care, education, safe drinking water etc. The role of public sector in the non-essential areas was reviewed and it was decided that: "The role of the public sector as a direct producer of goods and services needs to be reviewed in the context of experience gained and emerging realities. The Eighth Plan saw the start of a process of disinvestments of government equity from public sector enterprises and the resources so generated were used to supplement available budgetary resources to finance development expenditure. Initially, disinvestments were undertaken subject to government equity remaining at 51%. There was no particular reason as to why government should retain a majority equity stake in public sector enterprises except for those that are in the strategic areas where national security was involved. For all other enterprises, the government announced that as a general rule it would dilute its holdings to 26 per cent as early as possible. The manner in which this was to be done would be determined on the basis of recommendations of the Disinvestments Commission. The Commission had made recommendations regarding several public sector enterprises, including recommendations to induct a strategic partner who would exercise full or joint management control, in some cases. These recommendations needed to be implemented expeditiously. The resources realised through sale of government equity in PSUs could be used to finance much-needed investments in the social sectors, especially health and education. At a time when resources are scarce, there was merit in unlocking resources embedded in public sector assets created through earlier investments in these enterprises and using these resources to invest in the social sectors, where the State have been seriously deficient. Reduction in the government's holding in public sector equity would not have any adverse effect on the health of the public sector units. On the contrary, the removal of government interference should give these units the corporate freedom they need to function efficiently in a competitive market".

The Commission felt that there had been inadequate investment in the areas like power, telecommunications, railways, roads and ports, during Eighth Plan period. These infrastructures, being key for rapid economic development, would require huge investment. Public sector, being the large supplier of infrastructure, has not been able to mobilize enough resources. Therefore, for infrastructure development mobilization of private investment, to supplement public sector efforts, is essential. While public sector would bear the burnt of burden in the areas such as roads, railways, and rural electrification, where scope for private investment is limited, this calls for far-reaching reforms in infrastructure sector like, State Electricity Boards and Railways to achieve higher operational efficiencies.

TENTH PLAN (2002-07)

The Planning Commission in this Plan period stressed the need for improvement in the quality of life of the common man. In the introductory paragraphs of the Plan, the Commission made clear its intentions by stating that mere expansion of production of goods and services, and the consequent growth of per capita income could not be the sole route for enhancement of human well being. While defining the concept of human well being, the Commission stated, "The notion of human well being itself is more broadly conceived to include not only consumption of goods and services in general but more specifically to ensure that the basic material requirements of all sections of population, especially those below the poverty line, are met and they have access to basic social services, such as health and education." For enrichment of quality of life, it is not the per capita income alone but the social indicators like health, longevity, literacy, and environment sustainability should be the governing factor. It has also been observed by the Commission that:

> "The Tenth Five Year Plan (2002-07) has been prepared against a backdrop of high expectations arising from some aspects of the recent performance. GDP growth in the post reforms period has improved from an average of about 5.7 per cent in the 1980s to an average of about 6.1 per cent in the Eighth and Ninth Plan periods, making India one of the ten fastest growing countries in the world. Encouraging progress has also been made in other dimensions. The percentage of the population in poverty has continued to decline, even if not as much as was targeted. Population growth has decelerated below 2 per cent for the first time in four decades. Literacy has increased from 52 per cent in 1991 to 65 percent in 2001 and the improvement is evident in all States. Sectors such as software services and IT enabled services have emerged as new sources of strength, creating confidence about India's potential to be competitive in the world economy."

The Commission did not forget the negative areas of development during 1990, less employment could be generated and infant mortality rate stagnated at 70 per 1000 for the last several years. There are certain states where the infant mortality rate has been as much as 100 per thousand. The pace of rural electrification was poor, and the target to provide safe drinking water in rural areas could not be met. In the words of Commission:

> "An important aspect of the redefinition of strategy that is needed relates to the role of government. This redefinition is necessary both at the Central Government level and also at State Government level. It is now generally recognized that government in the past tended to take on too many responsibilities, imposing severe strains on its limited financial and administrative capabilities and also stifling individual initiative. An all-pervasive Government role may have been necessary at a stage where private sector capabilities were undeveloped, but the situation has changed dramatically in this respect. India now has a strong and vibrant private sector. The public sector is much less dominant than it used to be in many critical sectors and its relative position is likely to decline further as

Government ownership in many existing public sector organisations is expected to decline substantially. It is clear that industrial growth in future will depend largely upon the performance of the private sector and our policies must therefore provide an environment which is conducive to such growth. This is not to say that government has no role to play, or only a minimalist role, in promoting development. On the contrary, Government has a very important role indeed, but a different one from that envisaged in the past. The current back log of unemployment around 9 per cent, equivalent to 35 million persons, is too high, and every effort needs to be made to not only arrest the rising trend, but to actually reduce it during the Tenth Plan period itself. The Prime Minister's vision of creating 100 million employment opportunities over the next ten years is taken as the basis for targeting the creation of 50 million employment opportunities during the next five years, which is about 14 million higher than the target mandated in the Approach Paper on the basis of additions to labour force during the Plan period. If this target is achieved, the unemployment rate is likely to decline significantly to 5 per cent by the end of the Tenth Plan. Similarly, the mandated reductions in the poverty rate of 5 percentage points during the Tenth Plan and another 10 percentage points during the Eleventh Plan, as stipulated in the Approach Paper, will still leave more than 11 per cent of the population, or about 130 million people, below the poverty line in 2012. There are other areas, *e.g.* infrastructure development, where gaps are large and growing faster. It is estimated that with a proper sectoral and regional focus, it may be possible to reduce the poverty rate by nearly 7 percentage points over the Tenth Plan period if the growth target of 8 per cent is achieved through the State-wise break down that has been drawn up in consultation with the States, the private sector cannot be expected to step in significantly. In these areas, the role of Government may have to be expanded and restructured. It will have to expand in some areas of infrastructure development, which are unlikely to attract private investment, *e.g.* rural infrastructure and road development. In others, *e.g.* telecommunications, power, ports, etc., the private sector can play a much greater role, provided an appropriate policy framework is in place. Here, the role of the government needs to change to facilitate such investment as much as possible while still remaining a public sector service provider for quite some time. In all these areas, the role of the government as a regulator ensuring a fair deal for consumers, transparency and accountability, and a level-playing field is also extremely important."

The Commission identified capital assets, which have been lying idle or had never been used to their potential and decided to utilise them productively. The first major area of idle capacity was in public infrastructural investment, which had been caused by the tendency to launch too many projects without the requisite financial provision or management capability, leading to a tardy pace of completion and sometimes even abandonment.

The second area of idle capacity stock was in the public sector enterprises where financial and managerial problems had prevented adequate investment in balancing and/or up-gradation, leading to inadequate utilisation of the capital assets or to the lack of market competitiveness. Prolonged periods of insufficient maintenance expenditures also had similar effects. Mere infusion of fresh funds was unlikely to solve this problem since the roots of the malaise go deeper, and usually lie in the domain of policies and excessive interference in the management of these enterprises. Measures to unlock such potential capacities through institutional change could yield rich dividends to the economy.

The third area was in the public sector itself, which accounted for bulk of economy where efficiency was vital. Therefore, in order to take advantage of whatever idle capital stock that exists in the economy today for accelerating the growth rate in the Tenth Plan; there are at least three categories of measures that would need to be taken immediately:

Measures to Reduce Idle Capital Stock

- Full emphasis to be placed on completion of partially completed or on-going projects and up-gradation of existing capital assets before starting new projects.
- Rapid privatisation of Public Sector Enterprises (PSEs), particularly those, which are working well below capacity.
- Legal and procedural changes for facilitating quick transfer of assets, including such measures as repeal of Sick Industrial Companies (Special Provision) Act (SICA), introduction of a bankruptcy law, facilitating foreclosure, accelerating judicial processes, etc.

Thus, the all-pervasive and dominant role that the public sector was playing in key sectors as well as consumer products area, during post-1956 Industrial Policy Resolution, and post-Second Plan period, with an over all intention to achieve a balanced economic growth in the country was completely changed in the Tenth Plan and the State was asked to concentrate in social sectors like, health, literacy, rural electrification, rural development and nutrition and allow the private sector to grow without any day-to-day State interference. Of course, the government have to play the role of a facilitator for investments as well as that of a regulator, ensuring fair deal to the consumers, transparency and accountability. It has been a great stride forward in liberalizing the economy that had been in the hands of the public sector for such a long time. Such a dominant role of public sector soon after the independence was indeed inevitable in view of the fact that either the private sector was incapable or unwilling for huge investments. Now that situation no longer exists, for which the private sector has to come in a big way for investment in infrastructure or in consumer products sectors.

A close analysis of various Plan documents would reveal that the public sector was given a dominant role till

Seventh Five Year Plan with a view to shape the economy of the country, to balance the regional disparity, to prevent concentration of wealth and economic power among the favoured few, and to make available more funds to the social sector. This dominant role to the public sector enterprises was inevitable keeping in view the inability or the unwillingness of the private sector to invest funds of such huge volume in the infrastructure or in the consumer product area. This being the definite policy of the government of the day, the public sector enterprises went on expanding constantly and to the commanding heights till the Industrial Policy Resolution 1991 was announced by the government. This was also reflected in the Eighth Plan document and for the first time the concept of restructuring and, if required, disinvesting public sector enterprises was mooted and various measures were initiated to modernize it. The Policy guidelines of 1991 and subsequent policies further enunciated a lesser role to be played by the public sector in areas like, consumer products as well as in some infrastructure areas like State Electricity Boards, communications etc., and play a bigger role in the social sectors. This is a significant change in the policy and a bold one too. In spite of this change in the policy, government have to go a long way to improve the productivity, profitability and capacity utilization percentage, efficiency and internal resources mobilization in the public sector.

7

Efficacy of Public Sector Undertakings

The analysis of the different Industrial Policies and recommendations of the Planning Commission in the post-independence era brought about many facets of the industrial progress in the country. Indeed, it was the need of the hour that government had to heavily concentrate on the industrial progress for the economic upliftment of the poor, downtrodden and have-nots. The fear of concentration of wealth with a few and unequal distribution of wealth, coupled with an urge for a socialistic pattern of society weighed heavily among the planners for envisaging a dominant character to the public sector undertakings. The perception that it was the public sector alone, which was capable of playing a major and dominant role in building infrastructure to bring about a sustained development, both in social as well as economic front, led to setting up of large and heavy public sector industries in the country. The State had to take on heavy responsibilities as the principal agency speaking for and acting on behalf of the community as a whole. The public sector had to expand rapidly. It had not only to take responsibilities in the areas in which the private sector was either unwilling or unable to undertake, but also to play the dominant role in shaping the entire pattern of investments in the economy, whether it made the investments directly or whether these were made in collaboration with the private sector. The private sector had to play its part within the framework of the comprehensive plan accepted by the community. The concept of 'the Socialistic Pattern of Society' was enshrined in the Preamble of the Constitution of India. It was emphasized that the public sector would be able to bring about a sizeable increase in national income so as to raise the level of living standards in the country; rapid industrialization with particular emphasis on the development of basic and heavy industries; a large expansion of employment opportunities; and reduction of inequalities in income and wealth and a more even distribution of economic power. The country had a very large pool of unemployed and underemployed work force. The standard of living of the people was extremely low, with a poor quality of life. Majority of the population were dependent on the agriculture, which was unremunerative. In the agriculture sector, the farmers were dependent on the age-old obsolete equipment, and there was complete dearth of modern technique as well as machinery. The agriculture sector had to be modernized in order to achieve Green Revolution. The communication facilities available were inadequate. It led to poor marketing of goods and services. The health and educational sectors were completely ignored. No nation could perceive progress without development of these core areas. These were the paramount requirements, which necessitated a new approach for the industrial sector. While framing the Industrial Policy of 1956, the Government of India in their own words, as narrated below, conceded the then socio-economic conditions for which a dominant role had to be bestowed on the public sector:

> "The growth of public sector in India had been guided by the Industrial Policy Resolution, 1956 which gave the public sector a strategic role in the economy. At the time of India's independence 1947, there were various problems confronting the country, which needed to be

tackled in a planned and systematic manner. India basically had been an agrarian economy with a week industrial base, low level of savings and inadequate investment and near absence of infrastructural facilities. A vast population was extremely poor. There existed considerable inequalities in income, levels of employment as well as glaring regional imbalances in economic attainment and trained manpower in various fields of management. It was thus obvious that the country was to speed up its economic growth and maintain it in the long run at a steady level; a big push was required from the government. As such, the state's intervention in all sectors of economy was inevitable because private sector had neither the necessary resources in terms of funds, managerial, scientific skills nor the will to undertake risks involved in large long gestation investment. They were also not willing to take up social responsibility. Among the imperatives were the removal of poverty, better distribution of income, expansion of employment opportunities, removal of regional imbalances, accelerated growth of agriculture and industrial production, better utilization of natural resources, and a wider ownership of economic power to prevent its concentration in a few hands. Given the type and range of problems faced by the country on its economic, social and strategic fronts and the various imperatives, it became a pragmatic compulsion to deploy public sector as an instrument of self reliant economic growth so as to develop a sound agriculture and industrial base, diversify the economy and overcome the economic backwardness. It emphasized the need for establishment of a socialistic pattern of society and the need for a planned and balanced industrial development of the nation. The State was therefore "to assume direct responsibility for the future development of industries over a wide area."

Different provisions of the Directive Principles of State Policy enshrined in the Constitution of India on social issues, development issues and issues relating to the public sector undertaking are as follows:

a. Article 38(2)

"The State shall, in particular, strive to minimize the inequalities in income, and endeavour to eliminate inequalities in status, facilities and opportunities, not only amongst individuals but also amongst groups of people residing in different areas or engaged in different vocations."

b. Article 39 (a)

"that the citizens, men and women equally, have right to an adequate means of livelihood."

c. Article 39(b)

"that the ownership and control of the material resources of the community are so distributed as best to sub serve the common good."

d. Article 39 (c)

"that the operation of the economic system does not result in the concentration of wealth and means of production to the common detriment."

e. Article 41

"The State shall, within the limits of its economic capacity and development, make effective provision for securing the right to work, to education and public assistance in case of unemployment, old age sickness and disablement, and in other cases of undeserved want."

More over the Preamble of the Constitution of India, among other things, asks for a socialistic pattern of society. Similarly, while planning for development, Government had to take into note of balancing the different regions of the country. These factors played heavily with the planners while framing the Industrial Policy Resolutions from time to time. As would be seen that in the first Industrial Policy Resolution enunciated during 1948, government recognized the need for a mixed economy and reserved national monopolies for only the munitions, namely, atomic energy, and railroad industries.

The government had the exclusive rights to initiate projects in six other industries namely, coal, iron, and steel, aircraft manufacturing, shipbuilding, telephone and telegraph, and minerals and yet could seek the aid of the private sector, if necessary. Moreover, the government could regulate and license 18 other industries of national importance. The extant industries were left to the private players. This resolution reassured foreign investors and the domestic business community that their holdings would not be confiscated or nationalized.

But at the time of framing the second Industrial Policy Resolution during 1956, the planners had to consult the Constitution of India that came to play on 26th January 1950. Besides, the scope and opportunity given to the private players could not be exploited by them at all. The private players were either not capable of, or were not keen on investing so heavily in the industrial sector. In the last eight years since the first Industrial Policy Resolution was enunciated, nothing much could be done by the private sector. Hence, Government had no other option but to take steps to build infrastructure in the crucial sectors. As such, the criticism by some that the theory of according commanding heights and the dominating role given to the public sector after 1956 was unnecessary, has been misplaced. Similarly, the other criticism now made that the present policy of liberalizing the economy is not based on the Constitution of India is also equally incorrect, in view of the fact that though the Constitution asks for a socialistic pattern of society, it does not bar any policy, if it sub serves the common good and does not result in concentration of wealth and means of production to the common detriment. (*emphasis given to the term common detriment*).

The issues before the Commission were not merely to evolve the method to enhance the standard of living, but to concentrate on the microeconomics and generate dynamism to improve the quality of life as a whole. The current levels of living in India are abysmally low. The production level is not sufficient to meet the minimum essential needs of the population. The population growth has been more than two percent, and at this rate the total population of the country would be more than 1.6 billion by the end of 2010. The infrastructure, the social sectors, and communication sector have been neglected since independence. There are large tracts or regions of the country, which are underdeveloped even in comparison to the rest of the country, and there are classes of the population, which are almost untouched by modern progressive ideas and techniques. Such crucial areas have to be dealt with on priority and techniques evolved for a faster growth. All kinds of efforts have to be mobilized and effective participation of the beneficiaries ensured to achieve the target fixed. Coordination among different functionaries is a key element. It need not be overemphasized that the material development of such people is linked to the microeconomics of the area, but a sustained development can be perceived only with improvement in the quality of life in general. Such improvement in quality of life is possible through a 'socialistic pattern of society' enunciated in the Preamble of the Constitution of India. A rising standard of life, or material welfare, as it is sometimes called, is, of course, not an end in itself. Essentially, it is a means to a better intellectual and cultural life. A society, which has to devote the bulk of its working force or its working hours to the production of the bare necessities of life, is to that extent limited in its pursuit of higher ends. Economic development is intended to expand the community's productive power and such a conception is feasible only when there is an urge to development and the institutions are moulded in that direction.

Tenth Planning Commission later on submitted its report underlying its view on public sector undertakings. Hence, we can make an analysis of the views, perceptions and the directions put forth by different Planning Commissions since their inception. In the First Planning Commission report, the underlying need and the objective of such a Plan was narrated as below:

- The central objective of planning in India at that point of time was to initiate a process of development, which would raise living standards and open out to the people new opportunities for a richer and more varied life. It is needless to say that in absence of a broader social environment, there could not be any progress in the economic front, for which the planning should not merely aim at development of resources, but also focus at development of human faculties and building up of an institutional frame work.
- Dynamism and vibrancy has been a key word of progress. Windows and doors have to be kept open in order to bring in fresh air. In order to develop to proceed further and to overcome stagnancy, a re-adaptation of social institutions and social relationships became necessary. In planning for a better economic order, the close interrelation between the technical and social aspects of the process of development had to be continually kept in view. Ground realities could not be overlooked. There was a need for concentrating efforts on the more immediate problems. Similarly, the community should also be in readiness to view the social process as one whole and to take action designed to shape the process along desired lines over a defined period.
- There had been considerable advance in public perception on the acceptance of such an approach to the problems of economic development and social change. Planning involved the acceptance of a clearly defined system of objectives in terms of which to frame over-all policies. It was considered that it also involved the formulation of a strategy for promoting the realisation of the ends defined. Planning was essentially an attempt at working out a rational solution of problems, an attempt to co-ordinate means and ends; it was thus different from

the traditional hit-and-miss methods by which 'reforms' and 'reconstruction' are often undertaken. Practical policy could not operate in terms of mere set doctrines; it must satisfy certain pragmatic tests. Policies have to be bombarded on the ground realities and synthesized norms/policies have to be evolved in order to achieve the desired results. This should be a continuous process.

- Primarily, the urge for economic and social change emanates from the reality of poverty and of inequalities in income, wealth and opportunity. The elimination of poverty could not, obviously, be achieved merely by redistributing existing wealth. It is another thing that equi-disribution of wealth is a utopian concept. Moreover a programme aiming only at raising production could not remove existing inequalities. The two had to be tuned, optimized and synergised, and only then a simultaneous advance along both these lines could create the conditions in which the community could put forth its best efforts for promoting development. The Directive Principles of State Policy enunciated in Articles 36 to 51 of the Constitution make it clear that for the attainment of these ends, ownership and control of the material resources of the country should be so distributed as best to sub serve the common good, and that the operation of the economic system should not result in the concentration of wealth and economic power in the hands of a few. It was in this larger perspective that the task of planning had to be envisaged.
- It was but quite natural that all-round and orderly development, would inevitably take time to come into full fruition. Large-scale changes in modes of production, in commercial and industrial organisation and in the institutional framework of corporate life could not be seen through within a

brief period of four or five years. It was perceived that in the initial stages of development, divergence in the economic and social interests of different sections of the community might create special problems. While recognizing such a situation, attempt should be made to give a new sense of direction and purpose to the community. An underdeveloped country, which had suffered long from the effects of cramped development, coupled with a very low socio-politico-economic infrastructure, had the desire to progress rapidly and in many directions; the aim of planning must be to make this possible. Of course, political independence and strengthening of democratic institutions should provide the needed opportunity.

- The rapid advances in science and technology over the last few decades have opened new vistas in the direction of abolition of want and the restoration of man to a new sense of dignity. Knowledge of the socio-economic changes and utilisation of these techniques is neither complete nor certain. No problem has a generalised solution. Conditions vary as between countries, and each country has to evolve a solution in the light not only of contemporary conditions but also of its traditions and culture. Geography, weather, size and the existing environment play a very important role in the formulation of economic plans. Parallels from past history or from contemporary conditions in other countries are useful up to a point, but they cannot provide a complete answer. All that can be said is that there is a need, on the one hand, for clarity in regard to basic values and, on the other, for readiness to adapt practical solutions to the concrete problems arising in the process of transition to a different economic and social order.

- It is in this context that there is a need to stress the essential political and administrative conditions fundamental to successful planning. Briefly these are:
  1. a large measure of agreement in the community as to the ends of policy;
  2. effective power, based on the active co-operation of citizens, in the hands of the State; and, earnest and determined exercise of that power with an inbuilt mechanism for checks and balances, in furtherance of these ends; and
  3. an efficient administrative set-up, with personnel of requisite capacity and quality. The competency of that set-up would need continuous updating, and the result should be visible.

A national plan had to be an expression of a basic unity of purpose in the community. It is this unity, which would constitute the ultimate sanction behind the plan, should give it requisite driving force and evoke the necessary sacrifice and effort on the part of members. Joined to this unity of purpose, there must be effective power in the hands of the State to be exercised, of course having in-built mechanism for checks and balances, with the necessary persistence and determination in order to ensure the furtherance of accepted ends. Constructive use of this power calls for integrity, efficiency and responsiveness in administration. The creation and maintenance of these basic pre-requisites of economic and social growth had to be considered as matters deserving continuous and careful attention.

The party in power has not only to carry public opinion with it; but it has to get the active co-operation of all sections. In a democratic country, every citizen is free to think and vote as he likes, and political parties have the right freely to canvass public support for their programmes and in the event of securing a majority in the legislature to form the government. Under these conditions, the greater the responsiveness of the party in power to trends of opinion outside, the greater will be its effectiveness for action. The smooth functioning of the party system rests on an underlying agreement as to objectives, though there may be differences as to approach or to the pace of change with reference to certain problems. These differences are a necessary concomitant of democracy; they ensure a continuous re-examination and re-adaptation of governmental policies. On various matters, different parties tend inevitably to come together and co-operate. For planning to proceed with the necessary momentum and continuity, it is essential that the country adopts a programme of action which reflects the unity of outlook and approach among the members of the party in power and draws forth at the same time the support and co-operation from shades of opinion outside the party. It is through enlargement of the area of agreement that conditions can be created for the most effective mobilisation of the community's resources towards the common objective of all-round economic development.

It is not to deny that democratic processes are complex, and they put large demands on the government as well as the governed. Real democracy means much more than adult suffrage and parliamentary government; it means a reordering of social relationships in terms of new values. It is not without significance that in several parts of the world, the emergence of a new leadership determined to carry through far-reaching economic and social changes in keeping with the needs and urges of the people. It has been accompanied by a great upsurge of public enthusiasm and a release of the pent-up energies of the community. The relationship between political forms and the spirit underlying them is a vast and intricate subject in which no easy judgments are possible. But, it must be emphasized that for democratic planning to succeed, it will have to energise the entire community and to place before it a goal of endeavour which will call forth all its latent creative urges. Even in deep crisis such as war, democracies have proved capable of effective action on a mass scale, and there is no doubt that once the community has come to appreciate the vital significance of the tasks in hand, it will rise to similar heights for constructive purposes also. The crucial factor in organizing the community for action is leadership, and, in a democracy, not merely leadership at the top but at all levels. Hence democracy is the mother to all solution in every country. Once democracy strikes root, other branches of the democracy also bear fruit.

India is a federation, in which the Central Government and the Governments of States have their assigned spheres of action, as per the mandate of the Constitution. There are certain concurrent subjects in which the Centre as well as the States can undertake legislation. Economic and social planning is in the concurrent list, as this is a subject in which the Centre as well as the States are interested and have to work in unison. The Centre has certain emergency powers, but normally coordination of policies has to be effected through mutual consultation. This system of consultation and of formulation of policies on the basis of over-all national requirements would have to be strengthened in the interests of planning. Care should be taken to see that the plan was implemented throughout the country as a single coordinated whole. The National Development Council which was set up and which comprised the Cabinet, Ministers of States and the members of the Planning Commission, with the Prime Minister as Chairman, was intended to secure this result. It was obvious that without complete coordination of policies and timely concerted action, there was danger of waste and misdirection of effort, which might have consequences extending far beyond the area of responsibility of any single authority, and this, it must be cognized, places special responsibilities on the Centre.

A planned economy aiming at the realization of larger social objectives would entail a vast increase in governmental functions. For these to be discharged efficiently, appropriate local, regional and functional organisations had to be built up and strengthened. Each of these must have a defined sphere of action and responsibility, and must be able to function with a measure of autonomy. Arrangements for the necessary coordination between them must be made at various levels from the village upwards. The activities of all developmental institutions in the country, official and non-official would have to be reoriented in terms of the requirements of the Plan, and in this process, due stress must be laid on the appropriate role of various local and functional organizations. The function of the Central Government was to evolve a national plan, to work out a coordinated policy for implementation of the same, to watch and assess the progress of major development schemes in the different parts of the country, and constantly to initiate and promote action in furtherance of the objectives and targets defined.

This was the intention behind which the first Planning Commission was set up. It was also this rationale, which formulated the first governmental policy on public sector. It is known that at the time of independence there was no public sector worth the name except railways and the postal system in India. No doubt, there were very few industrialists in the country capable to set up large scale industries. Many of them were also in need of governmental support in terms of capital base, subsidies and protection from foreign competition. It was already indicated that there was cramped development during the pre-independence times, which resulted in unequal distribution of wealth, marginalisation of the poor and the needy, and complete lack of infrastructure. Poverty was writ large everywhere. The social distortions bred economic inequality. Democracy was considered to be the panacea for the poverty. In spite of this, in the first Industrial Resolution Policy enunciated in 1948, it was laid down that besides arms and ammunition, atomic energy and railway transport, which would be the monopoly of the Central Government, the

State would be exclusively responsible for the establishment of new undertakings in six basic industries except where, in the national interest, the State itself found it necessary to secure the cooperation of private enterprise. The rest of the industrial field was left open to private enterprise, though it was made clear that the State would also progressively participate in this field. It reveals that government allowed the private players to set up industries in all sectors except the above eight areas. But in the second Industrial Policy Resolution enunciated in 1956, wherein government, in order to fulfill its obligations, laid down in the Directive Principles of State Policy an endeavour with a purpose that the citizens, men and women equally have the right to an adequate means of livelihood that the ownership and control of the material resources of the community are so distributed as best to sub serve the common good; that the operation of economic system does not result in the concentration of wealth and means of production to the common detriment; that there is equal pay for equal work for both men and women; that the health and strength of workers, men and women, the tender age of children are not abused and that citizens are not forced by economic necessity to enter vocations unsuited to their age or strength; that childhood and youth are protected against exploitation and against moral and material abandonment there was a complete turn around. The Industrial Policy Resolution of 1956 clearly spelt out its priorities, and embodied that in order to achieve the above objectives, the public sector must play a dominant role in the society. Thus the advantages available to the private sector in the First Industrial Resolution Policy were removed in the subsequent one.

The public sector grew from strength to strength in the subsequent years and in the subsequent policies. It got tremendous governmental support in terms of capital formation, marketing support, protection from foreign competition and subsidies. Except some minor modifications here and there, in every industrial policy resolution, the intent and the conception that public sector would play a dominant role, continued till 1991 when the government of the day pronounced a new policy which has been a complete departure from the previous ones. The government while recognizing the benefits of the past policies also admitted the pitfalls in the system. There had been a desire to unshackle the industry from the bureaucratic control and associate the private sector in a more vigorous way. While correcting the distortions or weaknesses that might have crept in in the system, it would maintain a sustained growth in productivity and gainful employment and attain international competitiveness. Government had indeed realized the weaknesses of the public sector and the consequences in according a dominant role to it way back in 1977. Hence while framing the Industrial Policy of 1977, Government of India admitted the weaknesses in the following words:

> "For the past 20 years, Government Policy in the sphere of industry has been governed by the Industrial Policy Resolution of 1956. While some of the elements of that Resolution in regard to desirable pattern of industrial development still remain valid, the results of actual policies in the industrial field have not been up to the expectations or declared objectives. The growth of per capital national income during the last 10 years has been about 1.5 per cent per annum and is clearly inadequate to meet the needs of a developing economy. Unemployment has increased, rural-urban disparities have widened and the rate of real investment has stagnated. The growth of industrial output in the last decade has been no more than 3 to 4 per cent per annum on an average. The incidence of industrial sickness has become widespread and some of the major industries are the worst affected. The pattern of industrial costs and prices has tended to be distorted, and dispersal of industrial activity away from the larger urban concentration has been very slow.
>
> The new Industrial Policy must, therefore, be directed towards removing the distortions of the past so that genuine

aspirations of the people can be met within a time-bound programme of economic development."

In spite of such realizations, the 1977 policy resolution did nothing much in terms of modernizing or bringing about a concrete policy that would have given a boost to the industrial sector. The concept of restructuring or disinvestments was completely missing. Rather draconian measures were introduced in 1977 policy in the plea of supporting and aiding the small-scale industries. While defining the role of large-scale industries, it had been outlined in the policy papers that in addition to small and village industries, there was also a clear role for large-scale industry in India. However, the Government would not favour large-scale industry merely for demonstration of sophisticated skills or as monuments of irrelevant foreign technology. The role of large-scale industry would be related to the programme for meeting the basic minimum needs of the population through wider dispersal of small scale and village industries and strengthening of the agricultural sector. In general, areas for large-scale industry would be limited to: (a) basic industries which were essential for providing infrastructure as well as for development of small and village industries, such as steel, non-ferrous metals, cement, and oil refineries; (b) capital goods industries for meeting the machinery requirement of basic industries as well as small-scale industries; (c) high technology industries which required large-scale production, and which were related to agricultural and small-scale industrial development, such as fertilizers, pesticides, and petro-chemicals etc; and (d) other industries which were outside the list of reserved items for the small-sale sector, and which were considered essential for the development of the economy, such as machine tools, organic and inorganic chemicals. Similarly, while defining the role of the large houses, the policy statement outlined that Government policies had not succeeded, in the past in restraining the disproportionate growth of large industrial houses. Moreover, while a certain measures of growth of existing enterprises was inevitable and also necessary for continued health of these enterprises, the growth of large industrial houses had been disproportionate to the size of their internally generated resources and had been largely based on funds borrowed from public financial institutions and banks. Hence, government desired that the process must be reversed. In order to achieve the goal, government outlined the following principles for the large houses in future expansions:

- The expansion of existing undertakings and establishments of new undertakings would continue to be subject to the provisions of the Monopolies and Restrictive Trade Practices Act. The provisions of this Act, including those relating to dominant undertakings, would be effectively implemented;

- Except in the case of industries eligible for automatic growth of capacity, the expansion of existing undertakings into new lines and establishments of new undertakings by large houses would require specific approval of Government; and

- Large houses would have to rely on their own internally generated resources for financing new or expansion projects. While an appropriate debt equity ratio will be permitted in the case of industries, like fertilizers, paper, cement, shipping, petrochemicals, etc., which were relatively more capital intensive in nature, the debt equity ratio in the case of other less capital-intensive or less sophisticated industries would be so fixed as to reflect the greater use of their own internally generated resources by the large houses.

Government in its licensing policy decided to regulate the activities of the large houses to bring them in line with the country's socio-economic goals. Where large-scale units, whether belonging to large houses or not, were already engaged in the manufacture of items since reserved for the small-scale sector, there would be no expansion in their capacity. On the other hand, the share of these units in the total capacity for these items would be steadily reduced and that of small scale and cottage sector increased. In licensing other activities of large-scale industry, particularly of units belonging to large houses, Government would pay due regard to the existing share of these units in the total domestic production of these items. It would be the policy of government to ensure that no unit or business group acquires a dominant or monopolistic position in the market. Government further decided that the present industrial activities of the large houses would be scrutinised so that unfair practices arising out of manufacturing inter-linkages could be avoided. This indeed, curbed the investment climate in the country and thereby reduced the production level in all industrial sectors. Such a decision also led to increased unemployment, social distortions and enhanced deficiencies in infrastructures.

Thus, it may be seen that stringent norms were prescribed by the government in 1977 industrial policy, keeping an eye on the development of small-scale industries, and to prevent concentration of wealth with a few individuals/ houses. The norms prescribed curbed the activities of the large-scale industries and large houses. Hence, the rigid regulations had its long term effect on the economy of the country, and the industrial growth suffered very badly. However, the government, during 1991, had to realize that unless such draconian rules were amended and friendly policies introduced, the industrial growth could not be achieved at a faster pace. However, the change in mind was also as a result of the change in the international scenario, during which the economy of Eastern Europe following rigid economic regulations started collapsing.

The pursuit of these objectives would be tempered by the need to preserve the environment and ensure the efficient use of available resources. All sectors of industry- whether small, medium or large, belonging to the publ (n)/V private or cooperative sector would be encouraged to grow and improve on their past performance. Government's policy would be continuity with change. In pursuit of the above objectives, Government decided to take a series of initiatives in respect of the policies relating to the areas like, Industrial Licensing, Foreign Investment, Foreign Technology Agreements, Public Sector Policy, and MRTP Act. At the out set, in the Industrial Licensing Policy that has been governed by the Industries (Development & Regulation) Act, 1951, three categories of industries were recognized. These were those reserved for development in public sector, those be permitted for development through private enterprise with or without State participation, and those for which investment initiatives would ordinarily emanate from private entrepreneurs.

Government decided to suitably modify the MRTP Act in order to remove the impediments to the industrial growth and expansion. Though the process of change started in the year 1982 and 1984, major changes were now proposed. The thrust of policy would be more on controlling unfair or restrictive business practices. The MRTP Act would be restructured by eliminating the legal requirement for prior governmental approval for expansion of present undertakings and establishment of new undertakings. The provisions relating to merger, amalgamation, and takeover would also be repealed. Similarly, the provisions regarding restrictions on acquisition of and transfer of shares would be appropriately incorporated in the Companies Act.

Government also decided to unshackle the Indian industry from the undesired bureaucratic controls and brought out changes in the Industrial Licensing Policy. It abolished Industrial Licensing for all projects- except for a short list of industries related to security and strategic concerns, social reasons, hazardous chemicals and overriding environmental reasons, and items of elitist consumption, areas where security and strategic concerns predominate would continue to be reserved for the public sector, in projects where imported capital goods were required, automatic clearance would be given in cases where foreign exchange availability was ensured through foreign equity or if the CIF value of imported capital goods required was less than 25% of total value (net of taxes) of plant and equipment, up to a maximum value of Rs. 2 crore, in locations other than cities of more than one million population-there would be no requirement of obtaining industrial approvals from the Central Government except for industries subject to compulsory licensing, the exemption from licensing would apply to all substantial expansions of existing units, and the mandatory convertibility clause would no longer be applicable for term loans from the financial institutions for new projects.

In the areas of Foreign Investment, the government took a bold policy and decided that in view of the fact that India had a significant development in industrial economy in the last forty years, foreign investment would bring about abundant technology transfer, production of quality products, bring about competitiveness, and boost confidence in the minds of the consumers, and so on. The government therefore, decided to welcome foreign investments. In the areas of high priority industries, requiring large investments and advanced technology, it was decided to provide approval for direct foreign investment up to 51% foreign equity in such industries. There should be no bottlenecks of any kind in this process. In the areas of Foreign Technology Transfer, government decided to provide facilities like, automatic approval for technology agreement related to high priority industries. Within specified parameters, companies would be free to negotiate the terms of technology transfer with their foreign counterparts according to their own commercial judgement, and the hiring of foreign technicians and foreign testing of indigenously developed technologies, would also not require prior clearance as prescribed so far, individually or as a part of industrial or investment approvals.

Similarly, government also modified the public sector

policy in order to cope with the changing international scenario as well as domestic compulsions. While recognizing the contributions of the public sector to the Indian industrial economy, government also had to address the other sectors of the economy for which the changes were paramount. Besides, there had been problems, which started to manifest itself in the form of inefficiency, lack of technological upgradation, excessive bureaucratic control, inadequate attention to research and development and human resources. Hence, it was decided to prioritise areas like, essential infrastructure goods and services, exploration and exploitation of oil and mineral resources, technology development and building of manufacturing capabilities in areas, which are crucial in the long-term development of the economy and where private sector investment is inadequate, and manufacture of products where strategic considerations predominate, such as defence equipment, which would be exclusive domain of public sector. Of course, at the same time, the public sector would not be barred from entering areas not specifically reserved for it. In rest of the areas, the private sector would be allowed to enter.

These steps taken by the Government appear to be insufficient. Government should open up the economy more vigorously and do away with the anachronistic rules. Reforms are needed in many areas. Reforms and liberalizations in economy should be always accompanied with a well organized control mechanisms and setting up regulatory authorities. In absence of regulatory bodies, reforms and liberalizations are meaningless. There has been complete lack of transparency and accountability in public sector. However in a detailed examination of issues, the following areas of positive gains of public sector emerge:

> The performance of the public sector cannot be judged on the basis of the yardstick normally applied to the private sector. The justification of the public sector lies in its contribution to fulfilling certain broader socio-economic objectives. Viewed in this light, the public sector as a whole

has acquitted itself reasonably well. But for the entry of the public sector in a major way in the development of these basic industries, the structural changes witnessed in the Indian economy could not have been achieved. It has also provided the necessary counter-poise to the private sector for supply management as needed from time to time in periods of crisis in vital sectors of the economy. The public sector has also devoted comparatively greater attention to research and development, so essential for achieving the goals of technological self-reliance.

In aggregate financial terms, the internal resources generated by the public sector undertakings for financing the Plan have been comparatively meager. There are many reasons for the vows of the public sector. The major factors responsible for these have been as follows.

- low return on investment on account of price constraints imposed on some public sector undertakings;
- considerable number of private sector sick units (particularly in the textile and engineering industries) which the Central Government had to take over in the interest of maintaining employment and production;
- the technological complexity of the industries which had to be promoted in the public sector where a longer gestation period and slower learning curve are inevitable.
- exercise of initiative, discretion, and entrepreneurship in public sector projects were discouraged by instruments of scrutiny *i.e.*, the Central Vigilance Commission with its network of subordinate formations; and the Central Bureau of Investigation (CBI). Vigilance inquiries, added to the fears of audit objections and CBI investigations. By the time an innocent executive clears himself of all these allegations, he becomes a broken man.
- borrowings of private sector business practices, such

as the introduction of corporate plans, mission and vision statements and strategic plans have not been worked out.

- lack of emphasis on cost cutting in many areas where cost cutting is required, and where efficiency needed to be upgraded with the reason that officers and the staffs working in the PSEs have not been able to cope with the new technology and ideas.
- complete lack of accountability while evaluating economic and financial performance. Such accountability relates to effectiveness of the policies formulated.
- transparency is an important element of good governance, but failure to share information in the public sector made the system incompetent and corrupt.
- Lack of consistency in public policy, which has a strong effect on investment climate, economics, and prices and so on, does affect proper functioning of the public sector.
- Lack of public participation adversely affects public sector as people are at the heart of development, the ultimate beneficiaries and agents of development, and with out their participation no project can be successful.
- resource crunch in the PSEs seriously retards the progress of the industrial out put, and PSEs have to depend fully on doles given by the administrative Ministries.
- erosion of net worth due to continuous losses incurred by public sector enterprises.
- reluctance of financial institutions to provide funds for revival of PSEs. Considering the track records of the PSEs no FI is prepared to lend funds for the revival of the sick and nonviable industries.

- heavy interest burden at high interest rate is one of the major factors for the failure of the industries.
- uncertainty in supply of raw material to PSEs is one of the major components for the survival of the industry as many a times the industry has to procure it at a very high price.
- continuance of large number of PSEs with the same old and obsolete plant and machinery results in frequent break downs and low productions.
- continuance with the out dated technology. The technological complexities of the industries, which had to be promoted in the public sector where a longer gestation period and slower learning curve, are inevitable.
- low capacity utilization resulting from management inefficiency and penchant to continue with the old and out dated know how and technology.
- excess man power caused by politicians' urge to rehabilitate party workers or that of top bureaucrats to acomodate his own kith and kin.
- reduction in import duty resulting from liberalization policy which facilitated swamping of market by imported goods and displacing indigenous products.
- stiff competition, weak marketing strategy, and price constraints imposed on some public sector undertakings causing in low return on investment.
- excessive ministerial and Parliamentary control on the PSEs exerted through many ways-like Parliamentary scrutiny, Parliamentary debates and Committees, which are inevitable in a Parliamentary democracy. Similarly, concerned Ministries and administrative Departments also exercise controls through budgets, circulars and office orders.

- lack of professionalism among Board of Directors in most of the PSEs which was anachronistic and detrimental to the survival of PSEs. Government indeed tried to infuse professionalism in the Board of Directors but such efforts, to a large extent proved unsuccessful due to political and bureaucratic apathy and negligence.
- multiplicity of audit: (1) by a firm of chartered accountants who audit according to a questionnaire given by the Comptroller and Auditor General; (2) a test audit on that again by the Comptroller and Auditor General; (3) a comprehensive review of public sector undertakings by the Auditor General, and (4) sometimes a direct scrutiny of public sector undertakings by the Committee on Public Undertakings (COPU), independent of Auditor General, which tended to stultify the decision-making process in a public sector. Almost all the committees and commissions have felt that the very system of dual audit is infructuous, and the audit by the Comptroller and Auditor General should be done away with totally.
- while decision-making executive is questioned by various probing agencies but a sluggish, negligent and apathetic executive goes scot free.
- relentless Parliamentary scrutiny, though inevitable in a parliamentary democracy, deters and delays decision making.
- special institutional arrangements, such as budget committees, calling attention notices, half-hour discussions, and so on, keep the senior executives busy adversely effecting the decision making processes.
- examination of the performance of PSEs by Parliament Committee on Public Undertakings, which originally functioned with reference to the

CAG reports, but of late, they have started independent investigations by themselves.

- writ jurisdiction under Article 12 of the Constitution which has led to a flood of cases causing fear psychosis amongst management as senior executives and bureaucrates are hauled up, admonished and sent to judicial custody in contempt of the court proceedings, on failure to comply with the court directions. At the same time several employees of PSEs prefer continuation of this. Though this provision is not a part of corporate governance in itself, it impacts building long term capabilities so necessary while competiting with private sector as also in cases where government control is below 51%.

Not withstanding these considerations, there is need for substantial improvement in the working of the public sector undertakings on the following lines:

- The continued growth prospects of the public sector, and indeed of the economy, are critically dependent on its ability to generate resources for its future growth.
- A substantial improvement in the efficiency of these undertakings, to provide a reasonable rate of return on large investments made on them is, of crucial importance. Pricing policy in PSUs needs to be reviewed to bring it in line with prudent commercial norms, to help them build their resource raising capacity.
- Improve management practices within the undertakings to impart a greater concern for optimal utilization of capacity and higher levels of technical efficiency.
- Inordinate delays in the implementation have not only caused loss of production but also significantly higher investment costs. Therefore, modern

techniques of project monitoring and construction management need to be introduced to avoid excessive costs due to cost and time overrun in construction of projects.

- Need for adequate delegation of authority to the public sector undertakings and also within PSEs at various levels. The authority and discretion of the public sector management, within delegated functions, should not be brought into question; and performance of the management should be judged on the basis of overall results achieved as distinct from the soundness of individual decisions taken by it.
- Promoting steadily induction of professional management and industrial culture inPSEs. An intensive institutionalized programme of induction and short-term training for senior public sector managers should be introduced to ensure continuous availability of a body of properly trained and motivated personnel for top-level positions in the public sector.
- Effective accountability mechanisms are made up of a series of interdependent parts: clarity of objectives, accurate and accessible performance information, an appropriate allocation of managerial decision-making responsibility, and effective ways of making managers accountable for results. The precise nature of accountability problems, and the proposed solutions, will vary in each part of the public sector. For instance, improving State Owned Enterprises (SOE) accountability involves, among other things, reasserting the armies length nature of the relationship between SOE managers and shareholders. For core departments, improved accountability will arise from stronger mechanisms for holding chief executives to account for under-

performance. The variety of functional forms making up the entity sector poses particular challenges for the design of accountability arrangements.

- From time to time, there are breakdowns in performance. Therefore, it is important to send a clear message to the system that poor performance carries adverse consequences. Accountability is the essential quid pro quo for managerial autonomy, and both are required to drive efficiency. Public service managers must expect to be held accountable, so accountability needs to be seen to be effective. In this context, it should be noted that chief executives are responsible for both direct and delegated exercise of power. Weak accountability also undermines high performance. Poorer performing public servants and others will come to believe that their performance is acceptable. There will also be a general loss of reputation associated with public service activities, reducing the ability of the public service to attract high caliber individuals. Chronic under-performance is potentially serious, and should be addressed before it produces high profile breakdowns. In the private sector, chronic under-performance increases the risk of bankruptcy or a hostile takeover. The absence of these exit mechanisms in the public sector increases the possibility that under-performance will be sustained for long periods of time.
- Concepts and methodology of PSEs given in different Five Year Plans allows in depth analysis of autonomy and accountability in public sector enterprises, where it has been indicated that to overcome the drawbacks of public sector, the executives should be allowed more flexibility in decision making and concentration of powers with the Government would make it more counter-

productive. Therefore, several of the industrial undertakings directly under the Central Government had already been organised as Joint Stock Companies with boards of directors vested with powers of management in the same manner as in any undertaking in the private sector. Similarly, industrial enterprises in some of the States reinforced desirability of organising these enterprises as entities independent of day-to-day governmental control. On similar lines Planning Commission also recommended State industrial undertakings with internal management entirely under the control of the board of directors but accountable to the public, which were their ultimate owner as well as beneficiary. Therefore, immediate problem is to see that the right conventions in these matters are evolved and also secure the right personnel for the boards of directors, the top executives and the technicians.

The Planning Commission observed that parliamentary interpellations and discussions on routine functions would stifle PSEs and constant public scrutiny, would frighten management making day-to-day decisions necessary and the enterprise will be stifled by red tape and bureaucracy. It was, therefore felt that a Committee of Parliament, which would enable informed parliamentary criticism to be brought to bear on public enterprises. Membership of the Committee was for a period of about three years to give time to members to master complex facts and to ensure some continuity. This would also result in a growing number of members of Parliament taking a specialised interest in these matters. As the Committee would assure Parliament of necessary vigilance, individual members would count on the judgements of the members of the Committee for proper and periodic evaluation of the public enterprises.

- Delegation of powers within the enterprise was a key area. Lack of delegation of authority was usually accompanied by a failure to define responsibilities and duties. Nobody could operate confidently or effectively or be held responsible for results unless he knew what he was supposed to do and had the authority to do it.
- Constant public scrutiny would push the management to the wall and they would be afraid to take initiatives and decisions involving risks but generally necessary in commercial undertakings. During 1959 the Krishna Menon Committee made various recommendations reconciling the accountability of public sector undertakings to the parliament on the one hand with their autonomy for ensuring efficiency on the other. The Administrative Reforms Commission had also gone into the subject, in detail. While Government had to ensure that the general policies pursued by the public sector organisations were in conformity with the national objectives and declared policies, the enterprises had to be given sufficient freedom in day-to-day operations so that the managements could run the organisations, both industrial and others, in accordance with commercial principles. This would help in increasing their profitability and efficiency.
- There should be reforms in civil service as a whole and improvement in transparency, accountability, honesty, efficiency, and sensitivity in public administration at all levels. The solution to the problem of corruption has to be more systemic than any other issue of governance. Merely shrinking the economic role of the State by resorting to deregulation, liberalisation and privatisation would

not necessarily be the solution to addressing the problem. All such procedures, laws and regulations that breed corruption and come in the way of efficient delivery system would have to be eliminated. The following are some of the steps that would need to be taken in this regard to improve the efficiency of the system:

(a) **Enforcing the right to information:** This must be the starting point. Free flow of information to the general public and to the consumers will bring about a sense of involvement in them. This will also make the public sector more careful in policy making as well as in the execution processes.

(b) **Greater transparency in policies and procedures:** The processes and the outcomes of policies, entitlements and procedures must be transparent, widely shared and well displayed.

(c) **Minimising discretion:** It is believed that less discretion would lead to a more equitable and less corrupt system.

(d) **Those who have the authority must also be made accountable:** Prevalent institutional arrangements have to be reviewed and changes made so that those vested with authority are also made accountable.

(e) **Revamping the system of rewards and punishments:** The present system of incentives in public life, which makes corruption a high-return-low-risk activity, needs to be changed. There has to be an incentive structure that rewards and promotes merit, at the same time disciplines and punishes malfunction and misconduct. Public examples will have to be made of people convicted or charged for misconduct/corruption.

(f) **Review of the functions of the Government and shedding of the redundant ones:** The functions of the Government change from time to time. We have come a long way from the days of famine management and quotas for industrial raw materials, etc. The opening up of the economy and globalisation has brought in many changes. It is necessary to review the situation and identity departments and functions within departments that were once essential, but are now redundant and would need to be done away with. A good example is the office of the Cane Commissioner in the Cooperative Department, which has become infructuous with the change in the cooperative law. In a bid to enhance the productivity of bureaucracy, it is important to make certain that each employee is performing relevant tasks.

Corporate Governance

As defined by Geeta Gouri, "It is clearly the system by which corporate entities are directed and controlled. It encompasses the entire mechanics of the functioning of a company and attempts to put in place a system of checks and balances between the shareholders, directors, auditors and the management." She further adds that "In a public enterprise, since there are no marketable ordinary shares, there is no market for corporate control. Corporate governance in public enterprises is by way of superimposed organizational structures as will be seen later. It is also a peculiar feature of the modern large corporation that owners of residual profits are not those who control the decision-making process. There is a division between ownership and control. Corporate governance is putting in place a system that ensures that the management of the company runs the firm such as to maximize objectives of owners (presumably profits) without abuse of its powers". Corporate Governance seems to be one of the major processes which could put the

PSEs in the right track. As experts conceive, it may benefit the public sector on the following core areas:

- The Board of Directors is made responsible for any low performance of the enterprise.
- The Board should set targets for themselves, keeping in view the overall interest of the enterprise and adopting the best HR practices.
- The aim of the Board should be to turn the enterprise from loss making to profit making and self sustaining one and free itself from the shackles of the government control.

However, to achieve the above objective, the following norms have to be adopted:

- Creating conditions for developing a sound business strategy in consonance with national/plan objectives.
- Ensuring that the enterprise has a CEO of the highest caliber, and that certain senior managers are being groomed to assume the CEO's position in future.
- Creating systems of information, audit, and control to oversee whether the enterprise is meeting its objectives.
- Ensuring that the enterprise complies with legal and ethical standards.
- Ensuring that the enterprise is able to manage crisis and that its actions come in handy in the prevention of crisis.
- Set goals for the CEO and functional directors separately and collectively to measure their performance. Written statements are ideal. Self-assessment or evaluation by an independent organization can be adopted.
- Each board constitutes a standing Audit Committee. The Audit Committee will have full

powers for appointing the chartered accountants and accepting the audit reports. The Audit Committee must have a special invitee from the CAG's office. The representative of CAG can initiate, suggest and recommend any type of audit as he/ she deems fit for the concerned public enterprise. The need for additional audit by the CAG will not be necessary. Each board constitutes a standing Audit Committee. The Audit Committee will have full powers for appointing the chartered accountants and accepting the audit reports. The Audit Committee must have a special invitee from the CAG's office. The representative of CAG can initiate, suggest and recommend any type of audit as he/ she deems fit for the concerned public enterprise. The need for additional audit by the CAG will not be necessary.

- Appoint committees/sub-committees to ensure transparency with regard to financial transactions, payment of wages/salaries, etc., and ensure full disclosure to creditors and suppliers.
- One-quarter of the Board must be drawn from experts, academicians, professionals and technocrats.
- Each Board must appoint from within them an Appointments Committee and a standing Audit Committee. Similarly, committees for Capital Expenditure and Compensation may also be created on need-basis. In the board managed situation capital expenditure decisions and compensation designs may be left to the Boards/AGM. These committees may co-opt external specialists, representatives of ministries, PESB (Public Enterprises Selection Board), CAG etc., as appropriate.

At the time of independence of India, there were only five public sector Enterprises with an investment of Rs. 29

crores. But the number went up to 242 as on 31.3.2004, with an investment of Rs.349209 crores. Against such a colossal investment, the retained profit has been only Rs.35925 crores. (Figure 1) Of course, the profit jumped from Rs.16917 during 2002-03 to Rs.35925 and the loss has gone down from Rs.10827 crores to Rs.8399 crores. Similarly, the total number of employees has gone down from 21.79 lakhs during 1991-92 to 17.66 during 2003-04. But the average annual per capita emoluments of the employees has gone up from Rs.56,508 to Rs.2,48,691 during the same period. Public sectors had been set up keeping in view the intention of the Constitution wherein it was enunciated to transform India into a socialistic pattern of society. The politico-economic scenario at the time of independence of the country was completely different from what it is now. The social and economic deprivations were writ large every where. Large percentage of the population was uneducated and did not have access to the minimum basic requirements like, food, shelter, clothing, safe drinking water, primary education, and medical care. Infrastructure in terms of communication, electricity, irrigation, school and hospital buildings were scarce. There was no social security system in place. Unemployment was the order of the day. Large percentage of the population was below the poverty line. The people in higher echelons of society did neither have the resources nor the ingenuity to set up industries requiring large capital investment. It was in these circumstances that the planners had to switch on to public sector investment and allowed them to play a dominant role in the economy of the country.

With the situation prevailing as indicated above, perhaps the Industrial Resolution Policy 1956, was the best possible panacea for the problems. The public sector created huge employment opportunities, especially for the people who are socially, economically and educationally backward. It created enourmous amount of national wealth, developed backward areas of the country by setting up new industries, irrigation and communication systems, gave free minor education and minimum health care, developed big urban growth centers, and last but not the least, brought about confidence among the general population.

In later years, Government entered into the areas of consumer goods sectors. The public sector gradually became huge and unwieldy. Incompetence, corruption, negligence in legitimate duties became the order of the day. Bureaucratic system overrun the professionalism, and took over the reins of the public sector. Decision making became more and more scarce and tardy due to the fear of anti-corruption departments and the Court directions. Procedures, rules, court rulings and government circulars were so numerous and self contradictory that enormous amount of confusion prevailed every where. Litigation increased manifold. The technology progressed fast. The existing staff with the obsolete machine and inadequate knowledge could not cope up with the invasion of the western modern technology and dynamic and vibrant work force. The investment increased every year, but the profit dwindled. Each enterprise suffered due to overstaffing, old and obsolete machines, labour unrest, lock-outs, mismanagement, lack of accountability, transparency, and so on. Inflation soared and crossed double digit mark. The rate of interest, both in borrowing as well as lending, went above 13 to 15 percent. The annual growth rate was hovering around only three percent. The situation was so bad that during seventies, the GDP growth rate was only 1.5 per cent. The country lost its prestige in the international scenario and had to mortgage its gold. It did not have foreign currency for more than three days. The purpose for which the public sector was allowed to play a dominant role gradually lost its relevance. Every one started searching for solution to the problems. Then came the fall of Berlin wall. The USSR and East European countries started disintegrating. Socialism took a back seat.

In the context of such a change in the national as well as international scenario, the Industrial Policy Resolution of 1991 was enunciated. The policy eulogised the contributions of public sector but simultaneously enunciated restructuring, modernising, and, if required, privatizing the continuously loss-making enterprises. There was a desire to upgrade the infrastructure. Huge investments were required to upgrade infrastructure and bring it to the international standard. Without massive inflow of FDI, upgrading the infrastructure would not be possible. The foreign investors want a congenial business atmosphere and liberalised rules and policies in the areas like labour, import, taxation, exit policy, etc. Inspite of protests, both in and out of Parliament, Government pronounced that the policy of liberalization was irreversible and would go on. Though the change is slow, it seems that every one was now realizing that such a change is good for the nation and should continue. Government has also delegated powers pertaining to financial management and personnel management in *Navaratna* and *Miniratna* schemes. The delegations in the financial sectors have been to incur capital expenditure on purchase of new items or for replacement without any monetary limit, to enter into technology joint ventures or strategic alliances, to obtain by purchases or other arrangements, technology and know how, to effect organizational restructuring, including establishment of profit centers, opening of offices in India and abroad, creating new activity centers, creation and winding up of posts, including and upto non-Board level Directors *i.e.*, Functional Directors who may have the same pay scales as that of Board level Directors, but who would not be members of the Board, to structure and implement schemes relating to personnel and human resources management, training, voluntary or compulsory retirement schemes, etc., to raise debt from the domestic capital market and for borrowing from international market, which would be subject to the approval of RBI/Department of Economic Affaires as may be required and should be obtained through the Administrative Ministry, to establish financial joint ventures and wholly-owned subsidiaries in India or abroad with certain stipulations. The above mentioned delegations have been subject to certain conditions and guidelines. But these delegations opened a flood gate of new vistas of change in the public sector undertakings. Similarly, the policy of Government on disinvestment has been evolved over a period of time. But the policy has been changing keeping in view the policy and the manifesto of the party in power or the one supporting to the coalition.

With the change in the policy, it now seems that the fruits of liberalization have a positive impact on the public sector as well. The public sector banks and other undertakings restructured the organizations, especially in the Human Resources front, floated policies like- VRS- spent more funds in training, professionalised the Board, made the executives accountable, and made the working more transparent. The general economic scenario has witnessed a sea-change. In the last several years, after the Industrial Policy Resolution of 1991, the economy has witnessed an upward swing. The rate of inflation has gone down to below five percent (Figures 3 & 4), the GDP growth rate has shown an annual increase of about seven percent (Figure 2), the interest rate has been reduced and is stable; the labour laws have been made slightly flexible though a lot has to be done in this area strikes and lock-outs have also reduced. India has now an economy of $ 700 billion which is third biggest in Asia after China and Japan. Interestingly, the stock market has also shown tremendous resilience and optimism with addition of millions of small investors and traders.

The following presentations in Fig. 1, 5 and 6 would show that there have been improvements in profitability as well as paying of dividends in the PSUs after the enunciation of Industrial Policy Resolution of 1991.But the Fig. 2 & 3 show the huge gap between the investment made and the retained profits by the PSEs. However, the Indian economy continued to exhibit strong fundamentals during the last six to seven years. The Central Statistical Organisation (CSO) has estimated that as per the advance estimates of Gross Domestic Product (GDP), the economy is expected to grow at the rate of 6.9% during 2004-05. The main drivers of growth in 2004-05 have been the industrial and services sector which did grow at a rate of 8.3% and 8.6% respectively. Fig. 2 would show that the GDP has steadied in the last decade. Thus, the new policy of liberalization has been successful in the revival and achieving profitability in public sector undertakings. Government should vigorously pursue the policy so that the public sectors would be able to create more and more wealth for the country and jobs for the youth. Of course, they should not forget that they have a social obligation and should not abandon the people who are socially and economically backward. Development without social obligation is meaningless in economic parlance and the ultimate aim should be to improve the quality of life of the citizens.

Figure 1

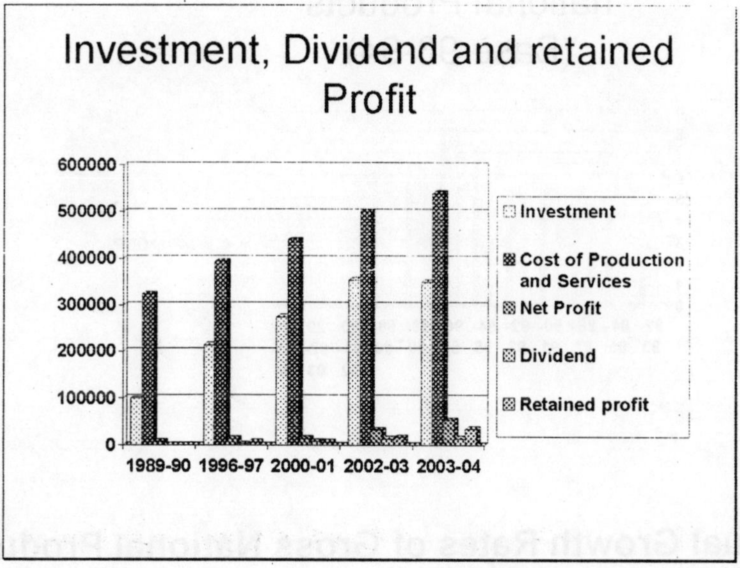

Investment, Dividend, and retained Profit

Figure 2

Annual Growth Rate of Gross national Products (Base 93-94)

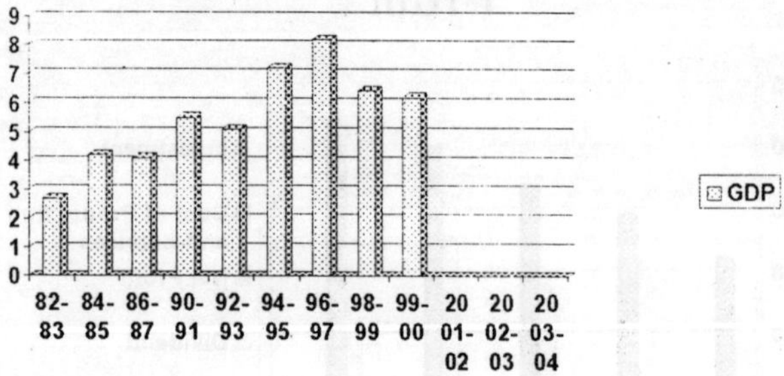

Annual Growth Rates of Gross National Products

(Base 1993-94)

Figure 3

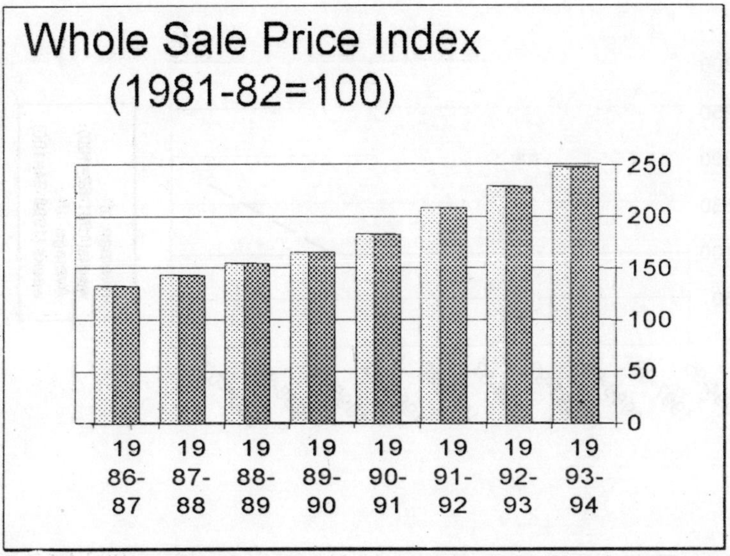

Whole Sale Price Index (1981-82=100)

Figure 4

WPI during 1986-87 to 1993-94 vis-a-vis during 1994-95 to 2001-02

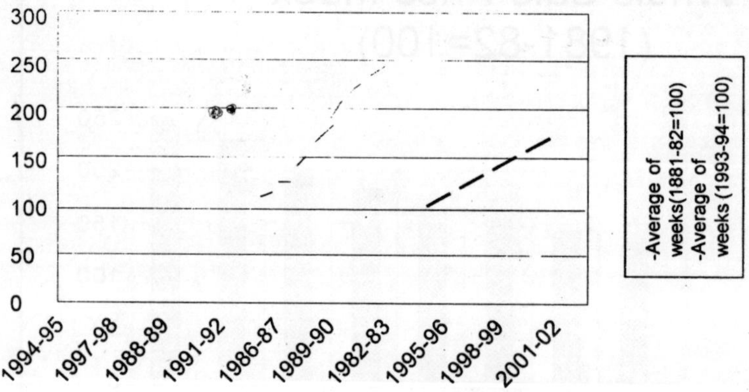

Note: The whole sale price indexes during 1986-87 to 1993-94 in red line reveals that the price index was going up at a faster pace in comparison to the WPI during 1994-95 to 2001-02 shown in blue line. This was the effect of liberalisation policy of Government. The prices recorded a down ward slide during post liberalisation era.

Figure 5

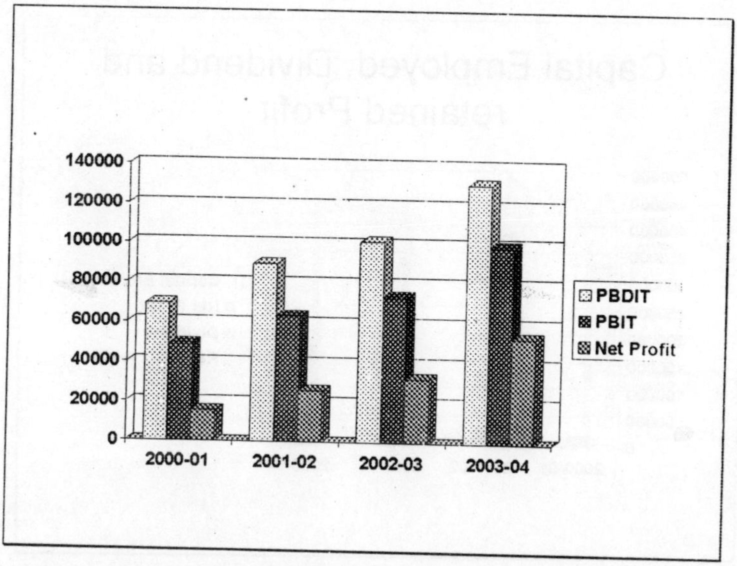

Net Profit, Profit before payment of Interest and Tax, and Profit before Depreciation, payment of Interest and Tax during 2000-01 to 2003-04.

Figure 6

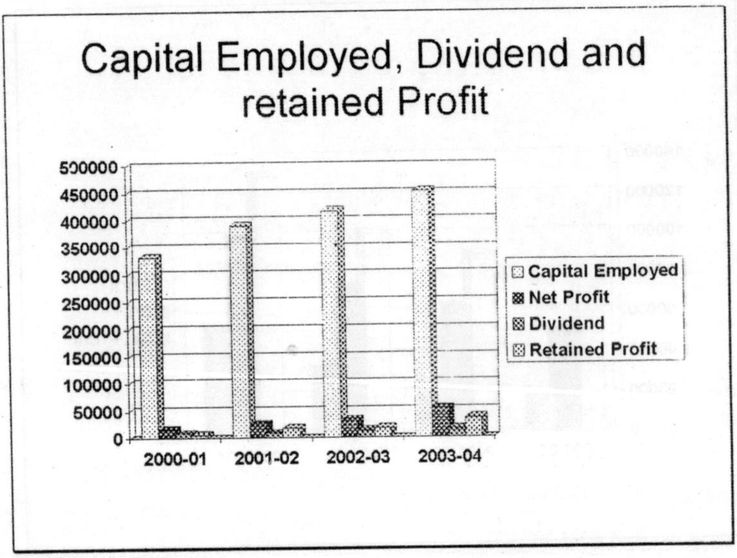

Capital Employed, Dividend and retained Profit

Bibliography

Growth of Trade and Commerce

1. For a preliminary discussion of public enterprise in antiquity, see Egyptian Study of Antiquities Chap.3.
2. ESoA, p. 168.
3. **For a recent translation of the Hittite Laws, Harry Angier Hoffman (1997),** *The Laws of the Hittites: A Critical Edition.* **Leiden: Brill.**
4. Bible (1 Kings 9.26-28; 10.1).
5. ESoA, p. 162.
6. ESoA, p. 57.
7. ESoA, pp. 173-74.
8. ESoA, Chap. 2.D.
9. 344 (*The Admonitions of Ipuwer*).
10. Bleiberg, Edward (1994), "'Economic Man' and the 'Truly Silent One': Cultural Conditioning and the Economy of Ancient Egypt." *Journal of the Society for the Study of Egyptian Antiquities*, pp. 24, 4-16.
11. An article by a professional economist, Morris Silver, devoted to the consideration of unsettled or disputed aspects of ancient economies, including the entire Mediterranean world. It builds on his books, *Economic Structures of Antiquity* (ESoA) (1995), Greenwood Press, Westport, Connecticut; and *Taking Ancient Mythology* Economically (TAME) (1992), E.J.Brill, Leiden.

12. **For an extended analysis of the commercial aspects of Herakles'career; Silver, TAME, Chap. 5 can be referred to.**
13. *Britanica Encyclopedia* ,deluxe edition 2002 "Public Enterprises".
14. Communist Manifesto.
15. Hans. (1999). "Ur-Dumuzida and Ur-DUN." In Dercksen (ed.), *Trade and Finance in Ancient Mesopotamia*.16. *sachirtu* ... (Wilcke cited by Powell 1999.
16. Powell, Marvin A. (1999). " *Wir müssen alle Nische nutzen: Monies, Motives, and Methods in Babylonian Economics.*" In J.G. Dercksen (ed.) *Trade andFinance in Ancient Mesopotamia*. Leiden: Nederlands Historisch-Archaeologisch Instituut te Istanbul, p. 5-23.
17. For a recent translation of the Hittite Laws, see Harry Angier Hoffman (1997).
18. For a translation of *The Eloquent Peasant, see* Miriam Lichtheim (1973), *Ancient Egyptian Literature*, and Vol. I: *The Old and Middle Kingdoms,* University of California Press, pp. 169-84
19. See Bleiberg, Edward. (1994).op.cit., pp. 24, 4-16.
20. For an extended analysis of the commercial aspects of Herakles' career, *see* Silver, TAME, Chap. 5.
21. Article by a professional economist, op.cit., Morris Silver.
22. A Commerce-and-Industry-Based History. By John G. Lankford 06.01.02;Exclusive to Roadhouse Sierra.
23. Thucydides wrote a *History of the Peloponnesian War*, a struggle that lasted, in two or three distinct phases.
24. http://members.tripod.com/adm/redirect/www.
25. **Chad Greenwood, *Economics of the Indus Valley civilisation,***
26. Basham, A.L. (1963), The Wonder That was India, New York: Hawthorn Books.
27. Hawkes, Jacquetta (1973), The First Great Civilizations, New York : Random House.

28. Heinz, Carolyn (1997), Asia, A New Introduction. 4th Ed. Chico: AS BKST.
29. Khan, Omar (1997) Hara Date. <http://www.csuchico.edu/~cheinz/syllabi/asst001/fall97/www.harappa.com> accessed: 12/03/97.
30. Wheeler, Sir Mortimer (1966), Civilizations of the Indus Valley and Beyond, New York: McGraw-Hill.
31. Rao, S.R. 'Lothal' (1985), Archaeological Survey of India
32. By Atreyi Maitra, Department of history, Bangabasi College, Calcutta.
33. Chattopadhyay, B., Kishana State and Indian Society, p. 195.
34. Thapar, R., Ancient Indian Social History, pp. 43 and 44.
35. Apastamba Dharma Sutra, 1.6.18.22; Baudhayana Dharma Sutra, I.S. 93-94.
36. Thapar, R., op. cit., p.44.
37. Kautilya, Arthasastra, pp. 106 and 107.
38. Rawlinson, H.G., Intercourse between India and the Western World, p. 101.
39. Wheeler, M., Rome, beyond the Imperial Frontiers, pp. 154 and 155.
40. Ray, H. P., "A Resurvey of Roman Contacts with the West", a paper in Athens, Aden, Arikamedu, ed. By Baussac and Salles, p. 103.
41. Chattopadhyay, B., op. cit., p. 191.
42. Wheeler, M., op. cit., p. 156.
43. Epigraphia Indica, XIX, p. 66; X. Nos. 1062, 1065, 1066.
44. Chhatopadhyay, B., op. cit. p. 191; Mahavastu, II.
45. Manusamhita, III. 158 ff.
46. Mukherjee, R., Indian Shipping, Chapter I.
47. Ray, H.P., op. cit., pp. 97, 98.
48. Reade, J., The Indian Ocean in Antiquity, p. 300.
49. Rawlinson, H.G., op.cit., p. 114.
50. Wheeler, M., op. cit., p. 120.
51. Reade, J., op. cit., p. 295; Ray, H.P., op.cit., p. 103.

52. Epigraphia Indica, VIII, pp. 75,90; VII. p. 52; and X. No. 1177.
53. Wheeler, M., op. cit., p. 125.
54. Rawlinson, H.G., op. cit., p. 123.
55. Ray, H.P., op.cit., p. 103.
56. Edward Baines, The History of the Cotton Manufacture in Great Britain, 1835.
57. Industrial revolution, web site- <http://www.historyguide.org/intellect/ind rev.html>.
58. Ben Frankline on Industrial Revolution, Web site- <http://www.english.udel.edu/lemay/Franklin/>.
59. Thomas Carlyle on Industrial Revolution, Web site- <http://www.victorianweb.org/victorian/carlyle/carlyleov/html>.
60. Arnold Toynbee on Industrial Revolution, web site- <http://www.cce.unifi.it/revista/toynbee6.htm>.
61. Lectures on Industrial Revolution in England, web site: <http://www.socserv2.socsci.mcmaster.ca/>
62. Jethro Tull on Industrial Revolution, web site: <http://www.britannia.com/bios/jtull.html>
63. Thomas Newcomen on Industrial Revolution, web site: <http://www.bbc.com.uk/education/archive>
64. James Watt on Industrial Revolution, web site: <http://www.history.rochester.edu/steam/marshall/>
65. David Landes, *The Unbound Prometheus*, 1969.
66. The India Handbook and Regional handbooks of economic development: prospects onto the 21st century. Chicago: Fitzroy Dearborn Publishers, 1997.
67. Department of Industrial Development, Ministry of Industry.
68. 1st Planning Commission Report, as approved by the Cabinet.
69. 2nd Planning Commission Report, as approved by the Cabinet.
70. 3rd Planning Commission Report, as approved by the Cabinet.
71. 4th Planning Commission Report, as approved by the Cabinet.

72. 5th Planning Commission Report, as approved by the Cabinet.
73. 6th Planning Commission Report, as approved by the Cabinet.
74. 7th Planning Commission Report, as approved by the Cabinet.
75. 8th Planning Commission Report, as approved by the Cabinet.
76. 9th Planning Commission Report, as approved by the Cabinet.
77. 10th Planning Commission Report.
78. Public Enterprises Survey, New Delhi 1990-91.
79. Public Enterprises Surve, New Delhi 1991-92.
80. Public Enterprises Survey, New Delhi 1992-93.
81. Public Enterprises Survey, New Delhi 1993-94.
82. Public Enterprises Survey, New Delhi 1994-95.
83. Public Enterprises Survey, New Delhi 1995-96.
84. Public Enterprises Survey, New Delhi 1996-97.
85. Public Enterprises Survey, New Delhi 1997-98.
86. Public Enterprises Survey, New Delhi 1999-00.
87. Public Enterprises Survey, New Delhi 2000-01.
88. Annual Report of Ministry of Heavy Industries, 1999-00.
89. Annual Report of Ministry of Heavy Industries, 2000-01.
90. Annual Report of Ministry of Heavy Industries, 2001-02.
91. Industrial Policy Resolution 1948.
92. Industrial Policy Resolution 1956.
93. Industrial policy Resolution 1961.
94. Industrial Policy Resolution Feb. 2nd 1973: Key Provisions, Department of Industrial Development, Ministry of Industry.
95. Industrial Policy Resolution , December 23,1977: Key Provisions, Department of Industrial Development, Ministry of Industry.
96. Industrial Policy Statement of July 23, 1980: Key Provisions, Department of Industrial Development, Ministry of Industry.

97. Industrial Policy Statement of 24th July 1991: Key Provisions, Department of Industrial Development, Ministry of Industry.
98. Industrial Policy initiatives announced in the budget 2000-01,Budget papers published by Government of India.
99. Letter no.1239-SCDN/65 dated 5th April 1965 of Department of C / oordination ,Government of India, setting up of Bureau of Public Enterprises.
100. O.M No.F20 (21)/69-BPE/Adm, dated 7th July 1969 of Ministry of Finance, constituting BPE as an independent administrative unit within Ministry of Finance.
101. O.M No.A-42011/13/85-Admn.dated 14th April 1986 of Ministry of Industry, Government of India, restructuring the Bureau of Public Enterprises
102. Govt. order No.A-42011/84-Admn.dated 27th August 1984, regrouping the functions of Bureau of Public Enterprises.
103. Public Sector Enterprises Survey, Govt. of India 1999-2000, Volume 1 page 194 on organizational structure.
104. 52nd Report of Estimate Committee of 3rd Lok Sabha on Board of Management
105. Report of 1st Planning Commission, Chapter 29, para 24, laying down the guidelines on management of public sector undertakings through a Board of Directors.
106. Report of 1st Planning Commission - Chapter 6, para 33 ,outlining the composition of Board of directors.
107. Letter No.2 (a)/70 -BPE (GM-1) dated 24th January 1970, farming a policy and issuing guidelines to improve the performance of public sector undertakings.
108. Letter No.2 (158)/70-BPE (GM) dated 13th October 1972, rationalizing the structure of Board of Directors.
109. BPE OM No.18/1/84-GM dated 19th September 1984, accepting the recommendations of Economic

Administration Reforms Commissions and conveying decisions with regard to certain appointments in PSEs and their Boards *viz*. appointment of Chief Executive, appointment of Part time Chairman, appointment and role of Government Directors, and number of Government representatives.

110. BPE OM No. 5/23/74-BPE(PESB) dated 3rd February 1975, agreeing to the views of the Administrative Reforms Commission that the number of the Government officials in the Board of Directors should be kept down and the possibility of drawing suitable persons from non-government sources should be explored. Besides, it also strongly recommended that experts from other public enterprises should be drawn.
111. DPE OM No.18 (6)/91-GM dated 16th March 1992 and vide DPE OM No.18 (6)/91-DPE (GM) dated 13th Nov. 1995, issuing guidelines on composition of Board of Directors of Public Sector Enterprises.
112. BPE OM No.18 (6)/84-GM dated 3rd January 1985 requesting the administrative Ministries/departments to advise the Public Sector Undertakings to amend the Articles of Association so as to include a provision for a spell of three years at a time with rotational retirement in respect of part-time non-official Directors.
113. DPE No. 18(6)/84 -GM dated 21st May 1986, bringing uniformity in regard to the tenure of part-time non-official Directors and enhancing it from one year to three years.
114. OM No. 18(4)/99-GM dated 15th February 1999, of BPE informing that there was no need to amend the articles of association with regard to the appointment of part-time non-official Directors.
115. Public Enterprises Survey 2000-01, volume 1, page 160-162 regarding board structure in PSEs.
116. DPE OM No.18 (6)/91-DPE (GM) dated 13th November 1995, Guidelines on composition of Board of Directors.

117. Recommendations of Committee of Secretaries in its meeting held on 25th June 1984 relating to tenure of three years for part-time non-official Director.
118. BPE OM No.18 (6)/84-GM dated 3rd January 1985 vide which the administrative Ministries /Departments were requested to advise the Public Sector Undertakings to amend the Articles of Association to include a provision for a spell of three years at a time with rotational retirement in respect of part-time non-official Directors.
119. DOPT Resolution No.27 (21) -EO/86 (ACC) dated 3rd March 1987 revising the policy relating to the functions, membership, methodology for selection and infrastructure of the Board.
120. Resolution No.6 (9)-EO DOPT Amendment No / 89(ACC), dated 6th September 1989, amending the resolution dated 3rd March 1987.
121. DOPT Amendment No.F. 27(8) EO/93(ACC), dated 2nd September 1993.In partial modification of Government of India, Ministry of Personnel, Public Grievances & Pension (Deptt. of Personnel & Trg.)Resolution No. 27(21) EO/86(ACC) dated 3rd March 1987, on Autonomy and Accountability.
122. Report of Third Planning Commission on Public Sector Accountability chapter 16, para18.
123. Report of Third Planning Commission on Delegation of Authority, chapter 16, Para(14.
124. Report of Fourth Planning Commission on Public Sector Accountability, chapter 6, para14.
125. Report of Tenth Planning Commission on Civil Service Reforms Aimed at Transparency, Accountability, Honesty, Efficiency and Sensitivity in Public Administration.
126. "Unshackling the Public Sector". Paper presented in the RGF Seminar on Reinventing the Public Sector on 22.9.2001,by N.Vittal, Central Vigilance Commissioner.
127. World Bank Annual Report 1998 on Decentralization/Autonomy as well as accountability,

Special Theme Governance in Asia: From Crisis to Opportunity, page 29.

128. Peter Evans and James Rauch, *Bureaucratic Structure and Economic Growth: Some Preliminary Analysis of Data on 35 Developing Countries* (Berkeley, California: University of California,1996).
129. John M. Cohen and Stephen B. Peterson, "Administrative Decentralization: A New framework for Improved Governance, Accountability and Performance," *Development DiscussionPaper No. 582* (Harvard University, 1997).
130. A World Bank Strategy: November 2000, *Reforming Public Institutions and Strengthening Governance.*
131. Minutes of Conference of Chief Executives held on 5/6 April 1983, on Autonomy and Accountability in Public Sector Enterprises.
132. The Bureau of Public Enterprises, Guidelines vide letter No.BPE/GL-0197/79/MAN/2(28)/79-BPE (GM-1) da ed 12th September 1979.
133. Designing Reform Strategies: Identifying 'Entry Points' to Enhance Accountability and Transparency, Para 27 of *Reforming Public Institutions and Strengthening Governance: A World bank Strategy, Implementation update Part 1: Overall Update,* April 2002.
134. Concept, genesis, growth and definition of Personnel Management from the study material prepared by National Institute of Labour Education and Management (NILEM), page 1 to 4.
135. Suggestion of Second Five-Year Plan to equip itself with personnel and to create organizations vide para 17 to 21.
136. Suggestions of Third Five Year Plan for building up of Management cadres, chapter 16.
137. The Fourth Planning Commission recommended that the enterprises of the public sector had a special obligation to follow labour policies, which were conducive to securing and keeping a competent working

force at a reasonable cost, vide chapter 16, para 37 of the report.

138. Workers, manager and society and responsible to the worker, an article, by *Encyclopaedia Britannica*.
139. Participatory management and flexible work systems and change in organization, an article, by *Britannica Encyclopaedia*.
140. The Industrial Disputes Act 1947, Section 2(k). Also the second and third schedules of the Industrial Disputes Act.
141. Ibid. Section 3.
142. Manik Kher, (1985) *Conciliation and Adjudication Today,* Pune, The Times Research Foundation, pp. 1-26.
143. The Industrial Disputes Act 1947, Section 10.
144. Ibid Section 4.
145. Ibid Section 5.
146. Manik Kher, *op cit*.
147. The Industrial Disputes Act 1947, Sections 12 and 13.
148. Ibid Section 10-A.
149. Manik Kher, *op cit*.
150. Ibid Sections 10 and 11.
151. Ibid Sections 7, 10(1), 7A, 7B and the second and third schedules.
152. For a detailed account of the debates, see V.D Kennedy (1966) *Unions, Employers and Government,* Bombay, Manaktalas.
153. Western India Automobile Association 1949, *I L.L.J* 245.
154. Bharat Bank Ltd. v. Their Employees, 1950 *II L.L.J*. 921.
155. Ibid
156. Ibid
157. See chapter titled "The Changing Function of Contract" in Wolfgang Friedman (1972), *Law in a Changing Society,* Middlesex, Penguin Books pp 119-160.
158. See, for example, T.C.C Thozhilali Union v T.C.C 1982, *I L.L.J* 425. In this judgement, it is explicitly stated

"Recognition by an employer of a trade union as a representative of its members and as their bargaining agent is a matter of volition on the part of the employer."

159. E.A. Ramaswamy and Uma Ramaswamy (1981), *Industry and Labour: An Introduction,* Delhi Oxford University Press pp 86-94.
160. Ibid.
161. Debi S. Saini (1993), "Reference Power of State in Industrial Disputes Adjudication: A Study with Reference to Industrial Disputes in Faridabad" 162. (Part II) Vol. 4, *Journal of the Indian Law Institute,* pp 233-252.
163. D.A. Desai (1994), "Industrial Adjudication and Social Justice in India" in Debi S. Saini (ed), *Labor Judiciary, Adjudication and Industrial Justice,* New Delhi, Oxford & IBH Publishing Co.
164. Debi S. Saini (1995), "Leaders or Pleaders: Dynamics of Brief Case Trade Unionism Under Existing Legal Framework," *Journal of the Indian Law Institute* Vol.37 (Part I) pp 73-91.
165. "Human Resources Development"- study material prepared by National Institute of Labour Education And Management, Adyar, pp 99 to 106.
166. Background material for the training programme on "Growth and Productivity-Blueprint of Organisational Success" prepared by National Institute of HRD and Advancement, Delhi; pp 73, 84,85,116 to 125.
167. Public Enterprises Survey 2000-01, Volume -1; *Investment in Public Enterprises-Analysis, Sources, Growth and Pattern.* pp 69 to 71.
168. First Five-Year Plan Report - chapter 29 - para 33 to 39.
169. Second Five-Year Plan Report - chapter 4 - para 3 to 16.
170. Third Five-Year Plan Report - chapter 6 - para 1 to22.
171. Fourth Five-Year Plan Report - chapter 4 - para 13 to 28.
172. Fifth Five-Year Plan Report - Chapter 4 - para 1 to 63.
173. Sixth Five-Year Plan Report -A Framework, Preface and Chapter VI,para 27.

174. Seventh Five-Year Plan Report -A Framework, Preface, Chapter 4, para 21, 22.
175. Eighth Five-Year Plan Report -A Framework, Preface, Chapter 5, para 10.
176. Ninth Five-Year Plan Report -A Framework, Preface, Chapter 3, para 1 to 60.
177. Letter No. BPE No.2 (32)/65-F1 dated 16th March 1967 of Bureau of Public Enterprises.
178. Letter No. BPE No.1 (49) Adv (F)/ 71 dated 24th June 1971 of Bureau of Public Enterprises.
179. Letter No. BPE-1 (49)/Adv- (F)/71 dated 27th September 1974 of Bureau of Public Enterprises.
180. Letter No. BPE/GL-030/76/Fin/1(21)/Adv(F)/74 dated 28th July 1976 of Bureau of Public Enterprises.
181. Letter No.F-No.4 (48)/96-ECB dated 19th June 1996 of Bureau of Public Enterprises.
182. An article titled 'Price' in *Encyclopaedia Britannica*.
183. *Pricing in Public Enterprises*- J. Felix Raj.
184. *Public Enterprisers Survey 2000-01*, Vol.1, Government of India, *On pricing policy in public enterprises*,-pp 91 to 100.
185. Government of India, Bureau of Public Enterprises, circular No.BPE/46/Adv (F)/68/25 dated 27th December 1968.
186. Government of India, Bureau of Public Enterprises, circular No.NPE/15(1)/Adv (F)/75 dated 3rd May 1975.
187. Public Enterprises Survey-2000-01, Volume 1, pp. 7 to 26.
188. Annual Report 2001-02, Ministry of Heavy Industries and Public enterprises, Government of India, pp. 71.
189. Report of Comptroller and Auditor General of India for the year ended March 2001.
190. Public Enterprisers Survey 2003-04, Vol.1, Government of India.
191. Economic Survey, Government of India, 2002-03; table 1.6 & 5.1.

❑❑❑

Index

❑❑❑